Yvonne Roberts has an impressive journalist career. Winner of the Young Journalist of the Year Award in 1971, she was one of the original team of LWT's 'Weekend World'. She has been a reporter on 'The London Programme' and Thames's 'This Week', and has made films for the BBC. She has written for the *Sunday Times*, the *Telegraph Magazine*, *New Statesman and Society*, the *Independent*, *Guardian* and *Standard*, and was most recently editor of the *Observer* Living Pages. She has written one other book, *Man Enough: Interviews with Men of 35*, published by Chatto & Windus in 1984.

For Zoe and Stephen and my parents,
John and Nancy Roberts.

MAD ABOUT WOMEN

CAN THERE EVER BE FAIR PLAY
BETWEEN THE SEXES?

Yvonne Roberts

Published by VIRAGO PRESS Limited September 1992
20–23 Mandela Street, Camden Town, London NW1 0HQ

*A CIP catalogue record for this book is available
from the British Library*

Printed in Great Britain by
Cox & Wyman Ltd, Reading, Berkshire

CONTENTS

ACKNOWLEDGEMENTS

I would like to thank Lennie Goodings, Ruth Petrie and Jo Tracy of Virago, who never questioned that the book could be researched, written and delivered in a frighteningly short amount of time. They gave unflaggingly of their enthusiasm, support and good advice, even when the deadlines dragged dangerously. And thanks to Gillian Beaumont for her keen eye. I would also like to give special thanks to Ann Treneman, who acted as main cheerleader. She has been an excellent critic and gave invaluable advice always when it was most needed.

Thanks too to many friends and colleagues who have exchanged ideas, shared laughs and, over the years, discussed many of the issues included in the book and experienced not a few of the problems, among them Sandra Horley, Frances Stathers, Carol Adams, Eva Kolouchova, Angela Neustatter, Anna Coote, Rosie Logan, Fran Bennett, Lynne Segal, Jean-anne Crowley, Julie Coole, Chris Tchaikovsky, Frankie McGowan, Frankie Rickford, Gail Somers, Judith Dudley, Geraldine Brennan, Renata Rubnikowicz, Adriana Whalley, Diana Quick, Sara Dunn, Nigel Horne, Jerome Burne, John Pilger, Billy Nighy, Ian Mayes, Nicci Gerard, Chris Oxley, Jo Green, Liz Cooke, and John Houston, king of the computer.

My thanks also go to all those who agreed to be interviewed and who lent so much of their time, and often their hospitality and friendship too.

Finally, special thanks go to my daughter Zoe, who waited patiently for the book to be completed and to my partner, Stephen. He was always willing to discuss ideas, challenge and criticise constructively. He also acted as chief maintenance engineer and managed to live for three months knee-deep in feminist literature without losing his sense of humour.

FOREWORD

It is impossible to extricate oneself from the questions in which your age is involved. You can no more keep out of politics than you can keep out of the frost.

Ralph Waldo Emerson

Jerome Robinson, a building surveyor, is thirty-one. He is an unmarried father fighting to maintain access to his two-year-old son Anthony after the break-up of a four-year relationship.

'I used to feel no stress and strain about women's rights,' he says, 'But now I'm just confused. I did my share in the house, I took her back when she had a couple of flings. I cared for Michael, I always played with him, bathed him, put him to bed. I vowed as a father I was going to be around. But none of it has been good enough.

'I don't know where men stand any more. I think men today are seen as sperm-bank donors and open chequebooks. Women have got the muscle but no respect. What I'm talking about isn't male ego, it's about me as a human being.'

Tom McCallan is an accountant in his forties. Friends describe him as 'solid' and 'a pillar of the Establishment'. He has a steady job, a semi-detached home of his own, and until he went on holiday in 1991, he also thought he had a relatively happy marriage: fourteen years, two children and a wife, Jennifer, forty-eight, with a part-time job and plenty of interests of her own.

'On the day we got back, she said she wanted a divorce. She said I was sulky and too controlling and that I must move out of the family home, see the children once a fortnight, and act sensibly.

'I felt as if I'd died inside. We'd had our ups and downs but I thought there was a commitment. Now I've lost my home, my kids, my wife, with no attempt at reconciliation. She says she wants to be free, to have a life of her own, to feel independent. And I honestly haven't got a clue what it's all about . . .'

Journalist David Thomas, in his thirties, is writing a book about the experiences of men in the 1990s. He too believes that the victims have become victimisers.

'Women are the new chauvinists,' he says. 'An entire generation of men has grown up in the same circumstances that women did in the fifties and sixties having to swallow a whole lot of one-sided ideology. [Men] are going to react in the same way that women did . . . when they burned their bras.'[1]

He argues that since (some) feminists have declared males as irredeemable and dismissed their efforts to escape the constraints of traditional masculinity, men must now concern themselves with their own agenda of needs. The moment has come, he says, to analyse the male version of 'the problem that has no name' first identified by Betty Friedan for white middle-class housewives in suburban America in *The Feminine Mystique*.

'Men are like housewives were twenty years ago. They'll tell you everything is fine, but why are they all taking Valium? Why are they pissed on a Friday night?' Fact is, everything is not wonderful. Fact is, men feel tremendous anger and hurt . . .'[2]

Then too there are the followers of Robert Bly and *Iron John*, who seek to avoid feminism's flak by fleeing from Ms to myths. They take to the woods in their men-only groups and drum and chant and attempt to find a new definition of masculinity, while seeking out the father they say they have lost.

'It is time for men to stop accepting blame for everything that is wrong in the world,' writes Douglas Gillette, Jungian analyst, author of *King, Warrior, Magician, Lover*, colleague of Robert Bly. 'There has been a veritable blitzkrieg on the male gender – what amounts to an outright demonization of men and slander against masculinity.'

In *No More Sex War: The Failures of Feminism*,[3] writer Neil Lyndon widens out the charge against women and particularly feminism still further. It is not just that they have inhibited and intimidated individual men and castigated his gender, he argues, but feminism has also destroyed the potential of a whole generation. The women's movement, he says, has put 'progress' in hock:

> I am disappointed to the soles of my boots that my generation, which promised so much, should have delivered so little by way of radical change in the institutions of the state, in the rights and freedoms of individuals, should have made so little difference to the slavery of worthless work . . . and to the privations and squalors among which we live . . .
>
> Much of the responsibility for that conspicuous failure I attribute to the influence of feminism and to the perverted account of personal relations and of social composition which feminism has fostered . . . The cardinal tenets of feminism divided my generation, effectively disempowering and disenfranchising its members . . .

Feminism is accustomed to opposition; no movement whose basis is radical change expects bouquets. It is used to the exhausted voices of complaint from those women who blame it because they now carry the burdens of home *and* work: a strange kind of 'liberation'. The fault for this may lie with those men who fail to provide adequate support, and a society that is still hugely ambivalent about the working woman, but feminism carries the can.

The women's movement is also used to the arguments of the traditionalists and the moral majority: those who urge women to heed their 'natural' instincts and return to hearth and heavily mortgaged home. But, in the 1990s, the objections being voiced by some men, appear very different in tone.

They admit they are confused by some of the consequences of feminism. They are bewildered by the actions of some women who demand new 'freedoms', only to fall back on old customs, such as 'the right' to be kept, when the going gets rough. At times, when it comes to sexual politics, they say, women appear consistent only in their contradictions.

These are men who, whether consciously or not, have fears about the loss of power that the slow crawl to equality between the sexes implies (or, more precisely, for too many, the evening up of the inequality) but who also insist that they are supporters of the principle of fairer play for women. What these men say they are attempting is to navigate a route through a geography which is constantly changing. And they are doing it, as they see it, without support. Feminism isn't the only catalyst in their lives, but as its influences have interlocked with further shifts and dislocations in society, it has become the easiest duck in the firing range at which to aim. At the same time, the women's movement has left its imprint in other ways. So these men are now demanding a recognition of their *own* disadvantaged place in society. They, too, claim the right to be judged as something other than a stereotype. Ironically, they, too, now want to be recognised as second-class citizens.

Mad About Women is partly about what has made these men angry and upset. It is therefore also about the state of feminism – neither dead nor dying, but – in Britain, at least – in need of some intensive care. This book looks at the mistakes it has made and the possible reasons why. It also reclaims some of the successes of the women's movement, particularly as reflected in the lives of many of the so-called 'ordinary' women and men in this country.

The book focuses on much of what Neil Lyndon has to say because his is the first attempt at a truly destructive attack on feminism in Britain from someone who is not on the right. It

is propaganda – and propaganda is ⟨...⟩
sells as opinion is often soon accept⟨...⟩
rebuttal is the provision of facts.

In addition, since he is of the sam⟨...⟩
those who govern space in print a⟨...⟩
arguably feel equally jaundiced about ⟨...⟩
receive a great deal of publicity. And ⟨...⟩
argument is a disquiet which I believe⟨...⟩
women share and which feminism cann⟨...⟩

An alternative approach might be to ⟨...⟩ ⟨...⟩ Lyndon
as the sole Luddite (Lyndonite?) of sexual politics in the
1990s. It might also be convenient but unfair to say of Neil
Lyndon, as some of his critics already have suggested, that
since he has been married twice and is now 'sick to the back
teeth of being fucked over by tiresomely angry women', his
problem is personal, not political.[4] But 'the personal is political' is precisely what gave feminism another kick-start in the
1960s. And who doesn't let some degree of private turmoil
invade their public actions?

A second approach might be to say of *No More Sex War*: so
what's new? The 'men's rights movement' has campaigned for
over thirty years in the States, and now claims to have more
than two hundred groups spread across the country. They
include Free Men, Men's Rights Inc., the Coalition of Free
Men and Men International. In Britain, a magazine, *Masculism
Monthly*, was due to launch in the autumn of 1992. Edited by
Terry Daly, author of *Masculism: A Militant Male Manifesto
for Men in the Nineties*, the magazine intended to present men
as 'militant, proud, assertive, strong – and on the attack'. The
backing failed to come through, but Terry Daly continues to
proselytise on the 'oppression' of men. 'We are living in a
woman's world,' he says. 'They are in the driving seat.'[5]

All these men share a common goal with Neil Lyndon: to
prove discrimination against men in law, in economics, in
personal relations and in society. They say they seek to expose
'the feminist conspiracy' in the courts. They also seek to

(as Neil Lyndon does) as unfair discrimination of gender, not as the various ways in which men women. Sexism in these terms, they argue, is visible, stance, in false accusations of rape, the plight of battered usbands and the lack of a say in abortion for potential fathers.

Neil Lyndon however would distance himself from the right-wing elements in the American men's rights movement. He argues again and again in his book that he is not against women, that he believes in equality, that he is in favour of emancipation for women – and for men. For feminism, in theory, he is the enemy within. So how should the women's movement react?

The opening up of a new front is a bonus. If nothing else, a backlash forces those under attack to examine what it is they wish to defend. *Mad About Women* argues the need for feminism, in spite of its present amorphousness, to acknowledge its errors, to reassess its methods and to move out of the honeycomb of politically correct ghettos some of its followers have occupied for too long. The women's movement needs to produce fresh ideas and sell some of the old ones better. It needs a strategy which is less like a New Age guide to self-fulfilment and more like an agenda which is relevant to the needs of the majority of women (and men).

For me, feminism is not about mystical bonds that I may or may not share with other women. I do not hold to the view that if women are in charge, all automatically improves – it depends upon which women and what they believe in and how they manage and with whom. For me, feminism is not about the creation of a new society of women. The notion that women have 'special' qualities that can bring peace and greenery to the world seems to me as sexist as the idea that they are all blonde bimbos or baby machines.

For me, feminism is about nothing if it is not about social justice: for women and men; in the First World and the Third.

Feminism can only ever act as a barb in society's bum. It will never seize power. It is the outsider among ideologies, since in Britain it has no leaders, no organisation, no conferences, no signed up membership. It is anarchic and that, in the past, has been both its strength and its weakness. Feminism is often defined by whoever speaks last – but it does have main strands of beliefs and goals which can be identified and shared.

Feminism has to be radical enough to force real change, yet populist enough to draw support. It is a challenge on which the Labour Party gave up many years ago. What works in feminism's favour is not the power of its rhetoric but the force of that one radicalising experience which affects each and every woman who is drawn to its cause. It is the one moment – or several – in her life which encapsulates the disparity between her rights and options and those of the man with whom she lives alongside.

In the 1980s, feminism worldwide was as affected by the swing to the right as was every other movement. In Britain, much of the local authority money which had funded a whole range of initiatives, including childcare and self-help projects for women in housing, refuges and health groups, dried up. The women's movement was also bruised by the dissensions which first appeared in the late 1970s – among them, those which divided radical separatists from women who chose to live and work with men.

Now, in the 1990s, can feminism evolve sufficiently in Britain to take on a more active role once again – or will it limp into the twenty-first century, a gentle hobby for retired feminist thriller writers and pensioned-off New Men?

I believe feminism *can* evolve. It has never been more necessary because women are at a crossroads. Capitalism is placing a high price on the skills of a few females while devaluing the rights and abilities of the many. Faced with low pay and casualisation, women often have no option but to work even on these terms. And while consumerism tries to hijack the idea of women's 'liberation' turning it into the gospel of the high flyer, it also attempts to portray those who uphold the principles of equality and social justice as hysterical and aggressive and man hating. It is time for feminists to go from the defensive to the offensive.

Feminism has also never been more necessary because we have a void on the left, a drive to privatisation on the right which hurts women most and a growing band of mothers, children and elderly women in the community who are impoverished, denied adequate money and all hope and status.

If feminism cannot speak of these concerns with passion and conviction because they are important not only to women but to the well-being of society as a whole, if it cannot find fresh audiences which include men, then it deserves to wither and die; but *Mad About Women* is no obituary. This book is about people and life as they see it, not as feminist theory would wish it to be. But it also argues that change is possible, in what areas it is needed, and why. And it tries to show where, in spite of (or even because of) the rise of the angry not-so-young men, the signs of hope may lie.

CHAPTER ONE

Tremble, tremble, the witches are back.[1]

> The necessity to do without illusions concerning one's own condition is the necessity to do without conditions that need illusions.
>
> *Karl Marx*

In the mid 1960s when I was seventeen, the only 'woman question' that concerned me was how to become a woman – officially, that is. All my closest friends had 'done it' (subsequently, it transpired that most of them were lying), so for several months I relentlessly pursued my boyfriend, Les, around his pink and grey Cortina. He wanted to 'save' me for marriage: I guessed (correctly, as it happens) that if I waited that long, senility would set in.

Les was an apprentice in the local railway works and bass player in The Untamed, a group not unknown in the backwaters of Bucks. In a gloomy light on stage, he looked like Wayne Fontana. He could also sing, in tune, 'A Groovy Kind of Love'. What more could a girl want? A husband, my mother said. Education, my dad said. Sex, my friend, Flo Stathers, and I decided.

Our zenith came, post-Les, in 1966, in the shape of Ron and Bob, two mods from Bedford. What they lacked in brainpower they made up for in money, the cut of their hand-stitched suits, and that most seductive of all ingredients: a car . . .

Every Saturday night for a month, Flo sat in the front with Bob; I sat in the rear with Ron. Bob's main topic of conversation was to recount, minute by minute, the plot of the latest horror – and I mean horror – movie he'd seen, in a voice not unlike that of the late Kenneth Williams. Ron was somnolent. Sex was out of the question, torpedoed by a mix of Black Bombers and Blues and too much Peter Cushing.

For me, the sixties were the same years that Michelene Wandor experienced:

> full of people I didn't sleep with
> joints I didn't smoke
> plays I wasn't in.

Two years later, by the autumn of 1968, I had begun to realise that the 'woman question' was not so much about what you wanted as what you didn't want: domesticity, babies, routine. At Warwick University, earlier that year, we had held our first sit-in to protest at the alleged business interests involved in the University. A group of us had dutifully helped by making dozens of cheese sandwiches: the little women at the barricades. Germaine Greer was a lecturer at the university, but we had no Women's Lib that I can recall. Che Guevara was on everybody's wall and most of the 'demon texts'[2] – *The Dialectic of Sex, The Female Eunuch, Against Our Will* – had yet to appear.

If this was the swinging sixties, permissiveness and Sergeant Pepper, then most of us were still worried about not doing 'it' too often in case we got labelled the campus bike. A friend had a backstreet abortion and bled and bled in one of the rooms in residents' hall, cooling the ardour of us all. At that time, what was personal wasn't political and what was political certainly wasn't personal: Ho, Ho, Ho Chi Minh!

In September 1968 I arrived in the USA along with forty other students from Warwick, as part of an exchange scheme. The whole of the States appeared to be erupting in student revolution, but I was allocated the one campus where the American flag was still honoured, respected and obeyed rather than transformed into tablecloths or T-shirts or treated as material for incineration.

If a woman really wanted to be treated like a 'girl', Newcombe College, on the campus of Tulane University, New Orleans, was the place to be. The female students were mostly bright, very rich, very conservative. Dresses were worn six inches below the knee; my miniskirts, *de rigueur* in Coventry, were considered 'cute' but as welcome as Janis Joplin at a church social. I had never before come across women so skilled at turning sex into an exchange and mart: intercourse for marriage. The only conversation I can recall about job prospects and careers and independence were those conducted by Newcombe girls about 'his' job prospects and career (law and medical students rated well) and his independence, an impediment to all well-laid matrimonial plans.

At Newcombe I shared a suite with Barbara from the Deep South. Barbara – 'Hush, mah mouth, what have I said?' – was a closet subversive. Marriage wasn't that great, she said, which in Newcombe was as revolutionary a cry as 'Storm the Bastille!'.

On my first day in the dormitory, I heard a tremendous roar: 'Man on the floor! Man on the floor!' Newcombe, it transpired, had a policy in which no man was allowed above the ground floor – if spotted, he was denounced. All women had to be in by a certain time; they had to account for whom they were with by recording names of escorts in the register (F. Ucker was a regular favourite). If they came in late or were caught lying about their whereabouts, they would be docked marks and, eventually, forbidden to leave campus. All this had quite recently also applied to undergraduate married women who had to live apart from their husbands, in residence. The suffocation I felt then speeded up my search for 'liberation'.

In September, a few weeks after I arrived in the States, while I was still trying to tackle the bizarre courtship rituals of the Deep South, the Miss America pageant was held in Atlantic City, New Jersey. Robin Morgan, the present editor of *Ms.* magazine, author of *Sisterhood is Powerful* and a former child star on television, was the catalyst in what was to become one of feminism's most formative examples of direct action. Florynce Kennedy, the lawyer who later bailed out the women arrested at the pageant, said it was 'the best fun I can imagine anyone having in any one day of their life'. Two hundred women had answered Robin Morgan's photocopied request for help, 'No More Miss America'.[3] In the afternoon, on the boardwalk, television cameras caught the women as they marched up and down with placards, shouting slogans: 'Atlantic City is a town with class. They raise your morals and they judge your ass!'

In *The Sisterhood* Marcia Cohen reports that the presidential candidate Richard Nixon had announced that he was going to let his children, Tricia and Julie, stay up to watch the pageant, so the slogans that didn't get screened included 'Miss America sells it' and 'Miss America goes down'. In a freedom trash can, the women threw dishcloths, false eyelashes, girdles, copies of *Playboy* and *Ladies' Home Journal* – and bras, but nobody did any burning.

Judith Ann Ford, Miss Illinois, aged eighteen, was crowned Miss America. 'Flashbulbs popped. Television cameras moved in,' Marcia Cohen writes:

> The pretty, teary eyed woman in the long evening gown
> began to speak, when shouts suddenly burst out in the hall.
> 'Down with Miss America!' 'Freedom!'.
>   Then it all came clear. A great, white bedsheet floated
> slowly down from the balcony, the cameras wheeled around
> and there (undoubtedly for the first time) most of America
> saw on the wavy banner, a *t* and an *i* hidden in the folds,
> but the message still unmistakable: 'Women's Liberation'.
>   And so millions now learned about the women's
> movement. Like it, of course, or not.

Two months later, I spent Thanksgiving with a friend, Robin, whom I had met at college. She, like my roommate Barbara, was a maverick. Her mother and father had very recently divorced. He was a colonel in the army, her mother had stayed at home, until the split. Now, in her forties, she was back at college and had plans to qualify as a doctor.

'It's time to do something for me,' I can remember her saying. I remember because Robin's response also stuck in my head. 'Oh Jesus,' she said to her mother. 'Give us a break.' And silently, I agreed.

Over that traditional, down home Thanksgiving, while we parcelled up cookies for Robin's brother, a helicopter pilot in Vietnam, and went duck-hunting at dawn with her uncle in the bayou, on the other side of the States, at Camp Hastings in Illinois, two hundred women from thirty cities were meeting for the first time, for one of the earliest of the women's liberation conferences.

In *Daring to be Bad*, a lucid history of American radical feminism from 1967 to 1975, Alice Echols reports that the conference was also a first in another way: it comprehensively exposed the divisions and attitudes which have continued to affect the women's movement to this day; the 'politicos', many of them mothers and living with men, versus the separatist radical feminists. She records that Marlene Dixon, who attended, called the radical feminists 'wildcat women' who demonstrated 'complete contempt' towards those who were unable to dismiss the 'invisible audience' of leftist male heavies. She was also critical of the 'Movement women' who rejected 'consciousness raising' as 'bourgeois counter-revolutionism'. And she blamed everybody for a suspicion of leaders which 'bordered on the pathological':

The conference ended in the atmosphere in which it had begun: suspicion, envy, arrogance bred from the sure knowledge that . . . consciousness raising or . . . socialist ideology was the single truth. No national organisation, no journal or newsletter, no communication network, nothing

5

of the structural framework for a movement did or could have emerged . . .

What *was* considered a success were the workshops, particularly one on sex organised by Anne Koedt, author of the highly influential *The Myth of the Vaginal Orgasm*. She argued that women have been fed 'a myth of the liberated woman and her vaginal orgasm' because 'women have been defined sexually in terms of what pleases men'. Women should, she said, 'discard the "normal" concepts of sex and create new guidelines which take into account mutual sexual enjoyment'.

(Cell 16, 'celibacy, separatism, karate', a New York Women's Lib group who were the first of the sisters to move into short hair, combat boots and khaki pants, took this a stage further a couple of years later in their radical journal, aptly titled *No More Fun and Games*. Cell 16 decided that sex was 'inconvenient, time-consuming, energy draining and irrelevant', and that 'happy, healthy, self-confident animals and people don't like to be touched, don't need to snuggle and huggle. They are really free and self contained and in their heads.')[4]

Alice Echols reports that during the Anna Koedt workshop, one woman revealed that she *did* have vaginal orgasms. Later she apologised to 'my sisters' for even considering such a heretical thought: orthodoxy, for some, was already beginning to matter more than the ideas people wished to explore.

Also under discussion were alternatives to marriage, but Naomi Weisstein and Marlene Dixon put the point – still valid – that the majority of single women were not in communes, they were not bisexual or lesbian: instead they would be returning from the conference, locked in a private 'struggle' to 'get a man'. The two suggested 'syndicates' in which women could make the first overtures. Any man who 'messes some woman up' would be blacklisted. (Ironically, at the same time, Helen Gurley Brown, editor of *Cosmopolitan*, the first of the vulva and Volvo magazines to achieve massive success, was also, in New York, tackling the same problem of the very real shortage of men. Her solution for a woman without a boyfriend or husband was to pinch somebody else's. 'Nice girls do have affairs and they don't necessarily die of them,' she wrote in *Sex and the Single Girl*.)

Back in England in February 1970, and hating every minute of a six-month graduate secretarial course in Oxford, I happened to walk by Ruskin College one Saturday morning. The first British Women's Liberation conference was under way. I went in and found myself, like many women present, both exhilarated and intimidated.

Women meeting other women, women making friends with women without much competition and rivalry, woman organising themselves without the shadow of men: that is – rightly – taken for granted today. Then, it was unprecedented. But even at Ruskin, a hierarchy was already developing; there was a certain look, a vocabulary, a credo which indicated you were more 'right-on' than the next person. No make-up, no men, no myths about finding true love (although as Rosie Boycott, one of the founders of *Spare Rib*, was to say later, most people secretly expected that at some point, preferably sooner rather than later, a man would come along to sweep you away in his BMW).

The conference took place before women's history had got under way; before there was a women's publishing industry; before women writers were reclaimed from the past; before women's experiences, working-class and middle-class, in the home and out of it, were sought out and recorded. So when woman after woman began speaking of such things, it was as if a missing piece of the puzzle had suddenly been found; the discomfiture of being thought 'peculiar' was suddenly explained. Others had gone before us.

In *Out of the Doll's House*, Sally Alexander, one of the organisers, explained:

We wanted to changed everything, absolutely everything. Every cultural value with which we'd been brought up . . .

We thought we could change the world and not just the relationships between women and men but everything that flowed from that – the way we brought up our children, the kinds of people that we would raise. That moment of complete optimism was quite shortlived, but that is what we wanted.

A year later, the optimism in me, at least, was alive and well, particularly since, as I was single and living alone, I had no one against whom to test the practical side of the theories. I was twenty-one and working on the *Northampton Chronicle and Echo*, an evening newspaper in an area more likely to believe that 'the problem that has no name' was something to do with a shortage of leather soles in the local boot and shoe industry than with the thoughts of Betty Friedan, author of *The Feminine Mystique*.

Five of us formed a women's group. One woman was in the Socialist Workers' Party, and married. While the rest of us were publicly impressed by the fact that if her husband didn't do the dishes and the housework, neither got done, privately, our mothers' voices spoke loud: 'How could she *live* in such a tip?'

Only one of our group was the genuine article: a young (twenty-two-year-old) mother of two, married to a traditional working-class man, who said she felt trapped at home. Sympathising with her was about all the feminist studying we did – the Northampton outpost of the female revolution was more about a gut feeling than about theory (but it was – and is – a very strong gut feeling); more concerned with lagers in the pub and chats about ourselves than with separatism and Marxism and *The Second Sex*.

Almost twenty years later, in January 1992, I was listening to 'Woman's Hour' on the radio. A discussion was introduced in which Neil Lyndon was ranged against feminists and a member of the men's movement. It was less the content of what Neil Lyndon was arguing than the tone in which he said it, the anger he expressed, that gelled with so many experiences I have had in the past of trying to conduct rational discussions with men about the 'woman question'.

I say 'rational' not simply because of the prejudices and lack of knowledge I may or may not have felt the other person revealed but also because of my own tendency, in the past, to hide behind the generalisation and clichés and truisms which become the grain of any movement, given time – particularly a movement constantly under siege, unsure of itself and divided within. (All aspects which can, with a different frame of mind, be viewed as strengths instead of weaknesses: a means of widening its support, not narrowing it.)

Since then, I have gone back to what I first read in the 1970s and 1980s, I have talked to people who were active at the time – and are still active now. I have examined much of the contemporary research on issues such as domestic violence, rape and the breakdown of the family. And throughout, my focus has been: are Neil Lyndon's criticisms fair?

I pose the question not because one man has such influence but because while some of what he says is absolutely justified, Neil Lyndon is also, I believe, a part of the first British male wave of malevolence towards the women's movement which is rooted in the right. The least women can do is to examine how such feelings have been roused and why and, if possible, to turn them into a constructive force for their own advantage – and to the advantage of the men whom Neil Lyndon professes to champion.

'If relations between men, women and children are to improve, attitudes to manhood must change. It wouldn't be a bad start if men ceased to be the butt of casual prejudice – expressed in half-witted habits of speech,' Neil Lyndon wrote with justification, in an article, 'Badmouthing', published in *The Sunday Times* magazine in 1990,[5] which launched his manifesto.

He continued:

But the most important job our legislators face must be to remove some of the systematic disadvantages of life for men

. . . there is one sense in which men, as a group and as a whole, can be described as a class in Britain: in a host of vital ways they are second-class citizens.

He went on to argue that women, unlike men, are no longer subject to 'institutionalised disadvantage'; instead, they suffer from 'general practice and custom'. Conveniently, these 'are hard to pin down and almost impossible to legislate out of existence'.

In contrast, among the examples of institutionalised disadvantage for men, he lists the unequal ages for retirement (women are about to be levelled up to sixty-five: a victory for no one); the limited rights of unmarried fathers (in part rectified, as Neil Lyndon acknowledges, by the Children Act); the difficulties fathers encounter trying to get access to their children (clearly, as I try to explain in Chapter Three a major problem and one in which the children suffer most) and the refusal to grant men the role of dependant in social security payments – an anomaly he believes will be resolved by the end of the decade.

A year later, in November 1991 in *The Spectator*, Neil Lyndon was on the attack again: 'the hoods' (Lyndonese for 'sisterhood') have tried to make the case that 'all men menace all women . . . that men, in their very being, have been represented as sub-standard genetic form, a mutation of life, which must be contained and ordered if it is not to threaten life on earth,' he wrote.[6] Sliding over the paradox of how a movement with so little support among women, as he claims – let alone men – could have influenced so much, he continues:

I can see few things more serious in our society than the presence among us of a totalitarian group, legitimated by fashion, office and place, whose wicked and vain orthodoxies are influencing the operations of the courts and of commerce and are inhibiting expression in all our most compelling forms of art.

(This could almost have been written by Kate Millett, author of *Sexual Politics*, in the late 1960s, about men.) And he warns: 'Men must keep their place according to the tastes and definitions of the hoods, or they risk public disgrace, humiliation and mockery.'

In publishing *No More Sex War: The Failures of Feminism*, Neil Lyndon has now clearly decided to take that risk. Other critics such as David Thomas may accept the basic premiss of feminism, but object to its methods and rhetoric; Neil Lyndon shuns it all. Yet at the same time, he says he shares many of its goals: equality of opportunity, better childcare, decent working conditions, more investment in housing, health and education, more attention to parental rights.

He nevertheless rejects feminism, 'that towering edifice of bullshit' on the basis that it first rejected him and all his gender. And despite the title of his book, this 'bleeding brigadier' in the battle of the sexes as he calls himself, is now conducting a war of attrition. 'My entire adult life has been spent under the influence of this poisonous orthodoxy . . .' he writes. 'Were my son's infancy and adulthood to be blighted by these poisons?' The disappointments and setbacks, for many, of the past two decades are not the fault of government or politicians or industry or national inertia, he argues; they are the fault of feminism.

In *Esquire* magazine in May 1992, journalist Sean O'Hagan, a decade younger (Neil Lyndon is in his mid forties) and weaned on the slogans of the women's movement, had an obvious suggestion: 'Maybe Lyndon's generation, who were in their early twenties when feminism exploded in their faces, has never really recovered from the shock, not to mention the indignity of having to have their consciousness forcefully raised – or at least restructured.'

Neil Lyndon's response is that O'Hagan has swallowed 'the cardinal presumptions of feminism', allowing himself 'to become a guilt-ridden second-class citizen who hasn't noticed how the inroads made by . . . feminist self-belief have undermined men's rights, not to mention their self-confidence'. (Ironically, this is again exactly the tone used by the radical feminist Andrea Dworkin to lecture women – with some power – that there is no such feeling as heterosexual love, only enslavement.[7] Orthodoxy is dead; long live the new orthodoxy.)

Neil Lyndon also argues that feminism is responsible for the cuts in family planning (because the sisterhood failed to 'squawk' loud enough in objection), the lack of opportunities for single mothers ('Feminism has failed to improve the circumstances and alter the minds of these girls'), the destruction of the role of the father, by implication the irresponsible use of abortion (he says he knows two hundred women who have had abortions for 'cosmetic social needs') and the widening gap between rich and poor. (He also throws in the Falklands War, but even he stumbles slightly over the connection: Women's Lib distracts the Left; enter Mrs Thatcher; move on to the Falklands War.)

The key to his thesis, 'the monster' of ideology he claims 'the hoods' begat is, in fact, a composite mongrel of his own making. In *No More Sex War*, he moves indiscriminately backwards and forwards across twenty-five years of feminist history, with no indication to the reader from which point in the timespan the view might have been plucked, or how it may have evolved since.

He argues that 'the false feminist picture can only be sustained through the exercise of intolerance, vulgar prejudice and totalitarianism in thought and speech'. He then goes on to display much of the same approach in his own polemic. For instance, he arbitrarily decides which of the experiences of women he will accept and which he will deny. (Job discrimination? Ridiculous. Marital rape? A successful con played on those unlikely allies of Women's Lib, the Law Lords, by 'the hoods'. Domestic violence? A case of too much booze.)

He is aware, he says, that his pick 'n' mix approach overlooks the many different strands of feminism, some of which advocate directly opposing views about women, men and the kind of society in which they might live – not least whether as separatists or heterosexuals, whether in a socialist or an alternative 'wimmin's' culture filled – for those who like that sort of thing – with spinning and weaving and praising the goddesses.

He argues that feminists share a common strand, and from this all ills flow. He defines this as: 'The belief that women share interests which are distinct from men's and that those interests can be advanced only by women acting collectively . . . No variety of thought or style of attitude could be termed feminist unless it involved these presumptions.'

This definition instantly cancels out those feminists who may argue that class is as strong an influence as gender; it also ignores much of liberal feminism, which has always believed in hitching its demands, where possible, to the male establishment, working within the system. In *An Encyclopaedia of Feminism* Lisa Tuttle runs through the many and various definitions of feminism, the simplest being 'the advocacy of women's rights based on a belief in the equality of the sexes'. She quotes the view of Donna Hawxhurst and Sue Morrow – a view which I endorse too:

Feminism has only working definitions since it is a dynamic constantly changing ideology with many aspects including the personal, the political and the philosophical. It can never simply be a belief system. Without action, feminism is merely empty rhetoric which cancels itself out.

I agree, too, with Charlotte Bunch, who believes that feminism is not about 'adding in' women's rights but about transforming society: 'Because everything affects women, every issue is a women's issue, and there is a feminist perspective on every subject.'

Above all, Neil Lyndon's definition also denies the mutuality of the needs of women and men and the fact that as an ideology, feminism cannot survive if, as he insists, it is all 'man-hating'. Feminism has to be based on humanism; its aims are in men's interests too.

Mary Robinson, President of Ireland, said in February 1992, giving the Allen Lane Foundation Lecture:[8] 'In a society in which the rights and potential of women are constrained no man can be truly free. He may have power but he will not have freedom.'

Neil Lyndon also denies that we live in a patriarchal society. He says this is because, 'if any individual man is denied a right by reason of his gender which is afforded to every individual woman, then it must follow that ours is not a society which is exclusively designed to advance and protect advantages for men over women.' I would counter his view: the 'advantages' women hold are mainly those which underline their traditionally inferior position. They are 'advantages' accorded to the so-called 'weaker' sex almost exclusively in the areas of reproduction and mothering. Feminists may differ on the precise definition of 'pariarchy' (literally 'rule of the father'), but they agree that it is universal but neither unassailable nor biologically inevitable.

In 1969, Germaine Greer was asked to contribute to the backlash current in that period (and there have been many throughout history). Would she write a piece for the fiftieth anniversary of female suffrage, explaining how women's own deficiencies had meant that since receiving the vote, they had got nowhere fast? Goaded, Germaine Greer sat down and wrote instead 'a direct rhetoric aimed at the viscera of womankind, not the babble of bluestockings'.[9] It was, of course, *The Female Eunuch*, a classic assault on femininity and those who benefit most from it: men.

'I shall have woman release her last clutch at man not to have her retreat into some absurd Amazonian society,' she wrote, 'but to . . . ally female with the male in a way which is not mutually limiting but, but what? I cannot know but I have a dream.'

Of course, neither her dream nor the dream of anyone else concerned with bringing women up to the baseline occupied, as yet, mainly by males has been realised. 'I do not wish women to have power over men,' Mary Wollstonecraft wrote two hundred years ago, 'but over themselves.' As part of that process, this book argues, it is time for the women's movement to exercise a little more honesty.

'For every woman trying to free women,' said the writer Brigid Brophy, 'there are probably two trying to restrict someone else's freedom.' The question is: why?

Criticism in feminism is not kosher. It is known as 'woman blaming'. While it is right to argue that it is always easier for the Establishment to point the finger at women rather than to change itself, feminism cannot afford infallibility. As powerful polemicists and early members of the second wave of feminism in the sixties such as Lynne Segal and Sheila Rowbotham have argued many times, if the women's movement refuses to learn from its own history, its own mistakes, how can it move forward in any sure-footed way?

Even when the analysis of such errors may itself be flawed, the very debate it provokes makes feminism, as a force, visible once again. In June 1992 the academic Ros Coward published *Our Treacherous Hearts: Why Women Let Men Get Their Way*. For all that sympathetic female journalists tried to cover the complexity of her arguments, the headlines said it all. Fairly typical was the headline in *The Standard*: 'Guilt: Why Feminism is a Failure'.[10] In her book, Ros Coward interviews 150 women, a number of whom are what she terms 'successful' (although it is not clear by what criteria – salary? A balanced home life and work life? Being top of the pile? Clearly, from what many of them say, it is not being happily bottom of the pile.) She also draws on her own experience.

Ros Coward dropped out of teaching when the first of her two children was born – partly to be with the child; partly, she explains, because she couldn't take the strain of the workplace any longer. 'At some deep level women seem to regard work and a career as dispensable,' she writes with the kind of generalisation that is sometimes difficult to avoid in discussions about sexual politics but, even so, appears a mite sweeping. 'If we are to gauge the strength of maternal feelings, we must try to understand what women are hiding from – as well as what they are seeking – in the bond they have with their children.'

Ros Coward goes on to argue that, in withdrawing into the home, these converted career women turn motherhood into a spectacle as competitive and bloodthirsty as any Roman Games (her underlying theme seems to be one popular in Victorian times: if the spirit of a child is not broken or subdued, then he or she, like a monster, will devour the adult).

Women's complicity in her own downfall does not end there. Ros Coward also argues that the 'loving' mother then projects on to her male partner her own hunger for power, status and success, and if he doesn't respond, she uses emotional blackmail and manipulation. (Her honesty and the honesty of some of her interviewees must be refreshing to critics such as Neil Lyndon and David Thomas, who with justification, in my view, have complained about the ambivalent messages being sent out by some women: messages about which, these men say, they are not permitted to complain or comment.)

Women do have power to demand changes in society, Ros Coward argues – I think correctly – but they have backed off. Women do have the influence to demand change in men, but instead they resort to the passivity which they think will rouse male desire. Rightly, she argues that it is not just the bias in society against women which holds them back, it is women's 'hidden complicity, a way of living our personal lives that protects men and reinforces their habitual ways of doing things'.

This portrait Ros Coward draws of the confused mess which is womanhood is not, of course, new. What is new is what appears to be her conviction that because of feminism, This Is

Not How Females Should Now Behave. The guilt is too much to bear – and it seems to me that she implies that the women's movement is to blame. 'Old-style feminism' has very definitely flopped, she implies, because in one generation it has failed to give birth, as Rebecca Fraser pointed out in a review of *Our Treacherous Hearts* in *The Times*,[11] to a new 'homogenised faultless person without illusions . . . without quirks or flaws and with no foolish dreams or ambitions for her offspring'.

Ros Coward goes on to argue that we are seeing 'a popular retreat into traditional values' (without presenting much evidence). And she rightly concludes that women should take responsibility for their own needs and recognise that bringing about social and political change requires collective action. Some might say that is exactly where the second wave of feminism came in, and that in prematurely bringing the 'old-style' movement before the firing squad, Ros Coward is simply assisting the women's movement to disappear without trace up its own orifice. Mary Wollstonecraft, author of *The Vindication of the Rights of Women*, was also aware of the gap between theory and reality. In 1797, having written much against the institution of marriage, she became a bride. In a letter to a friend, she wrote: 'What charming things would sublime theories be, if one could make one's practice keep up with them.'

In short, Ros Coward has asked too much of feminism, too soon. When it 'fails', it stands condemned. 'There is a belief that the "correct" analysis guarantees the "correct" experiences,' Janice Winship argues in *Inside Women's Magazines* –

> That is to propound feminist arguments is, in itself, to have already transformed our ideological feminine selves who enjoyed 'the bad old things'.
>
> Unfortunately, ideologies cannot be changed only by the assertion that they should be. Feminists we may be, but as individuals, our emotional responses and our sense of ourselves have been learnt within older codes of femininity

. . . It is important we recognise that contradiction not as a sign of weakness, to be pushed behind our public feminist veneer, but exactly that which feminism has to deal with . . .

It was in trying to absorb rather than examine and understand these contradictions in the 1960s that damage was done to feminism, a movement which ever since has become increasingly prescriptive.

In the States, in the main, the Women's Liberation groups that formed in New York, Boston and Washington, DC were white and middle-class. They were also anxious to become downwardly mobile. They wanted to prove that they were as oppressed as the next woman, simply because of their gender. As Alice Echols – a co-founder of the Women's Lib group Redstockings, now an academic – explains (quoting Ellen Willis, a fellow founder of Redstockings), this had long-term consequences. 'We no longer had to see ourselves as privileged people wondering where we fit into the revolutionary struggle; we were part of an oppressed class with a historic identity.'

Consciousness raising was the method by which some feminists reassured themselves that what they had in common was greater than any differences. The term was put into currency by Kathie Sarachild, an activist feminist who had been an organiser on the Summer Voter Registration Project in Mississippi in 1964. She adapted consciousness raising from the Civil Rights tactic of 'telling it like it is' and the approach of the peasants in the Chinese Revolution who 'speak pains to recall pains'.[12]

The anxiety to stress similarities, however, meant that issues of class and race were omitted, and the genuine tensions which existed were suppressed. At the same time, the importance of gender became overrated, while the obligation always to be non-judgemental spawned its own problems.

'Despite their sincere efforts to identify with those women

most victimised by the system,' Alice Echols points out in *Daring to be Bad*:

> the movement remained largely white and middle class.
> The vast majority of working class and third world women
> were not 'turned-on' by feminism . . . Their declaration,
> 'We will always take the side of women against their
> oppressors,' ignored the possibility that women's interests
> might in fact be oppositional. Their insistence in pursuing
> 'only what is good for women' rather than what is
> 'revolutionary' or 'reformist', echoed Stokely Carmichael,
> who in 1968, had declared 'It is not a question of right or
> left, it's a question of black.'

The idea that 'the personal is political' also has its problems, as Neil Lyndon points out. When it is divorced from action, instead of initiating change in society, it can become self-indulgent; a subordination of politics to lifestyle.

In Sweden, according to feminist academic Gisela Kaplan, consciousness raising, self-help groups and slogans such as 'the personal is political' have always been treated with caution:

> Swedish women believe that self-help groups are
> counterproductive because they take away from
> mainstream political focus by relieving pressure on the
> government. By and large, although this attitude might
> have delayed the establishment of crisis centres, it has
> continually ensured that . . . as part of a major political
> platform, their concerns are not merely social but questions
> of state, of government, of the country.[13]

Some of the members of the same groups involved in the debates about consciousness raising – Redstockings, New York Radical Women, Cell 16 and The Feminists – were also influential in the 1960s in developing and debating ideas to do with 'the female principle', the association of all that is 'good' with women – and most of what is 'bad' with men. It is, of course, an essentially sexist argument, but it continues to have an impact.

Cell 16 argued (without apparently seeing the contradictions) in favour of separatism and maternalism, 'the liberation of the female principle in all human beings – the worldview which is maternal, materialist and peaceful (noncompetitive)'. The group also held that women, by having children, marrying, having sex with men, wearing attractive clothes and using make-up, identified themselves as collaborators. Valerie Solanas, the woman who, in June 1968, won her fifteen minutes of fame by shooting and nearly killing Andy Warhol, provided inspiration in her SCUM (the Society for Cutting Up Men) manifesto. According to Roxane Dunbar, a Cell 16 member, this was 'the essence of feminism'. In truth, it was, as Alice Echols says, 'an unabashed example of misandry'.

'Sex is not part of a relationship,' Valerie Solanas argued, with no great show of appreciation from many women at the time:

> . . . it is a solitary experience, non-creative, a gross waste
> of time. The female can easily – far more easily than she
> may think – condition away her sex drive, leaving her
> completely cool and cerebral and free to pursue truly
> worthy relationships and activities . . . When the female
> transcends her body, rises above animalism, the male,
> whose ego consists of his cock, will disappear . . .

The Feminists, of whom Ti-Grace Atkinson was a member, also advocated separation from 'the enemy'. Ti-Grace Atkinson, described by Betty Friedan as having a 'main line accent and ladylike blonde good looks', had been elected president of the New York branch of the mainstream feminist, National Organization of Women, in 1967. Almost instantly she moved to a more radical stance, and subsequently resigned.

Flora Davis, in *Moving the Mountain*, tells how Ti-Grace Atkinson and The Feminists invaded the New York City marriage licence bureau in February 1969, armed with leaflets to advocate the destruction of marriage and the communal raising of children. Love was 'the psychological pivot in the persecution of women', asserted Ti-Grace. This presented problems when she later developed an attachment to Joe Columbo, a Mafia gangster who dealt in women and drugs. When he was killed in 1971, she explained that she valued 'Sister Joe', his working-class 'revolutionary spirit' 'in spite of his maleness'. The sisterhood was not impressed.

Also active in Washington, DC in 1971 were The Furies, who included the writer Rita Mae Brown. Political lesbians, they argued that heterosexism was 'a cornerstone of male supremacy'.[14] Charlotte Bunch suggested that straight women who didn't understand what heterosexual privilege was should 'try being queer for a week'.

Flora Davis explains how Adrienne Rich, years later, took the ideas of The Furies further:

> She suggested that because of the strong connection between mothers and infants, a female's first and most fundamental attachment was to other women. She asked: why, then, would women turn to men?
> Rich also conceived of lesbianism as a continuum that stretched from sexual relations at one end to intense nonsexual experiences such as 'bonding against male tyranny' at the other.

Many of the ideas of the radical separatists in the late 1960s and early 1970s go to form Neil Lyndon's view of feminism in the 1990s. They had impact, but even then they never held the stage alone. Betty Friedan, in her forties at the time and the mother of three children, continued to argue for co-operation. 'To achieve real victories, not just headlines,' she wrote in 1972, 'we have to make alliances with men.'

Ellen Willis also believed that an economic revolution would come only through working with men, while Gloria Steinem, editing *Ms.* magazine in 1970, said: 'Men will have to give up ruling class privileges but in return they will no longer be the ones to support the family, get drafted, bear the strain of responsibility and freedom.'

In Britain, too, the early 1970s saw feminism often working with men and at its most positive and active, setting up, for example, refuges, rape crisis centres, training projects, women's groups, nurseries and crèches, anti-nuclear and peace campaigns, most notably Greenham Common, as well as journals, magazines and publishing companies. It also began to use the experiences of women to challenge received professional wisdom on issues such as women and mental health, anorexia, rape and barbiturate addiction.

Still, it was – and is – the radical separatists who provided much of the 'inspiration' for the caricatures of feminism which passed for journalistic coverage during that period. It was an inevitable price to pay and perhaps, at the time, a small one. It was the separatists, the 'man-haters', who acted as midwife to the movement as a whole, forcing it to give birth, I would argue, to a far healthier, far louder, far more bolshie baby.

It was the radical feminists who helped to clear a space so that women could find a voice of their own. They also challenged prevailing orthodoxies about sexuality and love and how 'nice' women should behave (while also locking some women into a new set of 'must-dos'), and they provided a vocabulary, not least in the term 'sexual politics'. But precisely because they helped to devise a structure which itself made any dissent appear an act of treachery and regarded diversity as a threat, they inadvertently, later, helped to put a lock on much of the further evolution of the women's movement.

They have also left an inheritance which, because it has yet to be adequately addressed, saps feminism at a time when what it desperately needs is revitalising.

Yvette Williams is twenty-seven, British and black. She

represents part of the neglect of feminism and some of the hope for a way forward. 'I would put my black identity ahead of my feminism,' she says. 'But another black woman might give the opposite answer. I believe it's just as likely that I share more in common with a black man than I do with a white middle-class woman – but even if the oppression is different, we can still share goals in common.'

Yvette's parents came from Antigua in the 1950s, at the invitation of Enoch Powell, then Minister of Health, who was seeking all the cheap labour he could get. The family (there are three children) settled in Birmingham. At school, Yvette was the 'bad' girl.

'It was a mixed comprehensive. I was disruptive, I was always in trouble. I was regarded as 'difficult'. I was suspended. I was academically very bright without much effort and I came from a happy family life, but I was angry. I still am, but I've learned to control it more.'

In the 1970s, when white feminists were at their most practical, organising nurseries and health groups and conferences, Yvette was more involved with Rastafarianism.

'I never had an identity crisis. I was always black and nothing else. We had our own dress and music and culture. I lived in an entirely black part of Birmingham. If you weren't part of the scene, you were 'English'. And there's no worse insult than that.'

Alex Haley's *Roots* on television was a bigger influence on her than any of the paraphernalia of the women's movement. 'I can remember I had a white childminder who was racist. She would often say to my mum, "I used to live here before the coloured people came, no offence to you, Jane". But there *was* offence.'

At sixteen, in 1981, with Thatcher in power, Yvette left school with O levels and was given the choice: secretarial work, nursery work or Woolworth's. She began an NNEB course to qualify as a nanny, and was deferred in her first year for bad behaviour.

'It was the anger again,' she says. 'The white girls were worried about sexist remarks in books about babies being dressed in pink, I was pissed off when I had to read comments such as "There are no books in black homes".

'I was told I had a chip on my shoulder, but I knew I was right: it was about racism.'

In 1984, Yvette moved to London and still lives in Ladbroke Grove. She worked in a women's collective which taught women building trade skills and also provided a nursery. It sounds like a version of Carry On Sexual Politicking.

'It was 90 per cent lesbian, some white, some black and every kind of sexual oppression. The Irish lesbian said she had to face a different struggle to the German. The working-class lesbian said she couldn't take on the struggles of the middle-class women. The middle-class woman couldn't identify with the Europeans.

'I thought: common oppression it may be, but clearly my struggle always overrides yours.'

Three years ago, Yvette began a degree course in communications studies and sociology at Goldsmiths' College, from which she has just graduated. She chose to do one of her main papers on sex and gender.

'I feel strongly that the black matriarch always takes the blame for the "sins" of the children. We've seen it again after the Los Angeles riots. And feminism has failed to take account properly of the history of slavery when for the black man, the white woman was just as much the oppressor as the white man. In the fields, the punishments for black men and women were almost identical.

'The issue of absent fathers takes on a different form in the black community because of the structures imposed by history.

'Black women too have had to cope with the idea that their sexuality is everything white female sexuality isn't supposed to be. And I think now, the struggle around violence which affects both young black men and women is important. You only have to tread on a corn and some young ragamuffin woman wants to take your life.'

Yvette Williams says she has no interest in establishing a hierarchy of oppression. She believes in a recognition of the multiplicity of experiences and the constantly shifting alliances which tug at the black community as well as the white. 'People say to me, "What about black women, what do they want?" And I say, which black women? My mother in church? A black lesbian? My sister the civil servant? Women, black or white, have a right to our differences too.'

What feminism has blatantly failed to do is heed the experiences of women who are not white. In the 1970s and since, black and Asian women have set up their own organis- ations such as the Brixton Black Women's Group in 1973 and Awaz, one of the first Asian women's groups, established in 1978.

Awaz campaigned around immigration cases, sexual harass- ment of Asian women, and domestic violence. It also worked through long-established male groups such as the Indian Workers' Association of Great Britain and the Asian Youth Movement. For four years, from 1978, the Organisation of Women of Asian And African Descent (OWAAD) also oper- ated and, after its demise, spawned many more groups such as the Black Pressure Group on Education.

In *Power and Prejudice*, Anna Coote and Polly Pattullo explain that OWAAD, in part, eventually foundered on the issue of feminism and men: 'Some black women refused to be associated with the term [feminism] . . . because it was part of a white supremacist culture and because it was (or seemed to be) anti-men', they explain.

In the States, the writer Alice Walker has helped to publicise the term 'womanism' rather than feminism because, she says, it is rooted in black women's culture. But the term hasn't yet become very visible in Britain – neither have the bridges between black and white feminist activists.

In *No More Sex War*, Neil Lyndon not only focuses on what

25

he sees as feminism's flaws, he also attempts to undermine its reputation as a radicalising force. He argues that women have moved towards 'liberation' not because of feminism but primarily as a result of the introduction of the Pill. And women were not the only ones to feel the benefit; men did too:

> At some moment, between 1966–69, it appeared that the most perfectly divine opportunity had been given to us. We did not have to be our father . . . Ours had become truly another world. None of our fathers had ever known the variety of sexual opportunity which was ours for the having – no mistresses, no kept women, no prostitutes, no servant girls. No babies. Our lovers were our equals and our contemporaries. They were women whom we might, in earlier ages, have wooed, affianced, married and monogamised for life.

(In *The Hearts of Men* Barbara Ehrenreich argues cogently that the flight of the breadwinner began much earlier. He was liberated not by contraception but, in part, by consumerism: encouraged to spend, spend, spend – on himself, by the daddy of the bunnies, Hugh Hefner. 'I don't want my editors marrying anyone and getting a lot of foolish notions in their heads about "togetherness", home, family and all that jazz,' Mr Hefner told his disciples, shortly after launching *Playboy* in 1953. Three years later, circulation was over a million.)

In 1987, in a survey in Belgium, quoted by Gisela Kaplan in *Contemporary Western European Feminism*, women were asked to name the three most important changes in their lives this century. They said: the Pill (70 per cent), the right to vote (29 per cent) and the washing machine (28 per cent).

The Pill, as Neil Lyndon says, clearly gave women control over their bodies on a scale not known before. Almost all Western countries have seen a drop in the birth rate to below zero since its introduction in the 1960s (but not in Ireland and Spain, where feminism is as influential as anywhere else – but so is Roman Catholicism). In Britain, however, women began to take the Pill in significant numbers only in the early 1970s, when feminism was already a force[15]. I would argue that the Pill was only one of several influences – and that the beginnings of the second wave are to be found not in the sixties, but in World War II.

In *Rules of Desire*, Cate Haste reports how Mass Observation noted how women relished the independence the war brought:

> 'The change of spending her days outside her own home, of making fresh contacts and seeing people, is actually welcomed by such women with something approaching ecstasy,' Mass Observation commented.
>
> When husbands were away for long periods, working women developed a new independence and a new authority in the family, as well as an ability to cope on their own which had previously never been tested.

Again, in *Women in Wartime*, Jane Waller and Michael Vaughan-Rees, pursue the same theme, using contemporary material:

> 'My husband has just been on leave; for five months I've had the baby tying me hand and foot. Now my husband has gone back bad friends with me because I told him he ought to get up and light the fire,' an irate wife wrote to Leonora Eyles, the agony auntie on *Woman's Own*, in January 1941.
>
> 'He even asked me to clean his army boots for him, which is a job no woman should be asked to do. He will be home again in three months. How can I make him see his duty?'
>
> Leonora told her she couldn't. 'You should be ashamed of yourself, my dear. Next leave, show him how pleased you are to have him home again. It would be nice if you gave him breakfast in bed . . .'

Jane Waller and Michael Vaughan-Rees quote Rosita Forbes who in 1942 had spent months lecturing to service women. She reported that 'few of them think that marriage alone will be sufficient occupation. All over the country I listen to girls saying, "I'll have to go on working" or "I couldn't do without a job".' She concluded that men would probably abandon the idea 'I don't like to think of my wife working, when I am quite able to support her'.[16]

Sexual taboos also were broken, because who knew if your lover would return from the battle? In *A Secret World of Sex*, Steve Humphries quotes a survey conducted by Eustace Chesser, published in 1956. The survey inquired into the sex lives of 6,000 women. Even allowing for a reluctance to disclose intimate secrets, Chesser estimated, in *Sexual, Marital and Family Relationships of the English Woman*, that 39 per cent of those born between 1914 and 1924 and 43 per cent of those born between 1924 and 1934 had indulged in pre-marital sex. This is not to say, of course, that sex was frequent, or with a number of partners, or even that it was satisfactory – but neither does it prove that it wasn't. The eroticism of the British woman may be a deep, dark well.

Churchill, too, did his bit for emancipated womanhood when, at the end of the War, he laid the foundation for a united Europe. This resulted, in 1957, in the Treaty of Rome and the one clause which established that there must be 'equal pay for equal work'. 'Even though the treaty restricted its interest to women and employment,' Gisela Kaplan argues, 'it actually created a starting point for a change in woman's status and self-perception well beyond the employment sphere.'

If events during and following World War II helped to prepare the way, the general mood of rebellion and the optimism of the young in the sixties gave feminism its trigger. Again, Neil Lyndon misreads the clues. He argues that it was in the general emotional mêlée of the sixties, as the sexual revolution took hold and 'commitment' became devalued, that women did not seize the moment; instead, they panicked:

Very many of the sisters were far from happy. They did not welcome or approve of uncertainty. They required moral rules and firm categories of gender definition . . . Moreover, [they were] going to make sure that their ideas should hit home and be felt there . . .

They had grown up with common and conventional expectations of adult life which little differed from the lives of their mothers and grandmothers . . . they had been taught to cherish their chastity and to give the prize of their maidenhead only to the man they would marry . . .

They had learned, in childhood, the vital women's business of pleasing a husband, from making a Sunday lunch to looking decorous at a cocktail party . . . They had been taught . . . if you didn't keep your hand on your halfpenny . . . all the hell of teenage pregnancy would be the instantaneous outcome.

One of the ironies is that far from being 'conventional', many of the women who were part of the second wave came from families marked by individuality (which Neil Lyndon will now probably seize on as confirmation of their neuroses: the argument can't work both ways).

Gloria Steinem was left as a child to care for a schizophrenic mother; Kate Millett's mother became a lone parent in 1948 when her husband left her for another woman (Kate Millett was twelve and lone parents then were rare); Lynne Segal's father in Australia was a Jewish patriarch and doctor (her mother, too, worked full-time as a doctor) who moved his mistress into the house to care for the children while his wife stayed away as much as possible; Sheila Rowbotham – who, along with Lynne Segal and Juliet Mitchell, has supplied many of the most long-lasting ideas in British feminism – came from an outwardly conventional home, 'a lower-middle-class back-ground in Leeds', but anarchy, a strong stand in feminism in this country, was close at hand.

'My father was an engineering salesman and on the extreme

right wing of the Tory Party . . . but my mother, although she was politically Conservative, really believed in people's individual freedom and lived in a state of constantly taking the mickey out of pompous people. She was always on the side of young people having a good time and rebelling and stuff,' she says. 'So I always had that attitude to life.'

Sheila Rowbotham says she had been 'swotty' at a Methodist boarding school to which she was sent to help cure her catarrh. She had read Bernard Shaw and Olive Schreiner and Mary Wollstonecraft: 'I was a rebel in an earnest nonconformist way.' At St Hilda's at Oxford, in 1961, she met Bob, who had got to the women's movement ahead of her.

'He'd been in the CND marches and visited the New Left in America and I think he had visions of emancipation being about scrubbed faces and short hair and walking up and down mountains vigorously. I wasn't like that at all. I wore mascara and high heels and tight skirts.'

Far from being panicked by sexual freedom, Sheila Rowbotham, then a beatnik, embraced it enthusiastically – and, in the early 1960s, sooner than most. 'Bob was very enlightened; he'd read the Kinsey Report and he knew about these things,' she explains. 'So he took me off to a woman who gave me a diaphragm. She was a Fabian and her mother had been a suffragette.'

Sheila Rowbotham's experience of feminism helps to explain how those who became involved in the 1960s were not liberating themselves simply from the fear of pregnancy, as Neil Lyndon would have it, but from a host of other limitations as well. In her first year at university, in 1961, a couple were caught in bed. The woman was kicked out altogether; the man was suspended for two weeks. 'We protested over sexual inequality, but I didn't think that had anything to do with feminism,' she says. After university, she moved to London and taught in a college of further education. She also became active in the politics of the Left. She began to write, working on *Black Dwarf* with Tariq Ali.

In January 1969, Sheila Rowbotham and Fred Halliday produced an issue of *Black Dwarf* devoted solely to 'the question of women'. It may sound mundane now; then, it was unique. Sheila Rowbotham, writing from a socialist–feminist viewpoint, produced a manifesto, *Women: The Struggle for Freedom*.

'We want to drive buses, play football, use beer mugs not glasses,' she wrote.

We want men to take the Pill. We don't want to be brought with bottles [bird and bottle parties were common on the Left], or invited as wives. We do not want to be wrapped up in cellophane or sent off to make the tea or shuffled into the social committee. But these are little things.
Revolutions are made about little things. Little things which happen to you all the time, every day, wherever you go all your life . . .
   [Women] are perhaps the most divided of all oppressed groups. Divided in our real situations and in our understanding and our consciousness of our condition. We are in different classes. Thus we devour and use one another. Our 'emancipation' has been often merely the struggle of the privileged to improve and consolidate its superiority. The women of the working class remain the exploited of exploited, opposed as workers and oppressed as women.

Countering the separatist line from the States, she also extended a hand to men: 'Men! You have nothing to lose but your chains. You will no longer have anyone to . . . peep at with their knickers down, no one to flaunt as the emblem of your virility, status, self-importance, no one who will trap you, overwhelm you . . .'

(In his autobiography *Street Fighting Years*, Tariq Ali describes how a young hippie responsible for laying out the women's issue attempted to get his revenge. Sheila Rowbotham's manifesto was 'overprinted on a naked woman with the most enormous pair of breasts imaginable. Our hippie friend had designed it so that the key denunciations of male chauvinism were imprinted on the two breasts.' The hippie still won. Ordered to redesign the layout at the last minute, he slipped in an ad which read: 'Dwarf designer seeks girl: Head type girl to make tea, organize paper, me, free food, smoke, space. Suit Negress, Phone . . .')

Sheila Rowbotham is now forty-nine, the single parent of a teenage son. She lectures and writes. *Woman's Consciousness, Man's World*; *Women, Resistance and Revolution* and *Hidden from History* were all published in the 1970s. She also – in 1979, with Lynne Segal and Hilary Wainwright – launched *Beyond the Fragments*, an attempt to find some cohesion on the Left in areas which included women's issues.

'At the time, we thought it was a beginning,' Lynne Segal says. 'We didn't realise it was the end, a postscript on all the activism of the seventies.'

'What prompted me in the sixties wasn't reading feminist books,' Sheila Rowbotham explains. 'There wasn't that much around. I'd just got fed up. I was fed up of always being treated as invisible by men on the Left. Or patronised. Or told to shut up.

'On one occasion in particular, I'd organised a jumble sale to raise money for the Vietnam Solidarity Committee. In a meeting, the men told me that this was really rather reformist.

'Every time I tried to explain, they kept trying to shut me up and I wouldn't shut up. Later, this American, Henry, offered me a lift home and he said the reason why they were trying to keep me quiet was because I was a woman. He told me his wife was involved in a women's group in Boston, and that's how he knew about such things. I suddenly felt much better; I thought, "Wow, it's not something about me after all".'

In her book *Contemporary Western European Feminism*, published in 1992, Gisela Kaplan dissects every country in Western Europe to show the growth, development and differences in European feminism. Even though, as she assesses, only a million women have been involved as activists out of the total West European female population of a hundred million, the arguments the feminists have articulated and the campaigns they have pursued have had a far wider resonance – not because of single issues such as contraception or a wage packet, nor through feminist witchcraft forcing ideas on to an easily manipulated audience. If there is any magic, it lies in detecting the indefinable unease which many women experience but cannot explain.

As Betty Friedan wrote in 1963 of her white middle-class world:

> If I am right, the problem that has no name stirring in the minds of so many American women today is not a matter of loss of feminity or too much education or the demands of domesticity.
>
> This is far more important than anyone recognises . . . It may well be the key to our future as a nation and a culture. We can longer ignore that voice within women that says: 'I want something more than my husband and my children and my home.'

CHAPTER TWO

Come into my parlour, said the spider to the fly

I'm beginning to
wonder if
the tactics
of this revolution
is to
talk the enemy to death.

Pat Parker, 1978

Capitalism is nothing, if it is not the most adaptable of ideologies. Hence its success. It can cut a couple of inches off here, add a nip and a tuck there. Emancipated women? Sure, we'll have them on board. A little bit of equality never did anybody any harm: but don't let it get out of hand.

Customising feminism and turning it into a servant of the marketplace has been one of capitalism's easiest and most successful coups. But the task isn't over yet.

The women's movement has been absorbed, amended, glamorised, robbed of its sexier ideas (how many more coffee-table books can we absorb on 365 ways to have an orgasm?) and transformed into a series of thirty-second commercials. Each time, the effect has been to neutralise the essentially radical message at feminism's heart.

The marketplace influences the women's movement and the women's movement influences the marketplace – but the traffic hasn't been consistently two-way. As a result, we have feminism with its nerve extracted – or almost. And all to push the merchandise.

Ads for company cars aimed at the female executive? Frozen foods for the wife who has her own life? Gold Blend for A Certain Kind of High-Flyer? Nothing wrong in all that, so long as the prophets (profits?) of postmodernism don't try to convince us that because we have the ads, we also have the reality.

Where there clearly has been improvement is in removing some of the more blatantly sexist images. Now it's men who cop the advertising industry's total inability to deal with any social change in the home. If there *is* a new male agenda in the making, it should sign up with the Movement for the Liberation of the Incompetent Man from TV commercials. No more dads/lovers/husbands seen tackling the dangerous science of boiling an egg/filling the washing machine/making the gravy – a unique challenge, this, since it comes out of a packet.

In popular entertainment, too, the women's movement has served its purpose, particularly recently since Hollywood discovered the psychofemme – as in *Fatal Attraction*, *Thelma and Louise* and *Basic Instinct* (with much more to come). *Basic Instinct* is about a rich, successful, sexually voracious, apparently amoral career woman who may or may not prefer her men with ice picks in their chests. The film's selling pitch is 'Beyond desire is something beyond control'. It refers to the suspected murderess, but it is exactly the same view that 'the gentle sex' in the 1950s were supposed to have of men's sexual appetites. Get too close to a successful woman, is the message, and you get bit. It's the first film that flaunts a woman's fanny as a lethal weapon; every man's nightmare – or fantasy?.

Does it matter? Not a lot, if this genre is one of a range in films and TV series, aimed at mass audiences, which show independent women, preferably without 'a problem'. Slowly, in the TV soaps and in the cinema, that is beginning to happen. This is not because emancipation has eaten its way into Hollywood, but because – the market talking again – some creative feminist women also know how to make money.

Susan Harris led the way, producing series such as *Soap* and

Golden Girls; Nora Ephron, Whoopi Goldberg, Jane Campion, Roseanne Barr – the list is growing longer.

One of the surprise hits in the States in the summer of 1992, for instance, was *Wisecracks*, a Canadian film made by Gail Singer which shows off that virtually unsighted tribe – not one, but a group of funny female comics. 'Premature orgasm', says one wisecracker, 'is a foreign concept to a woman.' It's not a revolution in popular culture, but it's a ripple. And it means that capitalism doesn't always win.

The marketplace has also infected the women's movement as a result of the market's appetite for privatisation. For instance, good childcare via a range of provision, much of it in the community and available to all, was a sixties goal. How far have we come? We have arrived at the individual solution: nannies for the few, childminders for more (at £1.50 an hour) and Mr Major's half-baked idea that private enterprise will fill the gap (at a price most parents, unaided, can't afford). Feminism set the hare running, but this government, so far, has it neatly trapped. The privatising drive goes further still.

Now, instead of consciousness raising and women's groups we have therapists, co-counselling and the chance, if you're really fortunate, to disembowel yourself emotionally as part of a mass audience on the 'Oprah Winfrey Show' or 'Donaghue' or 'Kilroy Silk'; what used to be done before half a dozen now demands an audience of millions.

Forget fighting for an improvement in whatever situation you happen to find yourself in; your only reward is to relive your five minutes of anguish/revelation/disillusionment courtesy of the rewind button on the video machine. 'We're gonna try to find the love in this situation,' Oprah tells her guests. In the sixties, it used to be solutions we tried to find . . . Voyeurism has become the opiate of the (female) masses.

Magazines have played a similar game. Feminism, the argument goes, has been absorbed into the mainstream, a trend seen most clearly in the field of women's periodicals. *Woman, Woman's Own*, monthlies – among them *Marie Claire*,

Cosmopolitan, *Elle* and *Options* – have tackled issues such as low pay, rape and pornography, but as Janice Winship points out in *Inside Women's Magazines*, a book based on her research conducted at the Centre for Contemporary Cultural Studies at the University of Birmingham, these issues are tackled in a very particular way – not least because they lack the political context in which they were originally raised in the women's movement. She gives as an example an article on rape in *Woman's Own* in 1983, but not untypical of what is published today:

> It offers sound advice on self-defence and the necessary and demeaning practicalities to adopt having been raped. But masquerading as 'a solution' the advice proffers only individual survival strategies . . .
>
> What relation rape bears to more common forms of masculine aggression, contemplating the social conditions under which rape might be eradicated, are simply not raised.

In this way, she charges, some magazines have 'the . . . liberal hallmark of seeming to stand for individual "freedom" while unknowingly blocking its realisation'. They offer 'a pragmatic approach [which] seems to offer answers but contains and blocks . . . potentially controversial argument'. Her analysis was published in 1987 – has the situation grown any better since? Feminism remains the F-word and the attention is even more firmly fixed on individual rather than collective solutions.

Take the June 1992 issue of *Cosmopolitan* – no worse and sometimes better than the rest: 'Disillusioned? Don't blame your career'; 'Round up: a woman can't win'; 'Are you equal to supporting him?'; 'Be honest! You're jealous – the dilemma of coveting a friend's success'; and the one political story, 'Who cares about women in sport?'.

Personal salvation is best sought through sexual technique, synergy (New Age, a highly reactionary philosophy of help yourself and sod the rest, grows in popularity) and self-advancement. Every magazine now seems to have its own sealed section with coy references to problems the reader might have 'down there'; while every other full-page photograph appears to be a cocks' gallery of rogues – or even the other way round. Women complain when their bodies are objectified, but it seems the right doesn't extend to men.

In addition, each magazine has adapted the *Hello* approach, peering into the lives of others without making any links to the society in which these people live. 'Every society has a keyhole to which its eye is pasted,' said the writer Mary McCarthy. Our particular keyhole appears to belong to the boudoir of Rod Stewart and a thousand lesser-known deposed Baltic heads of state.

The mix fits precisely the definition of post-feminism provided by writers Susan Ardill and Sue O'Sullivan: 'an appropriation of the cultural space feminism opened up – minus the politics'.[1] It may go some of the way to explain why in *Cosmopolitan*'s twentieth birthday issue, in March 1992, a self-selecting pool of over 3,000 of its readers, 71 per cent under thirty, 'the majority . . . ambitious', 25 per cent with professional qualifications, felt overwhelmingly that equality has not been achieved (84 per cent), but 39 per cent said they would not call themselves feminists. (Two months earlier, in a demonstration of polls apart, an *Elle/Guardian* poll, presumably drawing on a very similar pool of women, had 59 per cent of women saying 'Feminism has nearly achieved its goal' and 57 per cent saying feminism is a good thing; 56 per cent of men agreed.)[2]

'The 60 per cent of you who don't wish to call yourself feminists', says the anonymous writer of the *Cosmopolitan* career survey, somewhat guilelessly, 'obviously don't see the link between feminism and equality.' Now that couldn't possibly have anything to do with what women see, hear and read – could it now?

This search for individual solutions holds inherent weaknesses. It offers women no sense of the power they wield if they stand together – solidarity, to use a jargon word; it offers no reassurance that what they experience is experienced by others. And it offers no clue to the fact that the problem itself may lie with society, not with them.

Apart from the women's movement's easy seduction by capitalism (and even at this late stage, it can still learn to say 'No'), there are other difficulties it needs to tackle. I would argue, for instance, that the rhetoric it has become accustomed to using around the issue of rape is no longer productive, and detracts from the real gains feminism has made in the treatment of this crime.

'All men are rapists,' writes Marilyn French. 'They rape us with their eyes, their laws and their codes.' Such a statement, while it clearly once held enormous power as propaganda, now, I believe, has a negative and counterproductive effect (as does the modified 'All men are potential rapists').

First, it hinders the flow of knowledge which can lead to the greater protection of women. If all men are (potential) rapists and masculine conditioning is the sole cause, the subtleties, the checks and balances which lead to different types of rape and the different types of 'ordinary' men who may commit the crime are rendered insignificant. Equally importantly, it ignores the reasons why men from apparently similar backgrounds to those of offenders do *not* commit the crime.

In 1981, research by N. Malamuth in which he integrated a series of studies carried out on North American students revealed that while a third say they would rape if they could get away with it, two-thirds said they would not rape even if they could be sure they would not be found out. (The men who said they would rape – just like convicted rapists – showed greater aggression towards women, more acceptance of rape myths – 'She asked for it' and so on – and a 'relatively high sexual arousal to rape depictions'.)

In 1990, 3,391 rapes against women were reported nationally. This may represent only 10 per cent of the actual total, according to Home Office research.[3] A new concern too is the rise in reported cases of male rape. In 1982 there were 516 cases; by 1990, again according to home office figures, the figure was 1,120. Neil Lyndon tries to argue that rape occurs rarely. Certainly, the fear of it, which appears to affect so many women and now perhaps men too – a fear which is fed almost daily by the press – may be out of proportion to the threat. But since, in rape, it is the unpredictability which makes women – and now men – feel vulnerable, that is hardly consolation. It also poses the issue of what do you term 'serious'?

In 1991, in South Africa, 22,000 rapes were reported. According to the National Institute for Crime and Rehabilitation of Offenders, which conducted a survey, 95 per cent of rapes are unreported. John Carlin, writing in *The Independent*,[4] said that if unreported rapes were included it would bring the figure to 1,205 rapes a day. Would Neil Lyndon consider that South Africans faced a serious problem of rape?

In Britain, in 1990, only just over a third of the reported cases of rape against women went to court. (A detailed research study of male rape has yet to be conducted.) Out of those 1,293 prosecutions, only 455 men were convicted – the average sentence: six years.

Sentencing reveals the difficulties in handling the only crime to involve the issue of consent – and a crime into which society's prejudices are so thoroughly threaded. Now, no ambitious judge considers behaving as Judge Bertrand Richards did in 1982, at Ipswich Crown Court, when he fined a rapist £2,000 and referred to 'contributory negligence' on the part of the woman because she had been hitchhiking. This change and the increase in the length of sentencing is, I believe, a tribute to the many feminists who have acted in court, lobbied, provided research and worked in rape crisis centres. Still, the uneven patterns of reporting, prosecution and conviction beg many questions.

Stranger rapes, for instance, receive a larger proportion of sentences of over five years than non-stranger. 'Even when consideration is confined to cases in which the attack is very serious and the victim badly injured . . .' says *Changes in Rape Offences and Sentencing*, a Home Office research study paper published in 1989. Bizarrely, rapists who commit the offence with others – a gang bang, as it's called – receive a lighter punishment than a single rapist.The report suggests that this may be because the latter has used violence. (This however, overlooks the fact that the trauma to the victim does not operate on a sliding scale.) The Home Office report also indicates that between 1973 and 1985, rapes on women became 'nastier'; there was an increase in the threat of violence and humiliation; a rise in sexual practices apart from vaginal rape, such as anal intercourse and oral sex; and an increase in the length of time a victim was held.

Pursuing further answers to the information thrown up by such research is vital – not just because it exposes police practice and the attitudes of the courts, but also because it fuels the debate over what to do about the different types of rape. Is there an argument, for instance, for keeping serial rapists in prison for life – not as punishment, but simply to keep them out of circulation so that women are safe? Are treatment programmes effective for first offenders – and how can we tell?

It also helps to maintain the pressure for a change in the judiciary. At present, an elite band drawn from the all-male, public-school, Oxbridge circuit sits in judgement, and it still often treats rape less in terms of the guilt of the accused and more with an eye to the respectability (or otherwise) of the accuser. (A female, not a male, judge, for instance, produced the report which led to legal changes in the questioning of rape victims about their sex lives.)

In 1973, I visited one of the first rape crisis centres in New York. It was still possible then to open up a copy of *Playboy* and read the standard rape 'joke'. 'Well, your honour,' says the woman in the witness box, with a look of bliss on her face.

'He raped me in the spring and then it was just rape, rape rape, all summer long . . .' 'Nastier' rape was already common in the States – with penetration by bottles and the use of knives not uncommon.

Since then, feminists have successfully campaigned with others (such as Ian Blair, an officer with the Metropolitan Police, whose study on rape in the 1980s helped to change some police practice) to introduce, for instance, the more humane treatment of the alleged rape victim, with the use of female police doctors and special suites for questioning and examination; a recognition of rape trauma syndrome; an awareness that the absence of physical abuse does not automatically mean that the woman consented; and an acknowledgement both of the seriousness of marital rape and of the likelihood that a rapist is likely to be known to the victim. Feminists have also challenged the view – once much favoured by some judges – that man is in the hands of a terrible beast, his lust, which, when tempted, rears up out of control.

In 1991, the trials of William Kennedy Smith and Michael Tyson threw open once again the question of date rape. A woman, it is said, says 'No' when she means 'Yes'. (You would imagine that the way her body responded might also tell a man whether she meant yes or no.) In the tabloids, typically, the issue, instead of being treated seriously, was used as a weapon against feminism.

In the *Daily Express*[5] Rosemary Carpenter quoted an anonymous 'woman who has written on feminism' who says, 'It has now got to the point where if a woman finds she doesn't like something, she says, "I've been raped" . . . It's a new tyranny . . .' Rosemary Carpenter then goes on to quote Ken Minogue, Professor of Political Science at the London School of Economics (although what political science has to do with date rape mystifies me). He, apparently, 'agrees that feminists are to blame for the current maelstrom. The significance of this [the Kennedy Smith] case shows the feminists' attempts to tie men up like Gulliver was tied up by the Lilliputians.' Rosemary

Carpenter might have done better to read the Home Office report *Concerns About Rape* before reporting such tosh. The report quotes unpublished work (presented at a conference in 1979) which examines how adolescents construct their sexual worlds:

> Half the male students thought it acceptable to force a
> woman to have sex under certain circumstances. These
> included: if the man had spent a lot of money on the
> woman; if he knew she had intercourse with other men; if
> they had been dating a long time; if the woman had
> changed her mind about sex or 'led him on'; and if the man
> was so 'turned on' that he couldn't stop.

One of the difficulties about rape is that underreporting leads to a distorted picture of the rapist. The majority of those who are convicted are poor, young and black. The Home Office report quotes one piece of research (published in 1979) in which S. C. Smithyman in California advertised for men who had committed rape (defined as non-consenting penetration of vagina, anus or mouth) to volunteer for a confidential telephone interview. (The report does not mention how he checked their authenticity.) The men who responded were different from convicted rapists. 'They were mostly white and had completed high school and/or obtained college or university degrees. Very few (12%) were unemployed, over two-fifths were white collar workers! Smithyman's study was small scale,' the Home Office report points out:

> Nevertheless, it is important in that it highlights that men
> who admit rape may be more evenly distributed through
> the male population than previously imagined. If this is
> true, then the role of the masculine culture, socialisation,
> attitudes towards women and the differences between
> men's and women's expectations of behaviour and, in

particular, of sexual behaviour should be considered if a fuller understanding is to be gained of why rape occurs.

A second argument against the use of the term 'All men are rapists' is that it causes offence. It offends the sensitivity of those men whom feminism needs, if the ambivalence that still exists in society towards the raped and the raper is to continue to be challenged. 'A little bit of rape is good for a man's soul,' Norman Mailer wrote in 1972 without too much comment from the literary Establishment. That ambivalence is still heard today, for example, in some of the 'slack' (sexist) lyrics of ragga, which originates in the clubs of Jamaica and is sung by artists such as Shabba Ranks:

> The girls dem want the jammer,
> Hard and warm
> Jammer; dem bawl out for it
> Jammer, a sit down pon it,
> Me a go kill her with it,
> Rammer fe the gal full of quality,
> So the gal bawl out 'pon it.
> (from 'Rammer Jammer' by Daddy Woods)

Third, 'All men are rapists' is the beginning and end of any discussion on sexual violence. 'Men were very definitely and stridently told to shut the fuck up and not to speak for themselves,' says Neil Lyndon, referring to the whole range of issues in sexual politics, including rape. 'Feminists said very categorically, this is our business.' As a result, men, when they do discover how pervasive the threat of sexual violence is in many women's lives, frequently express surprise. (By 'sexual violence' I mean a threatening act which uses sex as a form of power; it may include flashers, frottage, obscene phone calls – fifteen million were made in 1991 – and Peeping Toms, as well as rape and indecent assault.)

Fourth, 'All men are rapists' reinforces the concept that the only role for women is that of permanent prey: the victim never in control of her own destiny. Survey after survey indicates how women often operate a self-imposed curfew at night and live in fear of attack. In 1991, for instance, a *Today* – TV-am survey said that seven in ten women expected to be attacked within a year; 34 per cent said it affected the way they lived and 32 per cent said it meant that they did not go out as often.[6]

The campaigning on the issue of rape clearly needs to continue. We need more research (very little has been conducted in Britain for almost a decade), we need more information about how widespread or otherwise, rape is, why some cases are not prosecuted and why some men are acquitted on a technicality. We need to know too how many false charges of rape are made and why. We need to monitor courts, judges and police. We need a much clearer statement from society that rape (now penetration without consent by a human being but which should include penetration by an object wielded by an assailant) is unacceptable in any circumstances.

We need to accept that the solution isn't 'women only' areas in society (how does that apply to your own home?) but a continuing radical examination of a society which spawns such violence. A society which designs public transport, shopping complexes, housing estates and car parks which make women (and men) even more vulnerable. (Involving women in planning and design might be a start.)

Now that more men are speaking out about the experience of being raped, affirming that it is about power and subordination as much as it is about sex, using terms familiar to many women, 'I feel unclean', 'I must have asked for it', 'I feel invaded', perhaps such change will be accelerated. Certainly, in the 1990s, we need to deal with rape using a language which clarifies rather than clouds the little knowledge that we already have.

Pornography too, I believe, has held the spotlight for too long in the women's movement. Revolutionary or radical feminists argue that this is how it must be, since in what Mary Daly calls 'a cockocratic sado-state' pornography encapsulates the power men hold over women. It also allegedly provides a continuous trigger for sexual violence, the 'domino theory of sexuality'. 'Pornography is the theory and rape the practice,' Robin Morgan once wrote.

'Women are defined, valued, judged in one way only: as women – that is with sex organs that must be used,' insists Andrea Dworkin, the evangeliser-in-chief of the anti-porn movement, who writes with the force of a power drill. For her, 'violence' begins with what others might call making love.

'I think feminism fundamentally identifies sexuality as the primary social sphere of male power,' said Catharine MacKinnon in the early 1980s. She is the lawyer who, along with Andrea Dworkin, has fought hard to change the law and bring in censorship on pornography.

The debate about whether there are links between pornography and sexual violence is still inconclusive,[7] but critics like Lynne Segal point out that that wing of feminism which advocates it most strongly, gained ground in the late 1970s, just as a pessimism about challenging men's power directly took hold in the women's movement. In contrast, in the early 1970s, Lynne Segal says, male sexual violence was not 'identified as the central problem'.[8] Women 'were, for the first time in their lives, meeting together in small groups . . . talking about sex and relationships, organising for nurseries, playgrounds, better jobs and training, and demanding more control over their own fertility.'

It was only as the women's movement developed that hitherto taboo issues began to be discussed and sexual violence took over as a main motif. Lynne Segal, Carol Vance and Ann Snitow are among those feminists (clearly not known to Neil Lyndon, although well known to others and as 'authentic' a voice of feminism as Rosalind Miles, whom Neil Lyndon quotes copiously) who rejected the reductionism about men –

all men – that followed, 'which takes ideology to be lived behaviour'.

'Male sexuality is almost certainly not any single shared experience for men,' Lynne Segal argues in *Slow Motion: Changing Masculinities, Changing Men*.

> It is not any single or simple thing at all – but the site of
> any number of emotions of weakness and strength, pleasure
> and pain, anxiety, conflict, tension and struggle, none of
> them mapped in such a way as to make the obliteration of
> the agency of women in heterosexual engagements
> inevitable . . . Male sexuality cannot be reduced to the
> most popular meanings of sex acts, let alone to sex acts
> themselves. It becomes intelligible only if placed within
> actual histories of men's intimate relationships with others
> – or lack of them.

One of the prices paid as a result of turning the women's movement into a single crusade against pornography is that it has heavily discouraged its supporters from exploring their own desires, passions and erotic needs.

('Despite a lifetime of service to the cause of sexual liberation,' Germaine Greer told *The Times* in 1973, just as a reminder of feminism when it was a touch more zesty, 'I have never caught a venereal disease, which makes me feel like an Arctic explorer who has never had frostbite.') The result of this prohibition for some is that they once again feel the pull between how they 'ought' to behave and what happens in practice (for example, women having fantasies about being raped).

'What arouses us sexually, at least in fantasy, is not quite what we feel it should be, leaving us ashamed of our fantasies and afraid to be honest about them,' writes Lynne Segal. 'Better to reject sex completely or at least to blame men for what goes on inside our heads . . . better to project sex and its contradictions on to men.

'But once we can separate sex from guilt, and have the power to refuse others the right to exploit us,' she argues cogently, 'there is always the scope for the playful enjoyment of the links between sex and power. So much remains unsaid about women's sexual fears and longings that the last thing we need, as Ellen Willis comments, "is more sexual shame, guilt and hypocrisy – this time served up as feminism . . ."'[9]

The pornography question will probably intensify as the legal attempts to ban porn already seen in Canada and the States continue to meet with success, and the climate for feminism becomes tougher. One of the aims of this book is to try to raise the importance of swinging the debate back to the wider arena; while sexual violence remains an important issue, feminism also needs to be seen to be addressing more of its energy to concrete objectives again, such as childcare and a minimum wage; mobilising women once more 'around their visions rather than their fears'.[10]

A final criticism of the central obsession with sexual violence (which brings with it strange allies from the moral majority, such as William Rees Mogg) is that its philosophy removes all optimism for relationships between women and men. 'The promotion of progressive sexual politics between men and women, let alone the struggle for any more general egalitarian relations between them, enters the dustbin of feminist history, replaced by the cheerless certainty of men's rapacity,' writes Lynne Segal in *Is the Future Female*?

What feminism needs to restore is the distinction between men as individuals and the power they hold as a group. Conversely, while women as a group may be economically and politically discriminated against worldwide, as individuals, in certain circumstances, they may exercise power over the men in their lives very effectively indeed. Because feminism has denied that truth too often, it is mistrusted by both men and some women.

Feminism needs to deal with life as it is lived, not retreat into a set of aphorisms, however satisfyingly succinct, when the complexity of individual relationships does not quite match up to the theory. 'All men are bastards' may offer instant healing to a hurt done, but it does not change the situation, it only aggravates it.

Another hurdle for feminism is that it has what the advertising agencies call a problem of presentation. In the early days of the women's movement, in the two-year honeymoon period from 1968 when much of the press in Britain and the USA were taking the movement seriously, some of the women were reluctant to become 'media figures'. Some, too, were wary of how charitable a hand was being offered by the press.

In *The Sisterhood*, Marcia Cohen reports on one of the turning points in the media's attitude. On 14 December 1970, *Time* magazine published 'A Second Look' at Women's Lib. Instead of mentioning the gains of the previous year – for instance, on sex discrimination and equal pay – it presented 'an acidulous sampling of nearly every opposing diatribe'. It included a scathing attack on Kate Millett's *Sexual Politics*, and 'a grotesque and ludicrous drawing of a grim, balloon-breasted woman idiotically attired in leather sandals and a lacy infantile pinafore that rode a foot above her knees . . . she was waving aloft . . . a formidably capacious brassiere.' *Time* also announced that Kate Millett was bisexual. 'I had come out', she recalled later, 'in ninety-seven languages.'

'The disclosure', *Time* said, without a shred of evidence, 'is bound to discredit her as a spokeswoman for her cause, cast further doubt on her theories and reinforce the views of those skeptics who routinely dismiss all liberationists as lesbians.'

Kate Millett herself said that she believed that the rubbishing began because the movement was growing too powerful: 'The media is governed by fashion at the lowest level and big corporate money interests at the highest. The women's movement began as entertainment, but then it became serious. It began to make economic demands. Here was a minority group, a pressure group, and they were getting someplace . . .'

The same pattern of response is true today. If the press isn't

49

downright hostile (see Chapter Eight), it is snide. Susan Faludi is author of the bestseller *Backlash: The Undeclared War Against Women*. Published in Britain in 1992, the book charts the attempts, mainly in the States, to inhibit and undermine women's emancipation. In the USA, unlike Britain, these attempts are strongly orchestrated by the fundamentalist new right. The book is a work in the best traditions of journalistic endeavour; it makes powerful arguments with facts, not rhetoric (Susan Faludi is a Pulitzer Prize-winning newspaper reporter).

In May 1992, she talked in *Socialist Review* to Hazel Croft about the predominantly hostile reaction of the British press. 'Overhyped, overrated and over here,' said the *Independent*. 'America's feminist imperialism' was the headline on Richard Gott's article in the *Guardian*.

'The feeling I get is that a lot of journalists haven't read the book properly,' Susan Faludi is quoted as saying. 'Many articles proclaimed that I treat women as passive victims of the backlash – but I don't. In fact what I point out is how, under enormous pressure, women stood their ground . . . I feel angry at the misreadings and the implication that I'm some kind of conspiracy theorist.'

In part, the mainly antagonistic approach to feminism may be a reflection of how few newspapers have women at senior executive level and the fact that what feminism demands inevitably involves men, in the short term, shifting their butts on to far less comfortable seats. To a lesser degree, the approach is also because feminism itself has yet to lighten up and find itself a populist patch.

'Since the beginning of the days of the second wave, women have heard from other women that they are exploited and oppressed,' writes Gisela Kaplan in *Contemporary Western European Feminism*.

The constant reinforcement of these bleak tidings worked at the height of the movements because it helped to keep up the level of anger and create cohesion and a sense of purpose.

It also worked as long as consciousness raising groups, fun and positive cultural events gave a healthy counterweight to the stories of gloom . . . With the disappearance of the strong action-orientated energies of the movement, the sole remaining story of oppression looms large and ominously for the successors . . .

At present, if sexual politics is handled at all in the press, it is second-hand, courtesy of 'authoritative' market research and endless polls which create the impression that never have we known so much about each other when, arguably, never have we understood so little.

Say, for instance, a survey shows that 80 per cent of married men in East Anglia never clean the bath. In this survey, no one seeks to question how many households in East Anglia have a bath, how many men have been contacted – ten, a hundred, the entire male population? Or how the question was posed (a free plastic duck for all those who say yes? A loofah for those who say no?). Behind every survey, somebody, somewhere is selling something. Extrapolation then takes over from common sense. The anti-housework tendency in the modern East Anglian man (not just his aversion to bath-cleaning duties, a serious issue in feminist circles) is duly recorded, publicised, turned into a tabloid mini-series, discussed on 'Woman's Hour', incomprehensibly dissected visually on 'The Late Show' and duly added to the pile of percentages which is part of our alleged contemporary history recording the male lack of involvement in childcare/their own emotions/the lavatory bowl.

In travelling around the country as a journalist for twenty-four years; in the research I carried out eight years ago, conducting interviews with over fifty men in their mid thirties for a book, *Man Enough*; as well as in the three months I have had to prepare and write *Mad About Women*, I have spent time with families and couples, singles and individuals, at home, at work and at play. Without the prop of a single poll for guidance, it seems to me that what much of the press coverage – so reliant on polls – fails to register is that men and women *are* changing – some more, some less, depending upon age and income and peer pressure and politics and inclination and fear of losing the one relationship that matters.

Perhaps polls and market research need to be used with more cynicism and certainly more caution (a rule I have tried to apply in this book). They are, after all, often only a vanity, a device to infuse generalisation with false precision.

In the 1990s, feminism is plainly at a crossroads. Its messages have been hijacked, its radicalism has been muted, its energy has been channelled into cul-de-sacs, it is portrayed more often than not in the media in an entirely negative light, while many of its followers are weary from working inside and outside the home – at times without sufficient support from partner, employer or family. If this is the undertow which feminism must fight, does it have any tides running in its favour?

'What's been forgotten', says Robin Morgan, active in the women's movement for twenty-five years, 'is that we are all older. And not only do older women have more experience of life and refuse to put up with so much, we also grow more radical as we age. We have a cup of discontent which is nearly up to the brim, filled drop by drop over the years. Who's to say that the next drop isn't the one that causes it all to spill?'[11]

In the States in 1991, the Senate hearings to consider charges of sexual harassment made by Anita Hill against her former employer, Clarence Thomas, may yet prove to be a milestone in the history of the women's movement. The hearing unquestionably filled the cup very much closer to the brim.

Even before the Thomas hearings, the issue of abortion in the States, had once again contributed to what the writer Angela Carter once called 'a yeastiness in the air'. In *Backlash* Susan Faludi gives a concise and powerful account of the scope and span of American pro-life propaganda, including the Catholic bishops who hired the country's largest public-relations firm to orchestrate a $5 million dollar campaign, while New York bishop John Cardinal O'Connor sent a twelve-page statement to Roman Catholic politicians saying they risked excommunication if they supported a woman's right to an abortion.

In April 1992, in Washington, DC, over half a million people – the largest rally ever held – marched for reproductive rights. No matter that public opinion (even Republican public opinion) is overwhelmingly behind a woman's right to choose, Mr Bush paid his dues to the Right and changed his mind in the 1980s. 'Get George out of my Bush', read some of the marchers' posters, and 'Get your rosaries out of my ovaries'.

In the first several months of 1992 the battle became tougher as the country waited for the Supreme Court to decide whether and by how much it would amend the original (1973) Roe v. Wade judgement, which recognised a woman's constitutional right to an abortion (individual States have already passed their own laws, imposing severe limitations in some cases).

In June, the Supreme Court finally decided it would hack a gruesomely large chunk out of its 1973 ruling. It upheld a 1989 Pennsylvania law which, for example, imposes a twenty-four hour waiting period on a woman who seeks an abortion, requires parental consent for women under eighteen (which must lead to an upturn in business for the backstreet abortion-ist) and requires doctors to provide 'information' so that a woman understands what she is undertaking.

Reggie Nadelson, commenting on the implications in the *Independent* wrote:

And there is this: in some quarters, the idea is promoted that the foetus is a 'person'. If so, under the constitution some states could be required to treat abortion as harshly as murder. No justice in the Supreme Court has endorsed this idea yet but the newest member of the bench has expressed support for an article with this view. His name is Clarence Thomas.[12]

According to the fragile authority of the polls, women were mostly against Anita Hill, a law professor from the University of Oklahoma. Still, the hearings have become feminism's best recruitment officer in over a decade. Why? Because they appeared to tap into the anger of millions of ordinary women – women who have no interest in ideology, but who suddenly decided they had had enough. If the right button is pushed, it could happen in Britain too.

'Sexual harassment was never a major issue as long as it only threatened the careers of millions of women,' said one reader's letter, typical of many sent to magazines and local newspapers in the States, about the Clarence Thomas hearings. 'It only became a major issue when it threatened the career of one man. Click!'

What appears to have galvanised many women was not necessarily the charge, but the manner in which, before the eye of the television camera, male society revealed itself. (Anita Hill's allegations, for instance, were not even going to be considered by the Senate judiciary committee. Only because of a massive impromptu lobby by women across America was it forced to reconsider.) The affair reminded women that they are 'double outsiders. Outside the club and outsiders because of their gender,' Republican pollster Linda Divall is quoted as saying in *The New York Times*.[13]

The National Organisation of Women, which usually signs up 2,000 members a month, reports that in the eight weeks after the Clarence Thomas hearings it recruited 13,000 new members, and membership continues to rise. In Pennsylvania, Lynn H. Yeakel won the Democratic Senate nomination from Senator Arlen Specter, as Republican member of the judiciary committee. In her election commercials, she ran a clip of him grilling Anita Hill, then she asked the viewer: 'Did this make you as angry as it made me?' Evidently, it did.

In Illinois, in November 1992, Carol Mosely Braun may well become the first black woman Senator in American history. She decided to run for the Democratic nomination, she said, out of anger that Anita Hill had been ignored and Clarence Thomas confirmed.

'Women candidates are the face of the change for the 1990s. They're the classic outsiders trying to break into the Congressional system and make it work,' says Ellen Malcolm of Emily (Early Money Is Like Yeast, a Democratic fund-raising organisation).

'This is one of those awakenings,' Irene Natividad told *The New York Times*. 'It's like before and we feel powerful again . . .'[14] But crucially for feminism, in the States at least, there are healthy signs that it may not be quite like it was before. At 8.15 a.m. one Friday morning in 1992 in early summer, commuters in Grand Central Station heard drums begin to beat, and a group of women began to chant:

> Mother dear, we're sorry,
> You live in the USA
> Of all developed countries
> Only this one won't pay
> For pre-natal care, or day care
> Not to mention a living wage
> Child support is not enforced
> And we are in a rage![15]

It was the newly formed Women's Action Committee (WAC) paying a tribute to America's Mothers' Day. WAC began in New York in January, again spurred by the Hill–Thomas hearings. According to reporter Karen Houppert, it has 450 active members and 50 new recruits each week. (In the sixties smaller groups than this laid solid foundations for the women's movement literally almost overnight.) WAC began as a group concerned with sexual violence, but – significantly – almost immediately broadened out to deal with issues such as poverty and discrimination. WAC is not interested in consciousness raising, say its members; it advocates direct action. For example: a New York Supreme Court justice indicated that he was considering a lighter sentence for a man found guilty of sodomising a mentally disabled woman on the grounds that the woman had been sexually abused before; therefore this assault was not as violent as it would otherwise have been (an argument not unfamiliar in British courts).

WAC and WHAM! (Women's Health Action and Mobilization, also relatively new and radical) sent him instructive letters and demonstrated at the court. The judge, Nicholas Figueroa, sought advice on a suitable sentence from a panel of judges, and quoted positively from the letters in passing sentence. Intimidation, Neil Lyndon might say; progress, the women's movement would counter-charge. The defendant was given a sentence one year short of the maximum. The sentence may or may not be a triumph for feminism, but it does illustrate the advantages of tackling the system head-on rather than eternally talking about the problems it causes.

WAC is, as always, mainly middle-class and bases itself on the methods of ACT-UP, the gay direct-action group. Asked by Karen Houppert if WAC will have staying power, a member says: 'I wouldn't be surprised if it was here until the twenty-first century or if it blew up and was gone tomorrow. Things are that volatile right now.' No matter – WAC, and the issues it is raising, are getting positive and extensive coverage in the media – and that alone, for women, is a coup. And it has already been labelled as a genre: it is called 'Feminism in your face'.

The summer of 1992, too, saw the launch of The Third Wave – an idea first discussed in Europe in the 1980s and now, it seems, a reality: it is predominantly middle-class again, but black and white, male and female. And, unlike the second-wave sisters of the sixties who, for political reasons, shunned leaders and refused to play with the media, The Third Wave know better. They are the children of the Hard Sell.

The founders are Rebecca Walker, twenty-two, Yale graduate, daughter of the writer Alice Walker, goddaughter of Gloria Steinem; and Shannon Liss, twenty-three, a Harvard graduate. In their methods, they emulate the Civil Rights movement of the 1960s (as did the second wave). So August was spent on Freedom Summer 92; 250 Third Wavers toured twenty cities by bus, visiting communities to persuade young people to register to vote (75 million are unregistered). They also received large-scale media coverage.

Interviewed by Kate Muir in *The Times*,[16] both the two founder members said the trigger had been the Clarence Thomas hearings and the rape trials of William Kennedy Smith and Mike Tyson. 'Here we are, children of the MTV age, the Terminator 2 age, with this media blitz playing on our minds,' Shannon Liss is quoted as saying. 'We don't have control of it, we lead this passive existence and I just couldn't sit and watch.'

'There is a passionate intensity about these young feminists which makes them sound as if they are selling brand-new ideas rather than resuscitating the old,' Kate Muir wrote. 'Because they are straight from college, in their first jobs, or still students, they have an optimism their older sisters lack – they will raise $1million and gain mainstream corporate sponsorship because they expect no less.'

It is too early as yet to tell whether those young women who were reluctant to call themselves feminists will now be prepared to say 'I am The Third Wave' – or how radical they may become when they do. A new name begets a new image (and one so far unsullied with the ideological fights that were part of the second wave's necessary labour pains). This time too, unlike the 1960s, The Third Wave won't shun being cast as a 'hot' media property.

Can it happen here? I haven't a clue. But the lesson that *can* be drawn from the States is that once a pebble is thrown, the ripples go on and on. It would be ironic if it turns out that in Britain in the 1990s, it's Neil Lyndon who has cast that first stone.

CHAPTER THREE

My heart belongs to Daddy . . . ?

Thirty or so men sit in a side room of a West London pub and each, in turn, identifies himself by his name and a potted version of his case history. Occasionally the others, whose age, appearance, colour and class span the spectrum, break out in applause at some particular detail; occasionally, there is a sharp intake of breath.

John's case receives a sharp intake of breath.

He says he is an unmarried father of a four-year-old daughter. He lives in Spain, and for three years he has flown home once a month to spend the weekend with his daughter. He also pays £700 a month in maintenance to the mother. She now wants to reduce the number of visits and increase the maintenance. 'I'm fighting,' he says. The others clap.

Paul tells the group that he has been divorced for over a year. It was agreed that he should have unlimited access to his two-year-old daughter. 'Within a week, it was down to two hours. Now it's back up to three. I've lost faith and money in lawyers. I've maintained the marital home, now the DSS wants £500 a month in maintenance and I haven't got a prayer.'

Mike has a daughter aged seven. Access went well at first, he says, then arrangements began to be broken, so his daughter was made a ward of court. 'Now, I haven't seen her for two years and I'm not even sure where she is.'

Dick says he is due to take his eight-year-old to EuroDisney on Saturday; if she isn't delivered by his ex-wife, he will be back in court. Fighting for access over the past five years has cost him £20,000, spent as a result of fifteen court appearances. 'I have all the legal rights, but my daughter is being turned against me. I record her telephone conversations and what she says just isn't her speaking. My ex-wife', he adds laconically, 'is married to a divorce lawyer.'

Charles is the angriest person at the meeting, and an hour or so later he leaves abruptly (a rare occurrence) because someone has tried to persuade him that conciliation is better than the courts. 'I'm separated from my wife,' Charles says, 'and I don't know about you lot, but she's the most aggressive woman I've ever come across.' This is received with smiles. 'She explodes, she threatens me with violence, I can't get any sense out of her. But I *am* going to see my child.'

Rula – one of half a dozen women present – explains that she is at the meeting 'in support of Charles'. She is 'almost divorced' with a twelve-year-old son, and her former partner lives abroad. 'I believe very strongly that every child has a right to see both parents.' Another cheer. Some of the men, the anchor to their disjoined sons and daughters visible in the form of plastic carrier bags at their feet full of documents and files of references and bits of correspondence, nod their heads in agreement.

The mood of the group is upbeat, joshing, but the stories told are of disappointment and pain and frustration and at times, they say, feelings of undiluted murderous hatred (however temporary). Whatever the absent ex-partner's version of events, the apparent commitment of these men to maintain contact with their children, in spite of so many thwarted attempts, is undeniably moving.

Bruce, a veteran, tells the newcomers that it can work out. He and his ex-partner have been separated for four years and have a nine-year-old daughter. 'By staying away from solicitors, by using common sense and give and take, it's generally amicable, even if it took a bit to get there. And my daughter's as happy as a sandboy. Try every tactic you can and stave off going to the courts. In the courts,' he says later, 'fathers lose.'

Families Need Fathers was established in the 1970s and now has over two thousand members and forty-three contacts around the country. It offers support, outside and inside court, and information and guidance to men seeking to maintain contact with their children after separation or divorce. The fact that it exists at all is a measure of some movement in the traditional views that men are alleged to hold on fatherhood, the family and wives. The fact that FNF has to fight so hard for access – which, it is commonly agreed, is usually in the child's best interests – is an indicator of how unwilling the (male) judiciary and many women are to acknowledge that change.

Britain has the highest divorce rate in Europe:[1] one in three marriages are expected to end in divorce (the breakdown rates in cohabitation are not known); 40 per cent of second marriages also fail; 400 children a day face the trauma of their parents splitting up.[2] A third of fathers lose contact within two years, 50 per cent within ten years. A report by the Family Policies Studies Centre in 1991 said that 750,000 children never see their father after the break-up of the family.

David Cannon, secretary of FNF, is collator-in-chief of statistics. There is an appalling lack of information about basic questions such as precisely how many men challenge custody cases and how the courts respond; how many men who have had full-time care of the child lose to the mother; how many mothers who are full-time carers lose to the father; how many access orders fail to be properly implemented and, crucially, what proportion of all fathers who are separated and divorced actually desire regular access. In short, is FNF the exception, or the rule?

What David Cannon *does* know is that in 1990, the courts made 88,600 orders for custody – 63,700 gave sole custody to the mother, 6,500 to the father, and 18,400 established joint custody. Fathers, he says, are usually given sole custody only when the mother is deemed 'unfit' or it is her wish. He reckons that the majority of fathers don't contest because they are warned off by solicitors; of the 10 per cent who do, only one in ten succeed.

Access orders may be more freely given, but the courts appear reluctant to have them enforced. As a result, a father may lose not only time with his children, but eventually all contact. John Cameron is forty-nine and lives in Suffolk. He has three children, aged eleven, fifteen and eighteen. Eight years ago, when his wife said she wanted a divorce, he was a well-paid section head of a group of computer programmers. 'My first solicitor said, "You won't object to your wife having custody?" I said I didn't because I didn't know the implications and it seemed a reasonable arrangement.'

Now he has not seen his children for three years. He believes from what friends say, that they may be in the Yorkshire area. 'It's awful,' he says. 'At least, if they were dead, I could look back, have happy memories and come to terms with it. This way, for me and other fathers, it's never, ever, over.'

In the first five years of his divorce, John Cameron went to court five times to try to impose a proper routine to access. Often, there would be several months' delay before his case was heard when he didn't see the children at all, and received no information about them from his ex-wife. On the sixth appearance, the judge told him he was making life difficult for his former partner. 'Even when the court does decide in the father's favour not to have full custody of his children but just to see them on a regular basis, judges seem reluctant to impose the order,' John Cameron says.

He has now given up his job to fight court battles. He spends all his time on FNF business. 'A number of us feel that even if we've lost our families we have enough expertise now to help others who haven't.' He also has debts of £40,000 (again not uncommon) accrued from legal fees.

Research on the impact of divorce delivers a simple tale. If it is handled badly, the children suffer and continue to suffer into adult life. One piece of research indicates that children of divorced parents are twice as likely to leave school without qualifications, half as likely to go to university; they are more likely to marry in their teens and more prone to unemployment in their mid thirties.[3]

A divorce handled well means that the children remain in regular contact with the parent who is not in their permanent home, and mother and father do not continue to wage war or – better still – are supportive of each other. A decent standard of living is also vital. Society has one culprit for the fact that this does not often happen: the father. FNF disagrees. It blames feminism and individual women whom the divorce laws, it claims, have made greedy and conniving and who use children as tools. Next in line are solicitors (particularly feminist solicitors) who have, they say, a vested interest in conflict, and alongside is an anachronistic judiciary who almost always decide not simply that the mother is automatically the best main carer but that a father can conduct a relationship with a son or daughter often on the basis of two hours a fortnight.

If feminism *is* to 'blame', it is because it has encouraged women not to endure relationships which destroy their self-respect and corrode their identity. Many relationships end however because the *man* has found somebody else – often younger – leaving a partner, who has invested all in the home and children, bitter, angry, hurt, and broke.

A woman may then use the children to punish. This is not feminism at work, but tradition. It has its roots in a society in which the economic imbalance makes it almost inevitable that the majority of women are financially disadvantaged by divorce or separation. More money in her pocket may not dry a woman's tears more quickly, but it does reduce the extra stress and it may speed the arrival of a truce.

Out of the mess which passes for the way we often conduct our marital affairs, pre and post-separation, few facts emerge. What we do know is that in addition to many fathers losing contact with their children, many also fail to pay for their maintenance. According to the largest and most recent piece of research, *Lone Parent Families in the UK*, conducted by Jonathan Bradshaw and Jane Millar and published in 1991,[4] only 29 per cent of lone parents receive regular payments from the father. In 1980, the figure was 50 per cent.

The Bradshaw and Millar study indicates that almost three-quarters of all lone parents are on income support and only 40 per cent have any income from earnings. A study by Dobash and Wasoff (1986) involved an examination of all divorces in Scotland in 1980 and a follow-up of 103 cases three years later. In 1980, 75 per cent of fathers were ordered to pay child maintenance at an average of £10 a child (but in some cases, this fell to as little as £5). By 1983, 54 per cent of fathers had defaulted; one-third had never paid any money at all. The DHSS pursued only a quarter of the defaulters through the courts.

The history of who has paid a higher financial price as a result of divorce and separation in this country and the States demonstrates the power that myths have when they marry with male prejudice in moulding public policy. In the 1930s, if a woman chose to break her marriage vows and commit adultery, not only would she be left penniless – she would probably forfeit her children too. By 1958, there were still only 23,000 divorces – in the words of one divorcee at the time, quoted by Cate Haste in *Rules of Desire*, it was a step which was seen as 'a grave social misdemeanor, agonizing, suspect and against the moral grain'. Such a stigma saved some men a lot of money in alimony, but it also kept many couples in a permanent hell of bitterness, quarrels and icy martyrdom (and no research was conducted at the time to discover the negative effects on the millions of children who were reared in that kind of atmosphere).

In 1969, the Divorce Reform Act changed the grounds of divorce from finding fault to irretrievable breakdown – divorce was granted after two years with mutual consent and seven years without it. Divorce rose from 27,000 in 1961 to 80,000 in 1971.

Still, the myth of the massed existence of 'the alimony drone' has never decreased in popularity. 'When the little doll says she'll live on your income, she means it all right,' said the comedian Phil Silvers, also known as Sergeant Bilko, in 1957. 'But just be sure to get another one for yourself.' Certainly, individual cases, then and now, appear to be unfair, leaving men so financially crippled that they are allegedly reduced in middle age to living in bed-sits. Stories also abound of middle-class second families under so much pressure from the financial demands of the first wife that they crack. For some men, a woman's claim on their resources may seem eternal. In July 1991, for instance, Helen Twiname, aged seventy, won the right to take the husband whom she had divorced twenty-one years earlier back to court to increase his maintenance. Alec Twiname had become a millionaire several years after the marriage had broken up, and Lord Justice Glidewell decided that his obligation to his wife endured.

In practice, however, in the States, the drone was the exception rather than the rule. (Comparable figures seem not to exist in the UK.) Only 19 per cent of women divorced before 1970 were legally entitled to alimony for themselves (whether the husband actually paid it was another problem) and 13 per cent since 1980.[5] In Britain today, in the Bradshaw and Millar study, only 23 per cent of women receive maintenance for themselves; the average amount is between £10 and £16 a week (although the study appears not to cover the small proportion of divorcees who come from the better off middle class).

In the 1970s and 1980s, no matter that 'the drone' was in deep decline (if she had ever been in the ascendancy) on both sides of the Atlantic, middle-class men successfully lobbied hard to have the divorce laws changed. So, in this country, the 'clean break' provisions of the 1984 Divorce Act often forced ex-wives out to work or on to income support. Two-thirds of divorces anyway take place in the lower income groups, and the result since has not been the rise of a nation of affluent divorcees but a growing army of the poor.

FNF insists that its members *do* pay maintenance – where there is a return; contact with a child is the key. Ian Bell has two sons – one is twenty-four, the other is three. Each is from a different relationship. Ian Bell split up from his older son's mother when the boy was five. Father and son saw each other every weekend and each holiday. 'We have a really good relationship,' he says. 'He comes to court with me now.' Three years ago, Ian Bell split up from his second partner when she was three months pregnant. 'I called off the wedding, so of course she is angry, but how long does that have to go on?'

At first, she allowed him to see the child once every three weeks, then once every two weeks for two hours on a Saturday in her flat. 'She would be there radiating hostility and my son would pick up on that.' Now, he is going through the courts to increase access to every Sunday in his own home. 'My ex-partner wants me to pay £60 a week for the childminder. That's fine. I work hard, I have two jobs and a mortgage to pay, but in return, I expect to be able to conduct a proper relationship with my child. Wouldn't you?'

In the Bradshaw and Millar study, significantly, while a quarter of female lone parents wanted their child to have more contact with an absent parent, in 40 per cent of those cases where the lone parent thought the absent parent was seeing a child 'too often' the father was actually visiting the child less than once a month. So why *are* some women so resistant to children maintaining contact with their fathers? Is it just bloody-mindedness, putting their own desire for revenge before the needs of the child – or are the reasons more complex?

It begins with the most basic of all responses. 'He wasn't interested in them when we were together,' says Denise Matthews, thirty-nine, the mother of two girls aged ten and twelve. 'Why should he bloody well start now? I think it's because he wants to have a go at me.'

Carol Rhodes's ex-husband, Nelson, a market trader, is supposed to pay £45 a week maintenance for his three children, who are thirteen, seven and five. He is also supposed to take them out for one day a fortnight. 'Sometimes the money arrives, more often than not he's on the phone to ask if I can lend him a fiver,' Carol Rhodes, thirty-seven, a part-time counsellor, says. 'I've also got to the point when I don't tell the children if he's promised to take them out. On too many occasions, half an hour or sometimes two hours after he's due to arrive, he phones to say the cat's sick or he's got a flat tyre or whatever. And I'm left to cope with the children's disappointment. It's not fair on them or me.'

Some women also have genuine fears to do with their own safety (if the ex-partner was violent) and/or the physical and sexual abuse of their children while they are in the care of their fathers. In the USA, there is mainly anecdotal but growing evidence that if a woman makes an allegation of sexual abuse, it will almost guarantee that the judge grants custody to the father. Sanctuary is one of a number of 'underground railroads' operated by men and women, set up in the 1980s. It provides women and their children with a passage across the States via a chain of safe houses to avoid obeying a court order to hand the child over to an ex-partner.

The best-known case of defiance of a court order is that of Dr Elizabeth Morgan, a plastic surgeon, who believed that her daughter Hilary had been sexually abused by her father. Thirteen out of sixteen experts who testified in the case in 1987 said that they had found evidence of abuse. The teenage daughter of a previous marriage also said she had been abused by the father – but still Judge Herbert Dixon ordered that Hilary should be given to her father for a fortnight's visit. Instead, the mother hid the child and was sent to jail, where she stayed for two years for refusing to disclose her whereabouts. Finally, Congress passed a Bill which forced the judge to free her or put her on trial. Elizabeth Morgan was freed and in December 1990, after yet another court battle with the father, a New Zealand judge awarded her custody.

Sexual abuse is almost impossible to prove in court – physical evidence isn't always available; a child may be too young to speak out; or she or he may disclose and retract. A false charge could mean that a man loses his daughter or son for life; a true charge which is dismissed can equally mean that a son or daughter loses the chance of a happy childhood and, in addition, blames the mother because she failed to protect. (Even where there is no abuse, both men and women have told harrowing tales of having to force reluctant children to visit or return to a parent because the court says so. The voice of the child still too often remains unheard.)

In Britain, we have no research to indicate how many charges of sexual abuse are made in custody or access cases, and which are taken seriously or proved false. At a conference held in Tayside early in 1992 to examine the issue of whether lone mothers and their children are more at risk of sexual abuse, it emerged that a number of lone parents said that when they made allegations against their ex-partners, they were simply not believed or the charges were dismissed as made out of malice to 'get back' at the man.

'This belief', writes Sarah Nelson in *Social Work Today*,[6]

has become unchallenged truth in much research literature . . . A high percentage of separated mothers' abuse claims is found to be 'false' with little or no proof offered, and with no exploration of an obvious possibility – that many complaints are dismissed without proper investigation just because professionals assume they are unfounded.

Another factor is that mothers often feel that while they perform the run-of-the-mill tasks, the father takes on the role of the deliverer of fun at weekends. Add to that a basic desire to wound because of hurt caused during the marriage, and the mother uses the one weapon she has: the children.

'We have to devise a way in which we can get away from the idea of the mother as the permanent harasser of the kids and the dad as Santa Claus,' says Kate Gardner of the National Family Conciliation Council. But that, of course, requires the removal of the fundamental inequalities which hamper women's earning power. More important still is the fear that while the massive social changes of the last twenty years have made women more independent, they have also made some poorer and less protected. What should have happened – flexible jobs offering decent wages and affordable childcare – has failed to materialise. At the same time, women see ex-partners, many of whom do have the advantage of a reasonable income, waking up to the more emotional side of parenting. So a woman's fear is inevitably aroused: she is being asked to risk the bond she has with her children for no very clear reward.

What this analysis fails to include is the needs of the child. If feminism is about social justice, then it must also argue for the rights of a son or daughter who has not one parent but two. Sons or daughters often don't care a jot how much or how little their father was involved in their care or whether he is a new man or, as far as their mother is concerned, a boring old fart. What many children seek is the right to negotiate their own relationship within the context of regular and routine access with each parent, free from the contamination caused by derogatory comments or emotional manipulation. I know from my own experience – both with my own daughter and with the son of my previous partner – that even with everyone working as one, offering love, support, regular access and as much understanding as possible – often when the adults themselves are more than bruised – separation and divorce are very, very tough on a child. To be asked at the same time to cut off entirely from a relationship with a father – which, even if it is flawed, will often be a central part of a boy or girl's life

– seems doubly cruel. Indeed, one bonus of separation is that often the father, who may not have been the main carer, is forced to take on domestic duties for however short or long a period access lasts – and the relationship can grow stronger. It is not much of a compensation to the child who has – as she or he sees it – lost a family, but it is a start.

Recently an issue of *Stepladder*, the magazine published by the National Stepfamily Association, illustrated the confusion and sadness that some children feel about the way family affairs are conducted at present. Too often, in divorce and separation, a child's emotions are not considered by either party; nothing is explained, but he or she is expected to shoulder the mystery of the anger of each parent towards the other. It is a barren land for a child to occupy, alone and unaided.

'There are two families and they fight over dad,' wrote one child. 'They have arguments and they have contests . . . We have competitions, like pool competitions, or throwing competitions. Our dad goes to the family who wins. He stays with that family for eternity. They've won. We can't get him back.'

Another child wrote: 'My mum got divorced to my real dad because he kept spending money down the pub and he says he will have me at the weekend but then he can't because he's ill or there's no spare beds. And my step dad gives me more than my real dad.' And again: 'My daddy's got a girlfriend and he lives with her. I go to see him once every fortnight. When I go there I play outside. I like all of it at dad's. My little sister doesn't always like going to our dad's. She cries for mum and my little brother cries for dad.'[7]

The system in Britain, when it comes to dealing with the needs of children, seems at best inconsistent – at worst, less mindful of the child's interests and more committed to maintaining the traditional status quo: the mother as full-time carer, the father as the man who provides the resources for it to happen. (The courts' traditional view of women carries a price. It adversely affects, for instance, lesbian mothers.)

First, the inconsistency. According to the 1990 court statistics released by the Lord Chancellor's department, in Neath, for instance, 83.9 per cent of applications for joint custody were granted, 50 per cent in Merthyr Tydfil, but only 2.4 in Salford, 3.8 per cent in Consett and 1.3 per cent in Gateshead. Likewise, in refusing fathers access, courts in Accrington, Bodmin, Weymouth and Kendal, issued no refusals at all. In contrast, the Family Division Court in London refused almost one in five (19.1 per cent). It seems daft that considering the constantly changing criteria by which society decides what makes a 'good' father, geography appears to play such a large part.

'What people don't seem to realise', says David Cannon, 'is that for twenty years, men have been encouraged to be at their child's birth and that's where the bonding begins. But then, they're forgotten. Survey after survey shows that men, but for the pressure from work, want to spend more time with their children, and yet that right is still denied.'

Second, the traditional status quo. In December 1990, Mr Justice Ewbank in the High Court said that magistrates in north London were wrong to hold that it was in the best interests of a two-year-old child born outside wedlock to get to know her father as well as she knew her mother.[8] 'It is not normally regarded as being in the child's interests to know the non-custodial parent as well as she knows the custodial parent,' he said, drawing from who knows what expertise.

Bruce Lidington, a council member of FNF, put his view in a letter to *The Times* (FNF members are inveterate contributors to the readers' letters pages): 'The judge's ruling does much to explain why, under our present system of divorce law, our courts so effectively manage to convert the much loved children of divided marriages into the problems of "single parent" children of broken homes.'[9]

What many of the judiciary appear to have is a Victorian idea of family life in which children are accustomed to only brief formal encounters with Father. Society today expects more. So, if a man accepts a minor role in his child's life, he is condemned, yet if he seeks to extend his influence using the courts, many judges appear to find this behaviour highly suspicious.

Hugh Mills is forty-six; he is a primary-school teacher in London. He has been divorced for nine years and has two daughters: Zoe, thirteen and Claire, twelve. He lives a mile away from his family, and for the first four years he saw them almost every day. 'We were walking down the street one afternoon, the children were playing and running ahead and I was holding my ex-wife's hand,' he explains. 'I said, "Anyone looking at us now wouldn't think we were divorced." That was it; it was like a watershed. I think she suddenly felt that I was having my cake and eating it too.

'I had a girlfriend. I was still seeing my ex-wife and I had the children. She'd always promised from when we first had the children that she'd never stop me seeing them, but she twisted away from that. She told me then, "You're going to see them when I say you can see them." And that was that.'

In court, the judge decided that Hugh Mills's two daughters should visit him for a weekend once a fortnight. He also now pays £150 a month in maintenance. In spite of living so close, the children are forbidden by their mother who is also a full time teacher to call in or to telephone. If they find that they have forgotten something during their weekend with their father, they are not allowed to go to their mother's home to pick it up.

A few months ago, Hugh Mills applied to the courts to have access increased to a Wednesday night as well; for the girls to be able to phone him freely; and to be able to receive information from their school. In the Family Proceedings Court, he represented himself and asked if the children could be called to give their opinion. The judge refused. The court welfare officer and Hugh Mills's ex-wife both acknowledged that Zoe and Claire had a very strong desire see their father more regularly, but the judge accepted the mother's view that this would be 'unsettling'.

Hugh Mills says: 'The mother said the girls could phone whenever they want, but Zoe and Claire tell me they ask and their mother says, "Do your homework first", and then, "It's too late now, it's time for bed", and so it goes on.'

The judge told Hugh Mills that his interest in his daughters was 'obsessional' and if he made a further application to the court, he would pay the costs (£4,000) for the present hearing and the costs incurred from any new hearing. Hugh Mills now has no choice but to accept family life as an unsympathetic judge has chosen to ration it.

'On a Monday, every fortnight, after the girls leave, I see their breakfast things in the sink and their odd bits of clothes lying around and I feel bereft. It's like the *Mary Celeste*. I feel they should have freedom to come and go as they wish. I feel that my ex-wife has stolen my daughters' childhood, and my enjoyment of it. Sometimes, when they're not here, I do wonder: "Have they any commitment to me?" And it shouldn't be like that.'

Most members of FNF, he says, at some point in the fight contemplate three possibilities: murder of their ex-spouse, walking away altogether, and abducting their child. Despite the tone of his conversation, Hugh Mills appears to be an amiable, easy-going man. What makes the court decision especially hard for him, he says, is that right from the birth of his children, he was always the involved father.

'My ex-wife used to like it because friends would say how good I was with the kids. I've learned – all that means is that you pay a higher penalty. I've always been child-orientated. I'd play with the kids. I'd put them to bed, take them out at weekends, take them swimming and cycling. My ex-wife would often go off on holiday with a girlfriend. She went to Canada one Christmas and to Hong Kong for three weeks. I had the girls and didn't mind at all. If they woke up at night, it was me they cried for . . . I think I was much easier than their mother. I gave them more physical affection. If they cried, she found that immensely distressing and would get uptight. She was proud of them and loved them, but she was happy that I got on with the basics.

'It was difficult because I realise now, she had a lot of anger inside her. I felt she bullied me; sometimes she'd fight me all night and in that respect, she's changed a lot now. For instance, on a Saturday morning, we'd both be exhausted after a week of school, so I'd get up and take the girls to the park to let her have a lie-in. When I got back, she'd attack me and tell me she had so much to do, why hadn't I got her up? If I did wake her, she'd say I was inconsiderate and didn't I realise how tired she was? I spent a lot of the time, towards the end, living inside my head, and eventually I found somebody else. My ex-wife felt rejected because she felt she was more attractive and brighter and she was right, but this woman was kind to me and it was peaceful and we worked well together.'

Four years after the divorce, Hugh Mills's ex-wife began a relationship with a teacher twelve years her junior. 'I was jealous. I didn't like the idea of this man playing happy fathers with my children when he hadn't put in the mileage of basic caring. I admit I behaved badly. I threatened him and he left London. It was wrong but I was angry.'

Hugh Mills's ex-wife called in the police, who decided not to press charges. The crisis was resolved, and it was decided that Hugh Mills should move into his ex-wife's house to care for Zoe and Claire while she went travelling for a year with her boyfriend. That fell through and since that afternoon walk, fatherhood has been limited.

For the past five years, Hugh Mills has been active in FNF. 'At first when you hear how welfare officers and judges and solicitors talk to you, you think you must be a crank to care so much for your kids. You begin to doubt yourself. You begin to think that perhaps children's rights don't include a right to see a father. You're also a difficult proposition for any other woman who takes you on because this is so central to your life and everything revolves around the children's visits or the next court battle.

'Coming to FNF, it was a relief to discover that you're the same as everybody else. We're also realistic. A lot of fathers haven't valued their kids, they haven't paid attention to their wives. They think that when the woman goes to the solicitor that's the beginning of her disillusionment, but often it's been germinating for a year or more – and it's too late. The woman's never really sat down and told the man to pull up his socks and the next thing, she's off.

'More and more women are developing their own careers. They don't all want to be full-time mothers. It makes sense to have flexible parenting and to move away from traditional attitudes, but it doesn't seem to be happening. Lord Mackay [the Lord Chancellor] has said that judges will be trained to have a different focus and this will bring in "a new dawn", but an awful lot of us think it's still the same old dark nightmare.'

A decade or so ago, the government decided that the system of family courts, which takes the adversarial element out of divorce, would be too expensive to implement. Instead, now, under the 1989 Children Act, forty-seven specialist court judges (who are to be trained, although this is voluntary rather than compulsory) have been appointed to take primary responsibility for hearing childcare cases at a network of fifty county court 'care centres'. The adversarial element remains, but the voice of the child is now, in theory, taken into account.

In theory, the Children Act should bring many other improvements too. The philosophy is that the state should interfere as little as possible. The court will make an order concerning a child only if it believes this will be better for him or her (a fairly open-ended idea), otherwise parents will be expected to work out their own arrangements.

What is recognised in law now is that not only children but grandparents also have rights. 'Winning' and 'losing' within the family concepts which are no longer supposed to apply. If the court is involved, 'contact' and 'residence' orders, which indicate where the child will live and whom he or she will see (including grandparents), will be decided. A child can apply for contact and residence orders, as can a grandparent to see a grandchild, even when parents are living together. The Children Act may well force on judges an idea they have so far appeared reluctant to embrace: joint parenting arrangements in which, for instance, a child spends part of the week with each parent.

The Act, if properly resourced, may mean good news for children – if not for all fathers. In July 1992, a nine-year-old girl established a precedent in the British courts. She and her mother had lived in France until the previous November, when the mother defied a French separation agreement and returned to England. The High Court and the Court of Appeal in London decided to listen to the girl, who said she didn't want to live in France. The judge, Mr Justice Ewbank, said that the girl had put forward 'a mature and rational view which seemed to be based on genuine and cogent reasons'. The decision broke with the Child Abduction Act and the Hague Convention on the grounds that this case was 'exceptional'.

It left her father very angry indeed with his ex-partner, a forty-eight-year-old former secretary, and with the courts. 'If this case is exceptional,' said the father's solicitor, David Sterrett, 'every case is going to be exceptional . . . The implications of the decision are frightening . . .'[10]

Some FNF members report an improvement in the attitude of the courts since the Children Act; many more say that women, still cast in the traditional role by judges, continue to gain the advantage. In Gloucestershire, for instance, FNF member John Hanson quotes the recent case of a man he is visiting in hospital who had attempted suicide. He had asked the court to increase access visits to his four-year-old daughter. The mother had opposed the application under the Children Act. The judge had decided that although the man was a 'good' parent and had 'excellent relations' with his daughter, it would be in her long-term interests if all contact should cease. 'He will appeal,' John Hanson says, 'but he hasn't got a chance. People ask how a man can kidnap a child and flee abroad. It should be obvious, it's desperation.'

Blaze Vesolowski has also expressed enormous anger: 'I am bursting inside. My entire life has been ripped from me. I have lost my wife, my home, my daughter. Everything I love has been taken away.'[11]

He and his American wife came to Britain three years ago. He gave up his job as a traffic controller to look after their daughter Irina, while his wife had a well-paid job for a computer company which often involved spending time working away from home.

'I have raised Irina single-handed since she was two,' Blaze Vesolowski told Hugh Dehn in the *Guardian*. 'I potty-trained her, cooked for her, put her to bed – everything. I took her to the mother-and-baby group, I took her swimming every week and to ballet. A very special bond developed between us.'

In May 1991, the couple separated. Blaze Vesolowski continued to care for Irina: his wife Rachel moved out and paid £1,000 a month maintenance. Three months later, arguments began over access. Rachel had Irina made a ward of court; Blaze continued to have care and control. In April 1992 Rachel lost her job and successfully applied to the High Court to take Irina back to America. The judge said there were merits on both sides but the mother had made more realistic plans for the future than the father.

Against legal advice, Blaze appealed. He had seventy pages of letters testifying that he was a good father, including letters from Irina's teacher, doctor and dentist, and one from a mother in his village, which read: 'Perhaps the court is still so antiquated in its sexual politics that it cannot believe a single man can be an adequate parent to a child. Perhaps, in some cases, they are right. In the case of Blaze Vesolowski they are terribly wrong.'

'The judge in the High Court said I was an outstanding

father,' Blaze is quoted as saying. 'But he felt Rachel had the potential to make more income. Yet I know that if it had been me who had been working and my wife had been at home I still would not have got custody of Irina. It is blatant sexual discrimination.'[12] Blaze Vesolowski has now also moved back to the States to continue his battle. Irina continues to live with her mother.

'Husband and wife, once they go to solicitors, find themselves caught in a system in which they're forced to take sides,' says John Hanson. 'One's going to win and one's going to lose. And that has to be bad law.'

Many FNF members are critical of court welfare officers who are responsible for interviewing parents and children and preparing reports for the judge. The charge is that they are not adequately trained to deal in matters involving family life, they have insufficient time to do the job properly, and they are biased.

'They are probation officers, which immediately criminalises the procedure,' says John Hanson. 'They are paid by the state and before they used to be called "judge's witnesses", which says it all. They are also almost always on the woman's side.'

Andrew Gerry, secretary of the Solicitors' Family Law Association (which two years ago set up its own disciplinary system to investigate complaints against solicitors), says of court welfare officers: 'I think they are not insensitive to needs, but it's difficult when you have two biological parents with competing demands and limited resources. They have to find the middle road.' On judges, he is equally generous: 'They have a difficult balancing act and they do try and exercise enormous care and concern. Some of my friends are now in these positions and I know how much anxiety some cases can cause.'

Peter Wood, thirty-four, and his partner, Pam, were married for four years; both were Cambridge mathematicians. Peter Wood's wife will obviously have her side of the story, but many of the men I spoke to were reluctant to let me interview their ex-partners – mainly, they said, for fear of upsetting fragile access arrangements. Some suggested that I interviewed their children, but I refused, as I thought this might bring unfair pressure. In addition, this chapter is primarily about the less-well-heard voices of the men affected by divorce and separation. So readers must make their own judgements about where the balance of truth lies. 'I used to work in the evenings so I did a lot of the babycare. I enjoyed it,' Peter Wood says. When they separated nearly three years ago, his wife asked him to look after their two children – Molly, now seven and Sam, five – because she had begun a new relationship and she wanted to go back to university. (Molly, in any case, elected to go with her father; Sam was too young to decide.) Pam remained in Cambridge; Peter and the children went to live in Southampton.

'About halfway through the year, I began to realise I had no clear rights over the children. I asked Pam if she would put something down on paper – she didn't like it and refused. A little later, she arrived out of the blue and said she wanted the children back. I felt I had a right to be a full-time father, but that I had no right to keep her children against her will. She took them, and then two weeks later she was back. She said she couldn't manage. I applied to the court for an injunction to keep them until the end of the school year, which was six months away, and the court said yes.'

Peter continued to care for the children full-time, and Pam had unlimited access. Two years ago, he decided to regularise the arrangement and applied for custody. A few weeks before the case was due to come to court, when the children were on an Easter holiday with their mother, the police arrived at his front door with a warrant for his arrest.

'The police were mean-faced and it was very traumatic. They said I was suspected of child sexual abuse and physical abuse.'

The mother had taken the children to the police station, where it was arranged that the two should have a physical examination, including the anal dilatation test. They were also later interviewed by a social worker, and the session was videotaped. Peter Wood faced both a criminal and a civil charge.

In court on the civil charge, the tape was produced in evidence. 'It was damning,' he says. 'Molly said, "Daddy did this, rub, rub, rub." The social worker was also seen to ask very leading questions, but not the crucial one: "Did anyone tell you to say this?"

'I would never dream of sexually abusing any child, least of all my own, and although there was no physical evidence, I could see it all unfolding before me. It was a truly horrific experience.' Molly's headmistress said that over the course of a year she had observed nothing unusual in the child's behaviour or any unevenness about her work. Then Peter's ex-partner was called to give evidence.

'She became hysterical and accused me of about fifty other crimes, from locking the children in a cupboard to beating them and rape in marriage.' After cross-examination, the judge dismissed the charges, and soon after Peter Wood won his custody battle. 'I couldn't find suitable and affordable child-care, so I gave up teaching to look after them both full-time and that was fine.'

Easter 1992, and the children went on holiday with their mother again. Once more, Peter was accused of physical abuse, but this time not of sexual abuse. The children were removed from his care and went back to live with their mother in Cambridge, visiting him only every second weekend. His hearing, due two months later, was postponed for a further four months (a not uncommon event).

'By the time I do get to court, Molly and Sam will have been in this new arrangement for six months and the first thing the judge will say is that they're used to it and it's too late to change.' Peter Wood says, 'You can't win either way. even though the children want to revert back to living full-time with me, nobody's listening. The one bonus is that superficially at least, they seem to have come through all of this relatively OK.'

Since all his money has gone on earlier battles, Peter has to remain unemployed until the end of the year so that he is entitled to legal aid. Pam is now living with Chris, ten years her junior, with whom she has just had a baby. Both Molly and Sam like Chris and are enchanted with the baby.

'I don't feel any animosity towards Chris,' Peter says. 'If anything, I feel "Poor swine, in five years' time, you may find yourself in the same position as me." Recently, Pam insisted that Molly should visit an art therapist. I think that's ridiculous. She's a terrific child and now we have a nightmare situation in which she's beginning to be defined as "a problem" when it's her mother who needs the help.'

Peter Wood has had one short relationship (sabotaged in part by the charges of sexual abuse), but he now lives alone. At university in the 1970s, he says, he was involved in helping with crèches and he was interested in feminism. 'Yet in my personal life it's ironic that I've had so little room to play out my ideals. All I want now', he adds, 'is to be an average father with regular weekly contact – not the sole parent or some idealised perfect father, just an ordinary dad.'

At times, it appears, fathers don't lose their battles just with the courts, but with their children too. 'I grew up from the age of ten with a constant refrain,' says Sandra Jackson, now twenty. 'My father was a selfish bastard. He didn't give a toss for us, he didn't want to know us. It was only six months ago that I found out from my brother, who's made contact with him again, that he used to write to us and send us presents and my mother would put the lot in the bin.

'I can understand why she did it. He went off with another woman when she was in her early forties and she must have thought she might lose us as well. I still don't want to know my dad, but I feel my mother should have given me a choice. And I feel angry now with both of them.'

Tom McAllan is still in the middle of this battle. He is

forty-nine, his wife Jennifer is forty-eight. He is an accountant; she was a book-keeper; and they married in their thirties. 'When we married, Jenny was told she couldn't have any children. I remember her telling me that the chances were nil. I was a bit upset. I've always been very keen on children, but I loved the woman.'

On honeymoon Jenny conceived, and William, now fourteen was followed three years later by Sarah. 'I had to work long hours, 7 a.m. to 7 p.m., but at weekends I tried to get involved with the children,' Tom McAllan says. 'I tried to persuade Jenny that we all needed time with each other, that it might be a good idea if she went off with Sarah and I went off with William, or vice versa. But she was adamant. We did things as a family or not at all.

'I feel particularly with William that I haven't got the same rapport that I had with my father. At one point, for instance, I suggested William might need some coaching. Jenny's reaction was that I was undermining him. She was always the authority on the kids and anything I said was stupid or negative or dismissed.'

In the summer of 1991, the day the family got back from a 'pleasant, if slightly tense' fortnight's holiday, Jenny announced that she had seen a solicitor; she wanted a divorce on grounds of his unreasonable behaviour. 'My solicitor says my marriage is no different from his, except in one respect,' Tom says. 'My wife wants a divorce and his doesn't.'

Tom has decided to stay in the family home even though the divorce is finalised and, as he says, he lives like a leper in the house. 'My children need licence from their mother to speak to me, and she doesn't give it very often. It's evil.'

In November 1991, father and son were in the sitting-room. 'William suddenly threw a slipper at me. I asked him not to do it and he did it again. I said if he did it a third time, he would have to go to his room. He did and said, "And I'm bloody well not going anywhere." My wife interceded and said I was bullying him. William still refused to obey me, so I smacked him and he literally went berserk. He fell over and I picked him up and asked if he was all right. I felt for him, I really did. Then the poor little blighter burst into tears.'

This confrontation happened on a Sunday. The following Friday, at work, Tom was served with an ouster order (to leave his home) and a non-molestation order covering his wife and children. 'I was appalled – it was telling me to leave my home of fifteen years and not go anywhere near my children.'

In court, Jenny refused to give an undertaking to allow reasonable access, and the ouster order was dropped. 'I'm in my own home but I hear my children say, "Why don't you leave us alone?" and it breaks my heart. I feel that not only has Jenny got everything she wants – the house, an income – but she's also stolen the children. And at fifty, I have to begin all over again. Beginning where? In a one-bedroom flat where I can't have my children to stay?'

In October 1990, the government published its proposals on the maintenance of children in a White Paper, *Children Come First*. The tone of the White Paper is hardly objective: the mother is described as 'the caring parent', the father as 'the absent parent'. Instead of the very many policies the government could have put into practice to encourage a change in the role of the father, it has chosen to focus entirely on the traditional one: the man as breadwinner.

In April 1993, the Child Support Agency (CSA) begins work. It has, at its heart, a principle with which few would probably argue: that a father should pay for his offspring if he has the resources. The issue is whether the CSA will be any more efficient at imposing maintenance orders than the state has already proved itself to be (in 1988 there were only 1,232 civil proceedings and 38 criminal proceedings, compared with at least 200,000 defaulting fathers) – and whether, without a number of other changes to policy, the CSA will impose an even greater cost on those whom it is supposed to help most: the children.

At the same time, if the CSA is supposed to help to inculcate a sense of responsibility in fathers (as Mrs Thatcher has said: 'Fatherhood is for life'), then in its workings, it is delivering a contradictory message. According to the 1991 Child Support Act, if he is in work a man will be expected to pay according to a complicated formula which even Roger Bird, the district judge of Bristol County Court who has written a textbook on the subject, terms 'baffling' and not 'reader friendly'.[13] The formula is based on a permutation of a man's income, which takes into account a personal allowance and 'reasonable' housing expenses, but not travelling expenses incurred as a result of access visits.

In addition, the law does not take into account any expenditure the man may incur as a result of caring for children of a new partner in a second relationship. (The law uses unfortunate phrasing, referring to a man's 'natural' children to differentiate from the offspring of his second family.) In short, the moral is that while a father is now being encouraged to act as the major breadwinner in one family, it is implied that he will sidestep that same commitment in his new family.

According to Roger Bird, a man earning £160 net a week in 1992 will be expected to pay 29 per cent of that – or £46 to his ex-partner as maintenance for two children. A man on income support will be expected to contribute 5 per cent of his benefit. Mike Williams lives near Reading. His wife has a part-time job; he is a painter and decorator, now on income support. 'I have the children every second weekend and during the holidays. Then my wife gives me her family allowance for the children,' he explains. 'If I start paying maintenance, I'm worse off, she is no better off because she loses on social security, pound for pound, and only the Treasury benefits.' Ask him why the taxpayer should meet the cost of his family obligations, and his reply is not atypical: 'If I could get a job, I'd shoulder it all. I can't, and in those circumstances I think society has a duty to make some investment in children for everybody's benefit. If anybody imagines we all live well on the state, they've got to be mad.'

Another flaw is that the CSA has no power to order reasonable access in exchange for maintenance (and the courts seem reluctant to enforce orders), so if men find themselves under increasing pressure to pay yet still remain out of contact with their children, the anger can only grow.

Paul Wallace has two sons under eleven from his first marriage. He and they live separately just outside Manchester. Four years ago, Paul Wallace says, he discovered his ex-wife in bed with another man and left home. He is supposed to pay £100 a month maintenance for the children. 'Every time access was arranged, my ex-wife would put obstacles in the way. I was reduced to talking to my sons bent double at the letterbox. Eventually, after a couple of years of effort and no return, I gave up.'

A few months ago, he also stopped paying maintenance. Part of the reason is financial. He is a skilled craftsman, building kitchens. 'More often than not now, on a Monday, the men are told it will be a short week,' he says. 'And you just have to accept it because there's no other work around.' His wage goes down from £140 net to around £100. His second wife earns £120 as a clerk – £80 a week goes on the mortgage, £40 on the part-time childminder for their eighteen-month-old daughter Amy. If Paul pays maintenance for two boys, his second family must exist on £80 a week, since the CSA is not built to cope with abrupt changes in income.

'What choice do I have?' says Paul. 'At least if I could see my kids I'd know why I was asking everyone to make the extra sacrifice.'

Members of Families Need Fathers frequently refer to the example of the USA when asked what might improve the present situation. There, in over thirty-two States, joint custody is either a presumption or a law. This move to what is known as 'gender-neutral' laws should be a sign of progress; the danger comes if they are interpreted without due awareness that we do not yet live in a gender-neutral society. Instead, we face inbuilt inequalities of power and money that could tip the balance entirely in a father's favour.

In the 10 per cent of cases where fathers contested custody in the States at the end of the last decade – according to Flora Davis in *Moving the Mountain: The Women's Movement in America since 1960* – half were successful. The grounds in some cases give cause for concern . . . On occasions, for instance, the judge gave the father custody because he had a higher standard of living or because he had a stay-at-home wife (while his ex-wife was forced to work), or because the man was considered excellent at fathering.

'Excellent', of course, often involves a double standard. A man who changes a couple of nappies a week may be seen as the best father in the universe, while the same rate of nappy changes for a woman would probably condemn her as the world's worst mother. 'That's not equal treatment,' Joanne Schulman, former staff attorney for the National Center on Women and Family Law, is quoted as saying in *Moving the Mountain*. 'That's ignoring reality, to give special treatment to men.'

'We must give up the illusion that the law is pure, objective, abstract, and principled, and recognise that although the vast majority of judges are committed to fairness, the vast majority of judges are upper-class white men whose perception of fairness is filtered through the lens of that particular life experience,' argues the feminist attorney Lynn Hecht Schafran of the American experience in *Moving the Mountain*. Exactly the same could be said of the courts in Britain – and that is an advantage neither to women nor to men. But what it is also possible to see at work in the States is a system of checks and balances which could act to secure a greater degree of fairness.

In 1982, Marilyn Loftus, a New Jersey judge, asked the State's Chief Justice to appoint a group to study gender bias in the courts. Now, more than half the States have task forces on women in the courts, while the National Judicial Education Programme to Promote Equality for Women and Men in

Courts (NJEP) attempts to retrain judges in seminars, using evidence of bias gleaned by the task forces.

In Britain, the training encouraged under the Children Act will not require the mainly male judiciary to overhaul their traditional prejudices, but monitoring could certainly spot when they came into play. Such evidence of bias in the family courts (or in any other court, for that matter) could help to increase the pressure for change. (More women judges would also help.)

If task forces and a training progamme were instituted in Britain; if the economic plight of women could be improved, tackling childcare, low pay and a woefully inadequate social security system; if conciliation was easily available on every high street and there was a public campaign to encourage couples to go for help earlier; if court orders, once decided, were enforced; if some born-again fathers discovered their commitment earlier in a relationship and if both parents could cease to see children as non-negotiable property, then some of the anger of fathers and mothers might be averted in the first place. At present, however, the political will to initiate such changes by the Conservative Government is nowhere to be seen.

To give a couple of examples: the National Family Concili-ation Council began in Bristol in 1979, prompted by the frustration of solicitors, social workers and counsellors at the failure of successive governments to implement the proposals in the Finer Report on One Parent Families. In 1973 Finer argued for the setting up of a family court with conciliation at its heart.

There are now fifty-three independent branches of the NFCC throughout the country, but there are significant areas where there is too little help on offer – Wales, the West Country, Hull. Conciliation (not to be confused with reconcil-iation) is strongly advocated in the Children Act – what is missing are the resources.

'We don't work miracles, we just try to help couples to

resolve their own difficulties so that they can come to a workable arrangement, particularly about the children,' says Kate Gardner of Swindon NFCC. 'We don't offer personal advice or legal advice, we mediate with the information we are given.' NFCC has a success rate of 65 to 70 per cent and follow-up monitoring indicates that the agreement usually holds. 'We don't say people love each other,' Kate Gardner says. 'But they're no longer at the point of feeling that they could kill each other either.'

The NFCC relies on contributions. It costs £250 to concili-ate each case (around three visits) and the government offers no funding at all except for an £18.50 referral fee from the Legal Aid Fund. The remainder of the NFCC's income comes from trusts and local authorities. In 1990, it counselled only 6,000 couples. More money means more help, and more anger – both male and female – abated.

Reunite, the charity which helps men and women whose children have been abducted overseas (1,200 a year), is also in financial difficulties. Home Office funding of £23,000 runs out in March 1993. Lucy Jaffe, co-ordinator of Reunite, estimates that £40,000 a year is needed if the organisation is to do its job adequately. FNF receives no help, and Relate, formerly the Marriage Guidance Council, is also struggling with funding. It seems all the more bizarre that, in contrast, the Broadcasting Standards Council, designed to monitor what we see and hear from a standpoint located somewhere in the middle of the last century, receives over a £1 million a year from the government. (Industry, too, needs to wake up to the wisdom of investing in the prevention of marital break-up, since according to one estimate in 1985, organisations pay £5,000 in lost time and efficiency for each divorcing employee.)

One pressure which may help to speed the recognition that fathers may deserve better treatment and encourage men and women to settle their differences away from solicitors, judges and the courts is the slow but significant change in the roles of some women.

John Hanson of FNF says that a new type of member is beginning to come forward: the career woman who has handed custody of the children to the father and then finds that she faces difficulties in obtaining regular access. 'The judges look upon these women just as jaundicedly as they look at men who try to step out of the traditional stereotype,' he says. 'We have a vested interest in working together.'

Instead, however, a new stigma is in the making: 'Why are mothers becoming less caring?' ran the headline on a story in the Bible of the backlash, the *Daily Mail*, in July 1992.[14] It tells the tale of divorced man, Adrian Cohen, who works all day and cares for his child in the evening. The piece practises all the prejudices and criticisms normally exercised against absent fathers – but this time, the target is mothers who are career women. Over 100,000 fathers are bringing up their children 'on their own', the feature says, so what does this say 'about women's attitude to motherhood'? The answer, according to the *Daily Mail*, is that a woman's sense of responsibility to her children 'lies in tatters', and the feature ends with a piece of emotional blackmail.

'I'm glad my second wife is there to talk to her about being a woman,' remarried Philip Windle, a former lone parent, is quoted as saying, referring to his daughter Samantha. 'I used to worry that she didn't have a woman's love, that softer kind of love, with a kiss and a cuddle.' (Didn't Samantha have grannies, aunties, adult female friends?)

It is precisely this kind of approach, predicated on no evidence whatsoever, that affects to record social change while actually trying to manipulate and hinder it. If divorce and separation are to be an inevitable part of modern life, then clearly we need to handle them a great deal better than we do now – for the sake of the children.

The anger of men and the fury of women is, in part, fed by stereotypes about both sexes which are long past their sell-by date. 'What we need', says Hugh Mills, 'is for fathers and mothers to be judged as they behave as individuals towards their children – not as society expects them to act according to tradition.'

FNF may represent a minority of men, or it could be the voice of the many who have been silenced by the difficulties placed in the way of maintaining a life with their children. Certainly the seriousness with which its views are considered is bound to be influenced by how men are seen to behave as fathers *before* separation or divorce takes place, and how willing they are to meet their continuing financial obligations to their children once a relationship has died.

'Men *can* be good fathers,' Hugh Mills says, 'but nobody yet seems prepared to give us the benefit of the doubt.'

CHAPTER FOUR

Just wait until your father gets home . . .

I f feminism has infiltrated any area of contemporary culture, it is in trying to mould the modern dad – so much so that this is no longer seen as the work of the women's movement, it has become the manifesto of Mothercare. It has also created a conundrum at the heart of fatherhood. A man within the bosom of his family, is often pilloried, castigated and generally done over for his failures in almost every aspect of caring, catering for and coralling children. But, if he's 'no good' when he's present, why do we also make an enormous fuss when he's not?

Motherhood too, of course, is eternally criticised. Many women may also be tormented by a feeling of inadequacy about their sense of maternalism – an inadequacy that is unnecessarily inculcated in them, not least by some men. But while parenthood may be just as much of a cross, at times, for women, this chapter is intended to focus on why so many men believe that when it comes to fatherhood, they never seem able to win.

If a father takes on none of the basic (and at times boring) parts of childcare, he is damned for his chauvinism. Yet, often, if he *does* try to become involved, this may arouse the most alarming territorial instincts in a woman.

'I don't know how many times I've been with very capable men and their partners and it's been time to change the baby's nappy,' says Jerome Burne, forty-six, a writer, father of four, who shares childcare. 'Suddenly, the woman is in charge. "Don't you know we never use that type of cream . . .? I told

you to bring the other romper suit. Goodness, you're hopeless
. . ." And the man just sits and takes it.'

'It was all done to her rules or not at all. She was like a
sergeant major. And somehow, she was always there, standing
between me and the boys,' says Dennis Jackson, a divorcee
with two teenage children, Dan and Stephen. 'Suddenly, I
woke up and thought I don't accept this in the office from
anyone, why do I take it from her? I'm an average sort of a
bloke, what's the big deal about looking after a couple of kids?

'Now, they spend a week with me and a week with her, and
I'm in charge when they're here. I know it's tiring, I know at
times it's bloody annoying, but I also know I like their
company and I was right: if you're easy-going, then looking
after kids isn't a big deal. I think that's the mystery women
have tried to con us with for too long – that there's some
special technique that only a woman "instinctively" has. It's
bullshit – but it took at least ten years of Dan's early life
before I realised it.'

The contradictory signals being sent out, consciously or
unconsciously, by some women – feminist and non-feminist
alike – are that, in theory, they want fathering to carry the
same pleasures, burdens and responsibilities as mothering;
they want men to be warm and emotional and caring – but in
practice, they appear much more ambivalent.

This prompts a more quizzical look at the endless surveys
which show the unequal (but very slowly reducing) burden of
childcare on women. According to a Gallup survey for baby-
food makers Farley's (July 1992), 50 per cent of husbands
help feed and change the baby; one in three bath the baby;
but one in four refuse to do housework or shopping, and one
in five never help at all. Undoubtedly some men are resistant
to doing anything more than impregnating a partner, but
perhaps there are other tensions and contradictions at work
too?

Some women, for instance, may mock and deride a man's
efforts until he is reduced to the role of a subcontractor in the

family, allowed to deal with the children only on certain conditions and for limited periods of time. (And once this is established, the man is once more open to attack – for doing too little. And so the cycle goes on.) It's fatherhood tailored for martyrdom.

Twenty years ago, the solution superficially appeared easy. The man shares childcare, he benefits in the long term as does the child and mother. Now, on many different levels, this is proving more problematic. Some couples slide easily into shared care but others face a number of obstacles, including the unwillingness of the man to lift so much as a fish finger, to the woman's frustration that 'he' just doesn't 'do it right', to the uncertainty of the mother: what she thought she wanted, she is now not so sure about. At the same time, in spite of the many more varied types of fathering, such as single parenthood fostering, gay, househusband, working part-time to share childcare, the older second-time-around father, fathering step-children – even fathering two children in the same family in a different style, the traditional stereotype of the distant, une-motional, uninvolved masculine father remains enduring. But why? In the 1990s, have we become confused about what a father is *for*?

Peter Gibbs is thirty-eight. He is married with three children aged ten, thirteen and seventeen, and medically retired from the police force. He is about to become a mature student at university. In an interview with David Cohen in the *Independent*,[1] he conveyed his not untypical confusion about the state of paternal relations.

In 1980, he explained, his wife Hannelore became interested in feminism. She accused him of not doing enough of the childcare, and of being a 'bad' father. She began to go out in the evenings and leave him to it: 'I was quite happy to take on more childcare responsibility, but I wanted Hannelore to take on a corresponding share of the financial burden, to develop a career and allow me to change my job, but she wasn't interested. I was expected to be macho in the day and come home and be sweetness and light.'

Martin Large, forty-three, a freelance management consultant with four children, also explained how he received contradictory messages from his partner, Judy: 'Feminism challenged men to get in touch with their feelings, yet when I cried, Judy felt uncomfortable and said things such as "Don't cry in front of the kids" and "My father never cried in his life". . . I'd get very hurt when Judy said I was just like my father. My father was a traditional Yorkshire farmer. He used to sit at the dinner table and say, "Salt". Just "Salt". And my mother would scurry off and fetch the salt . . .'

Tony Kemp has been married twice and is now a single-parent father; his son Kevin is eleven. The two live in Bradford on an income of £83 a week (which includes a mobility and invalidity allowance because Tony has a crumbling spine). In Tony's second marriage he also became close to the two daughters of his ex-partner, but 'Kevin missed out a bit,' he says. 'His mum had remarried and it wasn't easy with his stepdad and my partner made it plain he wasn't her child.'

Finally, Tony Kemp decided that for Kevin's sake, and because his second wife had had several affairs, he and his son should set up home together. 'We manage well because Kevin is a really good lad,' says Tony, who is an active member of Gingerbread, the lobby group for one-parent families. 'I make sure we have meat on the table a couple of times a week and he has holidays with his mum on a farm in East Anglia, so I'm not bothered if we don't go out much. I'm always here when he gets home. I don't find it a problem because I've always loved kids.'

What has surprised him, he says, is the reaction of some women. 'It's as if they're a bit threatened. I asked one woman I know if she'd babysit for me once. "I told you men were no good as fathers," she said. "You want to be out every night." I never asked again.'

In the last forty years, the parameters of paternity have

clearly changed. In the 1950s, child guidance 'experts' such as John Bowlby insisted that rearing babies was Mother's work; Father's job was to pay for it all. Then, the average American and British family reared around three children (in Britain now it's more like 1.8), and while Father wasn't in at the birth, he certainly spent many more months than men do now in close proximity to pregnancy and, as the sole breadwinner, worrying about how to feed the many and several mouths afterwards.

In return, Father, on the rare occasion when he was home, expected to have a fuss made of him: 'his' chair ready by the fire, shirts ironed, supper on the table, housework done, kitchen out of bounds – ('After all,' I can remember my Auntie Meg, mother of three with two part-time cleaning jobs, saying, 'He's done a hard day's work.") – and the kids in bed: all part of the head-of-the-household routine.

In the 1950s, marriage was an obligation, fatherhood a duty that came with a wife, and those who didn't fall into line were given short shrift. In *My Life as a Man*, Philip Roth conveys graphically the pressures on the 1950s young bachelor:

> The great world was so obviously a man's, it was only within marriage that an ordinary woman could hope to find equality and dignity. Indeed, we were led to believe by the defenders of womankind of our era that we were exploiting and degrading those we *didn't* marry, rather than the ones we did.
>
> Unattached and on her own, a woman was supposedly not even able to go out to the movies by herself, let alone perform an appendectomy or drive a truck . . . If we didn't marry women, who would? Ours, alas, was the only sex available for the job: the draft was on.
>
> No wonder then that a young college-educated bourgeois male of my generation who scoffed at marriage for himself, who would just as soon eat out of cans or in cafeterias, sweep his own floor, make his own bed and come and go

with no binding legal attachments . . . laid himself open to the charge of 'immaturity' if not 'latent' or blatant homosexuality. Or he was just plain 'selfish'. Or he was 'frightened of responsibility'. Or he could not 'commit himself'. . . to a permanent relationship. Worst of all, most shameful of all, the chances were that this person who thought he was perfectly able to take care of himself on his own was in actuality 'unable to love'.

In short, children in the postwar period helped to prove that a man was a *real* man. Since the 1970s, the father is much less likely to be the only breadwinner in the family. According to the 1987 General Household Survey, 30 per cent of mothers of children under two, 46 per cent of mothers of children aged three to four and two-thirds of mothers of children aged five to nine are in full- or part-time work. This change is reflected in public attitudes. In 1965, 78 per cent of people thought that a woman with children under school age should stay at home. By 1987, that figure had dropped to 45 per cent (*British Social Attitudes*, 1991). The father is also, in many cases, the chief childminder while his partner is in her job.

The Women in Employment Survey, conducted in 1984 and – shamefully – the only major piece of research on how women in work cope with childcare, indicated that 47 per cent of women with pre-school children and 57 per cent of those with school-age children rely on the father to mind the family. (He is followed by the grandmother who provides childcare for 34 per cent of mothers with pre-school and 25 per cent of mothers with school-age children.[2]) According to Dr Sebastian Kraemer, child psychiatrist at the Tavistock Clinic in London, 'Men are prepared neither by nature nor civilisation to make genuine attachments to their children . . .'[3] For many families, whether fatherhood comes 'naturally' or not is an irrelevance – Dad just has to get on with it. But how well?

At Nottingham University, one study indicated that 50 per cent of mothers did not like leaving the children with their fathers regularly, 38 per cent discounted the idea altogether and 18 per cent thought it a good idea – but not for them. If women are critical of fathers, then that may come in part from the belief that they fail to do the job properly but also from an even deeper-rooted belief that Father is muscling in on mother's job.

In the late 1960s and early 1970s, it was the turn of the New Men in the embryonic men's movement to trash the dad. In 1983 I went to Leeds to interview Jack Dorset, whom I included in a book I was writing, *Man Enough*,[4] based on interviews with men of my own age at the time, thirty-five. Jack, a science teacher, had a son, Matthew, aged three, who split his week between his mother and Jack. Jack's ex-wife lived in a nuclear family; Jack shared his house with two single people, one male, one female, and they all cooked together.

Jack was trying very hard to rear Matthew according to the non-sexist book. His bedroom was painted shell-pink, there were a number of dolls in the toybox, Matthew saw Jack cooking and the woman next door, a carpenter, doing odd jobs. The house seemed to me to be a child's paradise: pets, projects, lots of amiable people, other children next door, a devoted parent.

Matthew seemed happy with the arrangement, then his mother asked for full custody because she had had a baby and wanted Matthew to be more a part of the new family. Jack turned to his men's group for advice. The consensus was that as women had suffered 2,000 years of oppression, Jack should forfeit his experience of being a father.

'They said if a woman wants to take a child, we should allow her to do so,' he explained to me. 'They argued that men have yielded too little in a patriarchal society and that that would be a small sacrifice to make. They felt that to insist on "being a father" was a hangover from a Victorian man possessing his wife and children.' Jack wisely, in my view, decided to leave such sacrifice to some other conscript and fought to retain the access arrangements.

In the early days, the letters pages of magazines such as the *Anti-Sexist Men's Newsletter* and *Achilles Heel* (established in 1978 after the first London Men's Conference) could easily have been renamed the masochists' mailbag as woman after woman berated the efforts of the New Man, and much of the opprobrium seemed to focus on childcare.

If help was offered running crèches at a women's conference, it was conceived as men trying to take over. If a man suggested bottle-feeding instead of breastfeeding so that he could take his share of sleepless nights, this was male manipulation; if a man attempted to open up discussions on fathering and mothering, he was accused of distracting women from the 'real fight' – their own. If a man was open about his feelings as a father, it was regarded as embarrassingly wet: the wimp effect in sexual politics.

To some men, it must have seemed that the more they tried to prove themselves as allies, the more roundly they were condemned as the enemy – sometimes rightly. In the *Anti-Sexist Men's Newsletter* no. 17, the organisers of the Men's Action Against Sexism Conference, held in Manchester in May 1982, turned on their brothers with gusto.

'This conference was a failure . . . Men who seek to "liberate themselves" are directly attacking and oppressing women. By blatantly aping feminist ideas men are using knowledge gained in women's struggle to increase their own power and advantages over women,' the anonymous organisers wrote:

Men have been talking about 'raising their consciousness' for the last ten years and it hasn't done anything to lessen women's oppression. It also hasn't changed the disgusting self-important sexism of men who stood around self-congratulating and tongue-massaging . . . and whose main worry about the conference was that there would be no heterosexual male-bonding session (commonly known as a party).

And here comes the crunch: 'An appeal was made by the Women in Ireland group for helpers at a crèche . . . but not one man out of 125 at the conference could be bothered. If you don't think these comments apply to you – think again.'

In 1983, Jeff Hearn, a veteran of the men's movement, published, through *Achilles Heel*, *Birth and Afterbirth: A Materialist Account*. (Jeff Hearn, a father of three, Amy, Tom and Molly, is now a Reader in Social and Critical Studies on Men at the University of Bradford, writing books and teaching an MA course on men and masculinities as well as being involved in a research project on violent men. For those who mock these early New Men, at least some of their efforts are now being put to practical use in work, for instance, with boys and young men in youth clubs, community projects, the probation service, and so on.)

In *Birth and Afterbirth*, Jeff Hearn describes how he felt the morning after his daughter Molly was born: 'I found myself lying in bed, knees up, getting rid of some of the wind by pushing down in the same way I had seen the previous night; then on the loo I had the very strange experience of momentarily believing/fantasizing that the slime sticking to my anal hair was a "show".'

On his wife Jay's return home with Molly, he writes: 'Inside the house Jay was confident and joyful. I just broke up. I just sobbed and sobbed and sobbed for a long time. I had no control over myself. I felt drained on behalf of others in the family, as Amy and Tom initially stood and stared, but at the same time celebrating all on my own in some way.'

If some women might feel that one more wailing individual – especially an adult – is one too many, then Jeff Hearn is undeterred. His self-exploration has led him to the conclusion that fatherhood should be opposed.

'The notion of fatherhood must be smashed or more precisely dropped bit by bit into the ocean,' he writes in *Birth and Afterbirth*.

Parenting yes, childwork, yes, crèches, yes, but fatherhood is the most pernicious part of the whole mess. Perhaps I should try and make it quite clear. I am not suggesting that men should not take responsibility for children, in fact I would urge men to do the absolute opposite.

What I am suggesting is that men should take as much responsibility as is necessary for children, whether they happen to be their biological father, live with them, be involved with them as friends, or on an occasional basis such as child-sitting or crèches . . . There is a need for new forms of relationships between men and children that are not fatherly or patriarchal or hearty but simply friendly and responsible. Most importantly, any attempt to assert father's rights, whether as part of some traditional notion of the father figure or more liberal variant of 'male liberation', is to be resisted . . . to do otherwise is to bolster male power by subtle . . . means.

In 1979, Paul Morrison described in *Achilles Heel* how he felt helping to care for his eighteen-month-old daughter Corey (he later discovered that she was brain damaged). A man who cares for his child does not often have the support of knowing other men in the same situation. Paul Morrison's feelings in the late 1970s – that full-time childcare isn't quite enough to feed the soul – are exactly those expressed by feminists at the outset of the second wave a decade earlier, in the late 1960s:

Different men that I know face these problems differently. One man seems to keep a firm control over his life and maintains a more disciplined structure for his 'external' work, against the threat of Engulfment. He compartmentalises his childcare more effectively. Another man is more easy-going. He lets his childtime flow around him more, doesn't fight the pressures. I find myself torn between these two ways of being. We are all juggling with our balance of 'internal' and 'external'. All our ways of finding what is best for us seem to have their different prices. And it becomes so easy to neglect ourselves . . . I don't appreciate the energy drain that a young child has had on me . . .[5]

This article – one of the first to mark out the 'new' fathering – also conveys the slightly self-satisfied air which gets up the noses of many women (who perform the same mundane tasks without acting as if it's an achievement akin to relieving Khartoum) and some other men, many of whom have the view that taking the kids to the park is about exercise, not existentialism.

In the early afternoon Paul Morrison describes how Corey finally has a nap:

Back to finishing my lunch. Now where was I? There's a number of calls I could make. Or I could go to bed and catch up on my sleep. Or I could do some 'productive' work.

When anyone tells me that it is an important and difficult thing that I am doing, that I am doing something good and right, I curl up with delight. I don't think to expect that kind of validation.

Eleven years later, in 1990, in a postscript added to the original article for the *Achilles Heel Reader*, Paul Morrison shows how the men's movement has moved from the defensive to the offensive in finding its own agenda – and in seeking its own definition of fatherhood, instead of accepting the one provided for them by women:

At that time, in the circles I moved in, it was unfashionable for men to admit to wanting to be successful in their work. We denied that side of ourselves. In retrospect, I believe it would have been easier for me to own up to my 'masculine' side and pursue it wholeheartedly in the time available to me to do that, than to try to persuade myself I wasn't really bothered. There's a danger that in substituting one set of right-on rules for the old ones, we create new straitjackets for ourselves.

Paul Morrison and Jeff Hearn were among the few in the men's movement to tackle fathering from a personal perspective. In the 1970s and 1980s, and even now, fatherhood is still often seen in New Men's literature and academic research as a theoretical technique, akin to learning how to strip a car engine; measurements are taken of how many nappies are changed, what quantity of time is spent in play, etc., etc., and fatherhood is tackled as a series of 'problems'. (It is the same approach that some feminists have to female sexuality – none of the joys, only the obstacles.)

In the April 1990 issue of *Achilles Heel*, for instance, Gavin Smith runs through some of the constituent parts of what he sees as a 'crisis' in fatherhood – how to cope with emotional dependency? What does fathering do to the male identity? What does childcare mean for male employment? Why do men shun childcare? And he adds some interesting insights on how the perspective of a man – in his case, a transport planner – can change as a result of having a child:

> Only on becoming a father am I more aware of the significance of what I vaguely knew before – that male transport planning does not mind that women and children have restricted mobility, that they are killed in disproportionate numbers, crossing our streets . . . Once a conscientious man has a child, his concept of male politics undergoes a transformation. He becomes less preoccupied with macroeconomics and geopolitics (perfectly worthwhile interests in themselves) and suddenly discovers an everyday politics of education, health and childcare (which so bored him before). He discovers a world normally occupied by women. I have the feeling that male 'politics' could be

characterized as male posturing, floating securely on the surface of a life support system sustained by women.

Keith Bremner, a former board member of the National Children's Bureau, described in the NCB's quarterly magazine how he set about re-creating the close relationship he had once had with his two sons and lost in their teenage years, partly because of the approach of traditional fathering. His sons are now twenty-nine and thirty-one, and he and they have become involved in twice-yearly workshops run by the Network for a New Men's Leadership:

> From early childhood, boys are encouraged to be independent, to be in control of their emotions, and to expect their emotional needs will be met by women – their mothers, sisters, girlfriends, partners and wives. As a consequence, it is taken for granted that men naturally find it easier to have intimate relationships with women, and that for two men to become closely involved with one another is unnatural.
> When the focus is on men's relationships with their fathers, feelings of anxiety, regret, anger and sadness are expressed. There is also an overwhelming need to express their love for their fathers and to receive love from them. The workshops have transformed the way my sons and I are able to relate to one another. We now feel there is a strong bond between us, we have no inhibitions about making close physical contact with each other and we regularly express our love for one another.[6]

This underlines the message delivered by feminist therapists such as Susie Orbach and Luise Eichenbaum:[7] that while men sharing in childcare is important for women's development, it also acts as a catalyst on the father himself, in many other areas apart from his relationship with the child.

Yet it is exactly for this reason, that a suspicion lingers

about the *nouveau père*: fathering for him is not just about being with the children or taking a fair share of the family burden, it is seen by some critics as a faddish means of finding (or furthering?) himself. And the fad can be fleeting.

In 1990, the then Norman Fowler announced his resignation as Employment Minister. He wanted, he said, more time to be with his wife Fiona and their three children, Oliver, Kate and Isobel. 'More time' is a relative term, of course. Sir Norman as he became, wrote his memoirs, joined a few boards as a director, continued to be an MP. In May 1992, his fling with family life was done; Papa had a brand new bag. He became chairman of the Conservative Party.

'People have this touching idea of him staying at home with me all day, holding my hand and making me cups of tea, but it wasn't like that at all,' Fiona Fowler told Jessica Davies of the *Daily Mail*.[8] 'We did go to the zoo and Norman taught our younger daughter to ride a bike . . .' but the rest was apparently much the same as it has always been – Dad dabbling in the fun bits while mother does the hard graft.

In *Fathers: Psychological Perspectives*, published in 1981, Judy Blendis conducted a small study (one of the few) of sixty men whose ages ranged from thirty to fifty, both working- and middle-class. The most striking aspect of the long descriptions of men's experiences with their own fathers, she noted, was not their uniformity (no authoritarian stereotype ruling supreme here) but the variety: 'From strong hatred and vicious brutality through indifference and lack of interest to close warmth, love and affection.' In terms of practical caring the fathers played a peripheral role, but they were often involved (sometimes negatively, setting impossible standards; sometimes not) in their sons' sports and school work.

Many of the men said their fathers had great affection for them but difficulty in showing it. In spite of having uninvolved fathers, Judy Blendis says, some research indicates that men become caring themselves as compensation or, if they had a highly nurturing mother, by emulating her. A less academic way of putting it might be to suggest that throughout the postwar years, no matter how a man was reared and no matter how strong the social taboos and attitudes, if the will was there, and his partner was co-operative, he could fashion his own idea of fathering – irrespective of how his own father behaved.

In 1983 I visited Sheffield to talk to Neville Wright for *Man Enough*. He had been without work for a couple of years. He and his wife, Diane, had married in 1975, when she was seventeen. In the next five years, they had four children. The fourth child was a girl, so they stopped.

Neville was then a full-time revolutionary and left the housework to his wife. Their two-up two-down was packed with Trotsky, Marx and Lenin. He was a member of the Centre against Unemployment, an active supporter of Militant, and he also spent two evenings a week on an applied social studies course. The family lived on £60 a week and had debts of £2,500.

In 1983, Neville said he had been forced almost from the outset to become involved in the basics of childcare because of the number of babies in the house at any one time. He said he had never had any problem showing a lot of affection towards the children, although his own father was more reserved. 'How else can you show them you care? They need to feel valued and I don't have any problem in supplying that.'

Almost ten years on, Neville's tale is perhaps a tale of the 1990s. Nevil (sixteen) is a British Rail apprentice, Michael is fourteen, Matthew is thirteen and Joanne-Sherri is eleven. Diane is about to go back to college and is a care assistant, and Neville has given up on the revolution. Leaving the barricades has given him more time for the family. Three years ago, he took a job. He moved to London and his employer now, ironically, is that arch-enemy of Marxism, Westminster council.

Neville Wright is an estate service officer responsible for 1,300 residents. A house comes with the job and a salary of

£17,000. In addition, Diana earns £9,000 a year and the house they still own in Sheffield brings in an income from rent. Since the dole, they've become a £30,000-a-year family.

'I wanted the kids to have more – it's a basic instinct in a parent. And I was growing disillusioned with the revolution. Now, I've even got to the point where I wonder whether a class doesn't get what it deserves.'

Partly because he and Diane worry about the effect of an inner-London estate on the boys, the family spend every weekend together – either in the caravan they've bought on the coast, or on day trips. 'I try and be available for the kids. I knock a football around with them, I help with homework. I want Joanne-Sherri to get a bit more confidence and give me a bit more cheek so then I'll know she's got the street cred to get by in London.

'All the kids give me stick if they think I'm short-changing them on time. And that's how it should be. Diane and I split duties and discipline between us, it's done equally.'

In 1983, Neville Wright had spoken warmly of his own father, in many ways a traditional father figure (he had died two years before). Neville said he was closer to him than to his mother: 'She always tended to be the family's dustbin for problems. My dad was very definitely head of the household.' His father had been a toolmaker and a professional football player until he had volunteered to give Neville a bone graft to help correct his son's contracted femur. He worked nights, so Neville and his brother David, who suffered from severe epilepsy, tended to see their father only for a couple of hours in the evening and at weekends.

'I loved my mum but she couldn't share my interests,' Neville Wright says. 'I got on very, very well with my dad. We were close, but I wouldn't take take my problems to my dad because I thought I ought to be able to handle them myself. 'He commanded a lot of respect for his macho image but at home he could be quite weepy about things.'

Neville's father never helped in the house and, he says, his mother would have taken umbrage if he had, since this was her territory. When she had a nervous breakdown, Neville was seventeen. His father took over the household chores and forced them on his son too. 'Up till then, I thought all I had to do was devour everything put on a plate in front of me. My dad decided otherwise. He managed as well as my mum really. It was a surprise to me.'

Asked how he rates himself as a father, Neville Wright gives himself seven out of ten. Given that men in domestic politics tend to score themselves higher than their partners reckon they rate, the opinion of Diane, a strong and independently minded woman, is sought. She agrees: seven out of ten.

'I put time in,' Neville Wright says. 'They know I'm interested in them. If I have to, I'll give them a clout now and then, but I think my kids know I put them first.'

If role models do matter, then what is available for the modern father is a strange mix. For instance, while no self-respecting 'women's page', family supplement or women's magazine is now without its contribution from a stepfather, father or father-to-be (in the tabloids, 'fatherhood' is still restricted to the occasional photograph of some faded pop star pushing a buggy), serious issues are rarely attempted. (An exception, to give one example, is David Cohen in *The Independent*[9] tackling life for the father once the baby is born, when he may be pushed to one side and sex is apparently put on hold for up to two years.) Instead, much is still along the lines: 'I may be the head of a multinational corporation but goodness me, which way up do you hold a tin of talc?' (also a popular theme in films such as *Three Men and a Baby* etc.). The subliminal message in the 1990s is that childcare is still women's work.

So, in the *Daily Telegraph*'s 'You and Your Family' supplement, we have Richard Ehrlich, A Man Who Cooks, telling us how to mix up cottage cheese, peas and carrots and 'two small leaves of fresh mint' for the children. (Please!)[10] While in the *Guardian* Saturday review, we are allowed sporadic extracts (not sporadic enough) from baby Jessica's journal, ghosted by her daddy, Philip Norman.[11]

'There are also the moments when my father, having been holding me quite happily, hands me to Jose the maternity nanny then steps back and gives an agonised wail,' 'Jessica' writes.

> 'God, no.' 'What is it?' My mother cries, rushing down the spiral stairs. 'I'm covered in goddam white fluff.' 'If you will wear only black and dark blue, what do you expect?' 'But do babies always have to be put in things that shed white bobbles over everything?'. . .

If this had been ghosted by a mother, it would have been a toss-up (so to speak) whether Jessica's journal would have hit the sick bucket or the spike first.

In spite of it all, men cope – often because, just like women, they must. Jonathan Philbin Bowman is twenty-three, his son Saul is four, and for three of those four years Jonathan has been his son's main carer. He occasionally refers to Penelope Leach's manual on childcare but otherwise, he says, he just gets on with it. Jonathan is a freelance journalist; he lives in Dublin. Saul goes to a crèche three days a week; he spends Tuesdays with his maternal grandparents, Sundays with his mother and 'paid babysitters, an aunt, helpful cousins, and friends' help out with the bits in between.

'I tend to do my socialising at lunch time. If I go out more than twice a week in the evenings, I feel that's once too many times,' Jonathan Philbin Bowman says. 'When my then girl-friend got pregnant with Saul, the only option I wouldn't countenance was adoption. But from the minute he was born, I felt connected. I've always liked children and one of my brothers arrived when I was eleven, so I was used to babies. It seemed quite natural that I should be involved with the childcare right from the start.

107

'I soon realised you have to have checks and balances. I have to earn a living, care for Saul, tidy up. I'm not the tidiest person in the world, but if I tidy up I can't be with Saul, so I don't. It's a matter of priorities.

'What's good about children, as everyone says, is just when you're growing bored with the routine, they'll suddenly take off in their development in a totally different way. One of the rewards is when he falls over, he always calls for me. That may sound egocentric but it gives enormous pleasure.'

Assumptions remain unchanged, Jonathan says. 'If I'm with Saul and a woman friend in a restaurant, people, if they're interested, always ask her what his name is and how old he is. The friend enjoys it when it gets to the point that she can say, "He's not mine, he belongs to him".'

Jonathan has a wide circle of friends and Saul is universally judged to be a happy, easy-going child (and if he wasn't, so what? Plenty of couples produce highly neurotic children too). 'I use Saul and work as an escape from each other,' Jonathan says. 'I escape from work into Saul and vice versa.'

At one point, for a year, Jonathan lived with a girlfriend who had a daughter. Saul got on well with them both, but Jonathan remained the main carer. 'I would be aware if a woman tried to take over, and cautious', Jonathon says. 'Computers, telephones and women, they are the only three causes for Saul to get cranky from time to time because he knows they – briefly – take me away from him.'

Jonathan says there is a crèche in Dublin which does everything for the parent, even to cooking food for supper in the evening and washing dirty clothes. 'I thought what is the fucking point? That's what it's about, doing things for him. Sometimes, a person will be critical because my standards aren't theirs – and that makes me furious. I do it my own way.' Does he have regrets? 'No, I'm delighted with the outcome,' he says. 'I'd do it again.'

John Dinsmore, at forty-six, comes from a different generation. He works a three-day week as a marketing consultant and shares childcare of his year-old daughter, Olivia, with his partner, Kate, who works in public relations and with whom he lives full-time. John also has three other children by two other women. Fatherhood involves a logistical set of hurdles each week, but John Dinsmore says he perseveres because the rewards merit it. He also believes that he has become closer to two of his sons, Joshua and Sam, only *since* splitting from their mother.

Fatherhood began twelve years ago. John had a brief affair. A month later the woman, Jane, said she was pregnant. She also said she was thirty-eight and intended to have the child. John said he didn't want to become a father and he didn't want to be involved. He refused to be at the birth. He has, however, paid maintenance ever since – now £50 a month.

'Friends split,' John says now. 'Some thought I was behaving very badly, others felt Jane was an adult and had made her own decision. Once Jack was born she kept bringing him round, but I resisted because I felt she was forcing me to become connected and that was not what I wanted.'

When Jack was eighteen months old, John conceded. He began taking the baby out every week. A year later, John married Sarah and had two sons, Joshua, six and Sam four. His marriage broke up shortly after Sam's birth.

Now, John spends Wednesday nights at Sarah's house looking after Joshua and Sam. They in turn spend each weekend with him and part of all the holidays (when he is the main carer) at his present partner's house. John sees his eldest son, Jack, only periodically. 'Kate is brilliant at coping and talking things through,' John says. 'Whatever understandable resentment she might feel at having her house taken over at weekends is mellowed by the recognition that my children, including our daughter, are important to me. Discipline is the only area where we have difficulty. She doesn't think I'm tough enough. I don't want to be the source of all authority.

'I never wanted children,' John explains. 'It was never my idea of what was interesting. It wasn't that I'd had a particularly unhappy childhood, babies just didn't appeal. Now, I recognise how a relationship develops. I wasn't with Jack in those early months, I didn't get up to him four times in the night, I didn't feed him or change his nappies, so the relationship is not so close, and that's sad.

'When the two boys were born, Sarah had her own idea of mothering. Her mother had died when she was eight, so she was quite tough on them and it was all about organising efficiently. I was treated, at best, like an incompetent assistant. We both worked, so we also had a nanny. With Olivia and Kate, it's been very different. I've got space as a father. On the first day Kate went back to work, she left me to it and didn't call once to see if everything was OK. I was pleased and amazed. Sarah would have been on the phone half a dozen times.'

John's own father was forty-five when he was born. He had worked overseas for an oil company and tried hard, John says, within the conventions of the 1950s, to be a 'good' father. 'He retired early and sent me at seven to the boarding school that he had attended and loved. He wrote me a letter every week. He was very conscientious, but it was all somehow a duty. My memory of him is of someone hanging around the house constantly trying to please my mother. She was always telling him the cream was in the wrong jug or the lawn wasn't mown quite right.

'I only found out when I was thirty, that my father was illegitimate and sent away by his mother to relatives at the age of five because she wanted to marry and the man wouldn't have my father as well. He used to tell me, "Trick cyclists say that's all very damaging but it didn't harm me." But it did, he was totally unconnected with his feelings.'

Several years ago, John began to be interested in various forms of therapy. 'I'd always assumed I was happy at prep school but what this unearthed was a very lonely, frightened eight-year-old who couldn't work out why his mother had abandoned him. I think that's made me very sensitive to separation from the children and I'm much more aware of their feelings of vulnerability.

'I'm always careful to explain when I'm coming and going. Our divorce clearly still hurts them. Sam the other night asked me at his house why I couldn't stay for ever.'

John's father taught him to box at seven, and John says he was very aggressive at school. He is sports-orientated and has a rough-and-tumble with the children, but 'I stay away from aggressive games. At heart, it seems to me about power. The father is really saying, "I'm in charge". When a boy steps out of line and throws a kick, as he's been encouraged to do, the father suddenly turns around and says, "I'll knock your fucking head off if you do that again."

'It's not about fun, it's about a form of violence, but then, having said that, at least I could cope in the playground. No father wants to think he's sending his children out unprotected against the school bully.

'I know all three boys are more open with their feelings than I was ever encouraged to be,' he says. 'I told Sam to apologise to Joshua the other day and when he resisted, Joshua said: "Sam always gets embarrassed when he has to say sorry."'

Asked if he is concerned that while he shares childcare, work opportunities are passing him by, John says: 'I'm not driven or ambitious by nature. I like being lazy, I like spending time messing about with the children, but what I do worry about is earning enough money to keep all the wheels turning. I'm also lucky in that I live with a very well-organised woman – like my mother – although sometimes I resent that attempt to control.

'I like the fact that my children have other adults who are important to them in their lives. I don't want them to see me as some power figure. Fathering is about the gentler side of love as well; being mates, not competitors. And I honestly believe that certainly for Sam and Joshua, because their mother isn't with me and so can't intervene, and isn't around so that I have an excuse to slip out of my responsibilities, both she and I have a better relationship with the boys. As for Olivia and Kate, it seems much more of a team effort. I don't feel suffocated as a father, I feel free.'

Fatherhood *is* changing. Yet ironically, feminism, which has pushed so hard to bring this about, is also often reluctant to acknowledge that the change is occurring. In truth, feminism and fatherhood have had an odd relationship. Look at most of the standard feminist tomes and there may be any amount on the patriarchy but, just as in the literature of New Men, hardly anything at all in terms of personal recollections of Papa (a couple of exceptions include Germaine Greer's portrait of her father). In a movement that relies so much on individual experience, it seems a strange omission (and, for that matter, it seems just as strange that the omission itself has hardly been commented upon).

In contrast, there is any amount on mothers – being a mother, mothers and daughters, cameos of living mothers, remembrances of dead mothers. The father remains faceless, without character, known only in the negative, symbolic, of course, of the patriarchy. And because of that, because there is a propaganda value in 'oppression' remaining undiluted, unchanging, the authoritarian stereotype continues to hold the stage.

In *Women's Estate* (1971) Juliet Mitchell wrote: 'Patriarchy . . . is the sexual politics whereby men establish their power and maintain control . . . Its chief institution is the family.' Liz Kelly, feminist researcher into sexual violence, wrote in 1984 that fathers 'lay the basis subtly, coercively or violently of our fear of male anger and therefore our fear of challenging men'. And as the women's movement has helped to expose incest, rape, domestic violence and child physical abuse, so the darker side of the father has been rightly exposed again to view.

In 1970 Shulamith Firestone, twenty-six, co-founder of

112

Women's Liberation groups in New York in the late 1960s such as Redstockings and New York Radical Feminists, advocated – in the highly influential *The Dialectic of Sex* – an androgynous future in which the business of having babies was left to the laboratories; the family was eliminated and romantic love discarded since it was, she argued, merely a tool to keep women subservient.

Neil Lyndon says he read *The Dialectic of Sex* when it was first published and was 'devastated'. It prompted him to write in *No More Sex War*: 'The elimination of the father has always been an essential purpose of the sisterhood.' In fact, *The Dialectic of Sex* did not advocate the end of men's involvement with children – simply the end of the status and power hitherto accorded to fathers as the head of the household.

In Shulamith Firestone's new model society, groups of ten or so, men, women and children, would apply for a licence to live together for a limited period of time, and the licence would be renewable. 'Adult/child relationships would develop just as do the best relations today,' she wrote.

> Some adults might prefer certain children over others, just as some children might prefer certain adults over others – these might become lifelong attachments in which the individual concerned mutually agreed to stay together, perhaps to form some kind of non-reproductive unit. Thus all relationships would be based on love alone, uncorrupted by objective dependencies and the resulting class inequalities.

In short, *The Dialectic of Sex* was a slice of Utopia, written by a woman who had presumably never felt the desire to have a child (a pull still to be adequately tackled by feminism). Her target was pregnancy as much as paternity. Shulamith Firestone believed that her ideas on alternatives to the nuclear family would free women from the slavery of reproduction. They were one of any number of theories being explored, written about and tried out at the end of the sixties – but always by a tiny minority. Ever since, however, some feminists have misquoted the book as a vision of an all-female future while some men have regarded it as *the* feminist anti-father tract.

Now, of course, science fiction has become fact. Women through artificial insemination, can and do have children 'alone', once again raising the vision of a society in which fatherhood is redundant. Older professional women are having children as by AID (artificial insemination by donor) single parents (about 2 per cent of the total, according to the National Council for One Parent Families). Some, of course, have become pregnant by orthodox means; while lesbians – and, in a flurry of publicity, virgins too – have opted for the twentieth-century version of the immaculate conception.

Three years ago in the course of making a film for the BBC, I interviewed several women who had taken or were considering taking that step of becoming pregnant by AID. Mary Dempsey was in her early thirties. She had a good job working in Liverpool with the mentally handicapped, her own house, and no permanent relationship – although she had had several relationships in the past. 'I was doing well,' she explained, 'but nothing mattered to me because I had this need and it was all I could think about.'

Her daughter Rebecca, conceived by AID, was fourteen months old when we filmed. She was happy and secure in an extended family with plenty of father figures in the form of uncles and friends – and Mary was still open to settling into a permanent relationship. Mary was happy with the ethics of the situation, arguing that Rebecca would have as good a life as a child born to two parents on a much lower income and with less support. 'It's the amount of love which matters,' she insisted, 'not who gives it' – a view supported by some psychologists.

'The whole history of child psychology has been a history of scares that don't exist,' Dr Charlie Lewis of the Psychology Department of Lancaster University told Linda Grant in a recent article on the subject in *The Independent on Sunday*.

> Certainly fathers make life easier and women who decide to do this should be careful about avoiding the spiral of disadvantage. There should be no hiding from the fact that you are likely to enter a poverty trap when you become a single mother. But as for the psychological development of the child, if you create a culture in which such families are accepted, they will thrive.[12]

As I hope to show in the next chapter, the 'culture' is not yet accepting, but even so, apart from some separatist lesbians, the overwhelming message is that this small minority of women are making the choice not as a radical political statement but as a result of that most traditional of urges, the desire to have a child. The father has not been found wanting – he simply has not been found at all. The dispensability of the father in these cases is more a triumph of medical research than it is a victory for feminist ideology.

In September 1991 Bryan Appleyard, in *The Sunday Times*,[13] tackled the issue of the fatherless family. Using the kind of intellectual rigour the Right often seems to employ when it deals with this question, he wove together several different social trends to support his thesis that 'the conventional family' (in itself changing all the time in its definition, a fact Bryan Appleyard overlooks) is 'seriously threatened'.

He began his piece with an observation by Anna Coote, a feminist, who was one of the co-authors of a report, *The Family Way*, published by the Institute of Public Policy Research, a left-of-centre think tank. 'The father is no longer essential to the economic survival of the unit,' Anna Coote was reported as saying. 'Men haven't kept up with the changes in society, they don't know how to be parents. Nobody has taught them; where are the cultural institutions to tell them that being an active parent is a good thing? They don't exist. At the same time, women don't have many expectations of what men might provide.'

Her views could have been criticised as a sweeping generalisation; they might have been condemned for being condescending. (Why do men need 'cultural institutions' to teach them to be good fathers? As I have tried to argue earlier, fathers, from whatever class they may come, can apply common sense.) Her opinions might also have been seen as counterproductive, since they allow men off the hook. ('Nobody's showing me how to do it, so I won't try.') But Anna Coote is absolutely accurate in describing men's demotion from the sole breadwinner, and about the expectations of many women. Crucially, what she went on to argue in the original IPPR report was not that fathers should be written off but that they should be given all manner of extra encouragement to remain involved with their sons and daughters because it is the father's absence, not the fact of living in a lone-parent family, that can do the most damage to the children. Nevertheless, she had already been quoted out of context in *The Guardian*[14] and in several regional newspapers before Bryan Appleby seized on the notion that this, once again, was a case of feminism versus fatherhood.

'I repeat: there is no respectable division on this matter,' he wrote, in generous mood:

All feminist and pseudo-libertarian raving on the issue should be treated with contempt. The family may be the source of many woes, but it is also the only source of our happiness and stability. Neither is there any serious division on the view that the conventional family is seriously threatened and that this is a threat to the whole of society.

The problem is not simply illegitimacy but the family itself . . . There is no longer any real political division among respectable thinkers on the key issue of the virtues

of the conventional family. Massive research programmes
. . . show as conclusively as can ever be shown that the
children of conventional mother–father families perform
and behave better than the offspring of unconventional
structures . . .

It is difficult to see how, in terms of income, this research can
be comparing like with like, as so many single-parent families
carry the added burden of poverty. In addition, there is also
research which reveals the extent of damage done by 'conventional' families (Bryan Appleyard's 'conventional' family must
include a working mother since only 5 per cent of families now
consist of a male bread-winner and a mother permanently at
home); it is not institutions but the individuals within them,
the attitudes they hold and the amount they have to live on, I
would argue, that make the difference.

The statistics Bryan Appleyard uses are often quoted to
show the alleged collapse of conventional families and the slow
exile of the father. On the contrary, they indicate a continued
optimistic belief in the nuclear family. Divorce and separation
rates may be high – but the overwhelming majority of men
and women remarry within five years.[15]

Illegitimacy rates may be high – over 28 per cent of all
births and still rising – but in 1987, 70 per cent of joint
registrations of births gave the same address for both parents.
The implication is that illegitimacy is no longer, in the main,
the mark of the single mother but of cohabitees. (In July 1992,
a study indicated that cohabitees who go on to marry have a
far higher failure rate than those who marry without cohabit-
ing. This may be for all manner of reasons, not least that the
cohabitees believe a wedding may salvage a relationship that is
already on the rocks. What we lack is any information about
couples who remain cohabitees.)[16]

As John F. Ermisch, Professor of Political Economy at the
University of Glasgow, points out in his sober, unhysterical
and highly rigorous book *Lone Parenthood: An Economic*

Analysis, the percentage of births outside marriage and registered solely to the mother has increased relatively little. In 1979, it was 4.9 per cent; by 1987, that had risen to 7.4 per cent. He reports that 60 per cent of these mothers were in a stable relationship by the time the child was five, a figure that rose to 70 per cent by the time the child was seven.

As Social Trends in 1989 pointed out, 'Just over 77% of people living in private households in Great Britain in 1987 lived in families headed by a married couple, a proportion which has fallen only slightly since 1961 . . .' Perhaps in this context, we might be richer as a community for a little 'unconventionality'?

Never the less, the majority in society still appear to retain a commitment to the idea of two parents rearing children, and the experience of single parenthood remains transitory for most. What *is* different, is women's refusal (and men's) to stay within relationships which are no longer tenable and may be emotionally and physically damaging. (In the Bradshaw and Millar study, overwhelmingly, the women said the 'best thing about being a lone parent' was 'independence' and 'freedom to do what you want'. Only 9 per cent of them said they regretted leaving the relationship.) What this represents is a threat not to modern paternalism but to patriarchy – but Bryan Appleyard prefers his own demons.

Where the main body of the women's movement has struck hardest against the father is not in fighting to remove him from the family altogether but in attacking the criminally 'bad' father whom society often still tries to protect or absolve from blame. (Consider the use of family therapy in the treatment of fathers who sexually abuse their children. Instead of squarely blaming the man, the interactions within the family have to share the fault – a policy which only adds to a child's pain.) Feminism too has focussed on criticising the influence of the traditional father, particularly on his sons.

In *Every Mother's Son*, published in 1983, Judith Arcana,

mother of Daniel, was not only damning of fathers but highly critical of women who want them in the lives of their boys:

> It is striking that so many mothers are willing to accept men as models for our sons. Despite women-hating and mother-blaming, despite man's creation and development of this murderous culture, mothers say that boys should be around men so they can learn what to be. What can they be thinking of, to say in one breath that most men are regrettably lacking, and in another that our sons need to spend time with them, to learn 'what they're supposed to do'?

More recently, in *The Rites of Man*, published in 1991, Rosalind Miles argues that today's conditioning of boys allegedly leads them into the same brutish, insensitive and violent behaviour as that practiced by their fathers, grand-fathers and great-grandfathers. What this view propounds is the belief that masculinity remains untouched, in spite of nearly three decades of feminism and economic changes, an opinion I don't share.

Clearly, some fathers, driven by their own insecurity and licensed by society's traditions, do continue exercise a primi-tive control through fear; they do abuse, batter, mentally destroy – and they do so on a significant scale because some still consider that this is part of a 'good' masculine upbringing. One woman I interviewed for the chapter on work (Chapter Seven) mentioned in passing for instance that even when she was eighteen, she had to be in by 9.30 p.m. If she was late, her father would heat a poker on the fire and burn her – a punishment she had received since she was a tiny child. But other men, either by force of circumstance or volition, *are* trying to create new patterns of fathering. It may not be, as yet, an earth shaking trend, but it deserved at least to be acknowledged and supported, not divided or ignored.

In the 1990s, I believe, if women are to be constructively

critical of fathers, they must also look to the behaviour of their own gender too. They might ask, for instance, how much a mother contributes to the idea of the all-powerful dad when she uses the threat 'Just wait until your father gets home . . .'? They might ask what form of conditioning allows mothers to terrorise or neglect their children, using just as many physical and mental weapons as a man can wield? The fact that this may be a symptom of women's oppression does not, in my view, always automatically absolve them of responsibility.

As Juliet Mitchell wrote in *Women's Estate* about the effects of women's inferior position within the family:

> It produces a tendency to small-mindedness, petty jealousy, irrational emotionality and random violence, dependency, competitive selfishness and possessiveness, passivity, a lack of vision, conservativism . . . to say that women have none of the above listed negative feminine characteristics is moralism not politics . . .

So where do we go from here? Whatever the efforts of individual men, the institutions which have shored up the traditional image of the father as the main breadwinner remain virtually unaffected. If the *nouveau père* has a genuine commitment to permanent change, there should be more evidence of a national strategy to bring that change about. Male parenting, like motherhood, is still very much a private concern.

In Britain, Gillian Shephard, the Employment Minister, fights to retain the forty-eight-hour week when what she should be doing is ensuring decent rates of pay so that no father or mother has to work overtime to make up their wage. (In the States, the pressure to work even longer hours is still more intense. In *The Overworked American: The Unexpected Decline of Leisure*, Juliet B. Schor shows how for some Americans, since 1970, the conviction that the working week would shrink from forty hours to thirty-five hours to less has gone into reverse. Instead, the average worker, male and female, puts in the equivalent of an extra month a year in overtime.)

In Britain, too, a higher proportion of men with children under five work fifty hours or more a week than in any other country in the EC. Paternity leave is either non-existent or a joke. The Ford motor company allocates three days for paternity leave – but it must be booked in advance. Compare this with parental leave in Sweden, where either parent can take up to eighteen months on 90 per cent pay. Once back, a parent can then work a six-hour day, on reduced pay, until the child reaches school age. And the economy has yet to collapse.

Concepts such as job-sharing, a thirty-hour week and parental leave to care for a sick child are still alien to the male work culture. The trade-union movement may have taken steps towards acknowledging the family (because it has been forced to do so by an increasing female and a declining male membership), but it still shows a marked reluctance to ask for terms which suit the father who happens to be a working man, not the other way round.

Meanwhile, it is left to individual men to challenge the notion that he who stays longest in the office is the best. In *What Women Say, What Men Say*, Ross Wetzsteon quotes the American lawyer husband of a prominent feminist editor: 'Feminism has changed most of the men I know. But its effect on the work ethic has been zilch,' the lawyer says. 'Hell! When I'm interviewing a young lawyer the last thing I'm interested in is his emotional openness or how much house-work he does. I want a tough ambitious son-of-a-bitch who'll stay at his desk until midnight.'

Victor McGeer is a Transport and General Workers' Union national official. He has four children under eight and his partner, Sally Gilbert, is national equality organiser for the National Union of Journalists. In *T & G Women* (Winter 1990/91), McGeer explains how he 'surprises male colleagues' when he leaves meetings at 5 p.m. to pick up the children from the childminder:

> Our kids go to . . . a registered childminder. We leave
> them at 8.30 in the morning and pick them up again at 5.30
> and I can only count one occasion when neither of us was
> there to do the picking up, tea, bath and bed in the
> evening. It can be done but it takes organisation and quite
> a bit of effort, but the rewards more than justify it. It's
> good fun.

Before joining the T & G as a full-time official, Victor McGeer was a bus driver and the long shifts made share-care very much more difficult: 'It's all very well having a nine-day fortnight or an extra week's holiday, but it means longer days. It means you're not going to be there if you've got people who depend upon you . . .'

Recognition of family needs has been slow to materialise so far in the workplace. Once men judge it to be in their own interests, as in so many other spheres, might change suddenly pick up speed? Already in the States, where benefits, rights and entitlements are far harder to come by, some companies are finding that, as an article in *The Director* pointed out:

> attracting the brightest and the best in a dwindling pool of
> well qualified recruits in the 90s has nothing to do with
> salaries and everything to do with family values.
>
> IBM and Pepsico were among the pioneers in what is
> known in the US as life-cycle benefits, offering a range of
> help through the different stages of family responsibilities.
> These include cash, time benefits such as special leave or
> flexible working hours, in-house service for childcare or
> adult day care and counselling for family problems . . .[17]

If corporations can do this for the highly priced, a government can do it for all (and after initial expenditure, save money).

Such are the times in which we live, once fatherhood is properly valued, so the artificially low price attached to mothering may belatedly rise too.

Even so, women – understandably – remain reluctant to concede some of their traditional role. Yet if they do not, as we are already witnessing, many will have to carry a double burden: a job both inside and outside the home. In addition, whether full-time mothers or not, they deny their children a route to what their father alone can contribute (just as the mother's contribution is unique). If fathers are not essential for status or protection or a guaranteed income, what they *are* for in the 1990s is potentially more humane. Research shows that children benefit not just from the caring relationship they have seperately with mother and father, but also from observing a loving relationship, free from resentment, anger and tension, developing *between* their parents.

For women to give up maternal power when, as a group, they already hold too little is a gamble, but there is the possibility of one further reward. The faster the traditional stereotype of the father is buried, and new models of fatherhood begin to be acknowledged, the quicker society may also be forced to accept that motherhood, too, comes in many different but equally valid guises, including that of the lone parent. As the black American feminist Florynce Kennedy said, 'Being a mother is a noble status, right? So why does it change when you put "unwed" or "welfare" in front of it?'

CHAPTER FIVE

I don't take the welfare to bed

I'd rather have my freedom than a freezer,
I'd rather be on welfare than be wed,
For though it's true,
There's a lot I've been through,
I don't take the welfare to bed.

*Written by Clair Chapman of the Women's Theatre Group
in 1974. This is a song about an unmarried mother who has
been accused by social security officials of being 'immoral'
and 'undeserving'*

Like the mouth of a crone, with every other tooth black-
ened, the main street in Goldthorpe in The Dearne is
distinguished more by its signs of decay, than by its prosperity.
The cinema which became a bingo hall and then a furniture
store is boarded up; the knick-knack shop is no more; the
church around the corner has a For Let sign; only the
Mediterranean fish 'n' chip shop seems to be doing good
business.

'You know the joke?' says a local resident.'When the pits
shut, every other miner put his money into fish 'n' chips. Even
us lot couldn't eat that many.'

A hundred years ago, the farming hamlet of Goldthorpe was
transformed. A shaft was sunk at Hickleton Main Colliery and
suddenly its seventy-five inhabitants, getting by in a dozen or
so houses with a dirt track for a road, no fresh water supply
and not much in the way of sewage disposal, were, relatively
speaking, in the money. Within a decade, Goldthorpe had a

Co-op shop, a working men's club, a hospital and a school. It had also had its first pit death.

On 19 April 1900 Henry Dyson, aged forty, was killed by slippage at the face. His wife would have been left a lone parent but for the fact that all three of the couple's young children had been buried in the previous two years. In the mining community, the single-parent mother has a very long tradition.

Local records show that as one local pit developed into two, then three (eventually turning into a network of eight in the stretch between Barnsley and Doncaster), the men and children in work did comparatively well (a shilling a week plus food for a ten-year-old spending thirty-one hours on household chores); but the poor went to hell and the boss couldn't lose. In 1900, among the cases in court – and not untypical – was a fine of ten shillings plus costs for quitting employment without giving notice: ten shillings also to be paid to employer for damages and costs. 'Culprit's pay is one pound a week.')

In the couple of years after the 1984 miners' strike (The Dearne is proud that it had only one scab in the area, 'And he came from Doncaster' – a foreigner), one in five male jobs went. Now, seven out of the eight pits are closed; so are the steel works. As a result, myriads of small cottage industries, mainly offering 'women's work' have also disappeared. Male unemployment is around 12 per cent (according to government figures fiddled several times over to reduce the number artificially); female unemployment stands at 6 per cent. Every post in the area, from street sweeper to factory worker receives several hundred applications – so much so that the skill of responding to a vacancy carries its own apprenticeship now, with advice on how and what and where to write.

It is one of the inequities of Thatcherism that in The Dearne, as elsewhere in Britain, so much talent and energy are now invested in the trade of just getting by; while one of the ironies is that if Goldthorpe has a growth industry, it is in the business of welfare rights. And it is the women – particularly that bogey of the 1990s, the single-parent mothers – who are helping to lead that fight back.

The Dearne Centre Against Unemployment and the Enterprise Centre, housed under one roof, was opened in 1986. Mid-morning, mid-week, the ground floor is occupied by a handful of small workshops, given seed money and space – among them businesses making embroidered badges, motorised golf trollies and stained-glass windows. Upstairs, older women who hope to return to work are in a typing class; half a dozen men are in the job-search section being given help with CVs and applications; also on offer are computer tuition, machine knitting, a writers' workshop, GCSE adult education classes (a recent 80 per cent pass rate in English); social groups, pressure groups such as a Child Poverty Action Group; and eighteen months ago the Centre acquired its own small urban farm, cared for mainly by volunteers. If the centre has a philosophy, it is self-help advocated not just for the individual but for the local community as a whole, pitted against a wider society which, Dearne people feel, no longer wants to know.

In the main room a small canteen offers chip butties and hot dinners and a team of welfare rights workers are on hand most of whom originally came to the Centre themselves for help. They now work as full-time volunteers. (Resources don't stretch to salaries.)

In the office, Jan Brooks, a divorcee with two children, who is the full-time organiser of all the courses, sits with Jan Gardner, aged thirty-four, a welfare rights volunteer. Jan Gardner is the unmarried mother of two daughters: Vicky is sixteen, Carla eighteen. Each has a different father. Vicky is taking her GCSEs and wants to be a journalist; Carla hopes to go to university if her A levels are good enough.

'I say to my mam, why doesn't she go to college?' Vicky says. 'But she won't, she underestimates her brainpower, she does.' Jan, an ebullient, direct woman, just smiles.

Jan Gardner left school at sixteen, pregnant. Her GP was a

friend of her mother and she felt she couldn't go to him for the Pill. Two years later, she had Vicky. 'It was the seventies, so there wasn't that much disapproval, but it still wasn't easy. Both my girls say they want to have careers first and babies later,' Jan says. 'I tell them they're right.'

In 1988, Jan came to the Centre for a tenants' association meeting. 'I don't think I've been home since.' She has been on several courses and specialises in debt counselling. Three days earlier, she gave her first public speech. 'I were nervous as hell but once I got going it were fine.'

The Centre's office is scattered with large multicoloured paper flowers, like the leftovers from some Hawaiian wedding. The flowers, it transpires, are for the forthcoming Lord Mayor's Parade. Jobs may have gone, but not the sense of humour. The smiles are prompted by the theme: the regeneration of The Dearne. 'Well, we've already got a bit of regeneration, and it's ecologically minded too,' someone says, tongue in cheek. 'The grass is growing over the pits all by itself, and it's ever so green.'

In the brochure put out to celebrate the first five years of the Centre's history, those whom it has helped bear witness. For instance, a woman in her forties with several children, who had no previous experience of adult education. She writes:

Courses – what courses haven't I done? Computing, farming, return to study, assertiveness. I'm on the urban farm group, the disabled club, I'm a street rep, I'm with the tenants' group. Before I came here, I'd never done anything, not since I left school. I never had time, I was just a mother with kids. It just shows you can learn even without qualifications. I've been to conferences and meetings at Gateshead, Leeds, Sheffield, Bradford, Liverpool and Bristol, it's much better than sitting at home. Just think, I wouldn't have got nowhere, if I hadn't come here.

Those who look at the rise and rise of the white middle-class businesswoman as a testament to the success of feminism aren't rewarding capitalism enough for its ability to recognise what is of value to the market. The true measure of the influence of the women's movement, it seems to me, lies instead in the network of self-help groups – non-professional, often anti-Establishment – which run from one end of Britain to the other – and of which the efforts in The Dearne are a part.

Around a coffee table in the centre, a group of women talk – all are single parents; some divorced, some never married. Susan is forty-seven and helps to raise funds for the Centre. In 1970, she fell pregnant with her daughter Janet. 'I didn't love him, so why marry him and get a divorce? I told him that she's mine, I'll bring her up my way. I didn't want a piece of paper from him that said I was his for life. It didn't bother me what anybody else thought. I was left to get on with it and Janet and me, we did all right.'

Susan says Janet's dad worked down the pit and contributed maintenance when he could. 'I had to take him to court a couple of times, but he's been OK.' He's usually paid between £6 and £10 a week. In the miners' strike it stopped and I gave him a hand with a soup kitchen. It was difficult for all of us then.

'When I first had Janet, I came home with the babby and about £2 on the social,' Susan says. 'People would offer you jobs and say, "Take it or leave it" and you always took it.' She earned money picking potatoes and tulips and turnips; painting and decorating for a tenner a room and following a tractor and trailer picking out the best stones for the farmer. 'Two pounds a day, that were.'

Susan's own father died when she was three years old. 'My mam worked as a caretaker and did a brilliant job with six of us. I remember one of my brothers paying for me to have a pair of proper shoes. I kept looking down on my way to school and thinking, "That's real leather laces there."

'If you're a single parent,' she says, 'you try all that much harder. You don't want your kid to be picked on because she's got less than the rest. I remember our Janet's friend had a leather coat for £120. Janet didn't say anything directly, she never did ask. "What do you think of it, Mum?" was how I knew.

'It took me a month to get the money together but I did it, working day and night. It was worth it when I saw her face. Janet did well, she got O levels and owt but she's got two kiddies herself now and a really good man. He works all the hours God sends and brings home £82 at the end of the week. Of course, I've got to help out. I've just bought her a fridge-freezer. They're still your kids, even when they leave the nest.'

May says that she has two daughters and two sons and her income has dropped by half since she left her husband, also a miner. 'You gave him the elbow, didn't you, cock?' says Susan. May is paid £5 a night working three evenings a week as a cleaner at the dog track. She also receives £50 a week maintenance; for every pound of maintenance, she loses a pound from her benefit. 'I don't have any regrets leaving,' says May, who was married for twenty years. 'He maybe earned a lot but what I got of it, I'm better off now.'

Once the new Child Support Act comes into force – and with it the Child Support Agency in April 1993 – many women who refuse to disclose the name of their children's father stand to lose between £5 and £8 a week. As with May, what they receive in maintenance if they do not co-operate will in any case be taken off their income support: the net gain for many will be nil.

'Vicky's dad is married and his wife has never known,' Jan Gardner says. 'Why should I wreck his life? I'd rather lose the money.' (The Bradshaw and Millar study indicates that one in four women will refuse to disclose for reasons ranging from fear to simply not wanting any contact.) Shelly, twenty-eight, a temporary welfare rights worker who has a baby son and who cohabits, says that women are already being subjected to aggressive interviews and the decision as to which women will lose income and which won't will be at the adjudicator's discretion. 'It's the same old story when it comes to single parents. The Agency will issue guidelines, but we're not allowed to know.'

What seems to set this generation of women apart from that of their mothers and grandmothers is not how hard they work to keep their families intact, nor their strength – both have always been strands in mining communities. It is the sense they seem to have of themselves and their rights: no matter how poorly valued they may be by the rest of society.

Jan says the black economy is alive and well in Goldthorpe (as it is everywhere in Britain). One single-parent woman says she earns £2.80 an hour cleaning – no sick pay, no holiday money, no rights . . . If it was taxed and she had to pay for childcare and lose her benefits, she might as well stay at home. As it is, she gets around £85 a week for herself and her two children from social security and benefits – and £28 on the fiddle: 'It means trainers for the kids and I'm queen of the karaoke night once every couple of months.'

Jan Gardner was also reared by a single parent. Her father was killed by cancer after nineteen years down the pits. 'They told my mam that she couldn't have free coal because he hadn't done his twenty years,' she says. Jan was ten when her father died and her mother, in her thirties, had a family of four to rear. 'She was always trying hard. She worked as a presser in a factory and as a petrol-pump attendant. People talk about a lack of discipline in single-parent families – they should come here. My dad was strict and my mum carried that on. And if she didn't do it, my older brother would give me a helluva pasting instead. I was brought up to have manners.

'I believe in chastising, not pasting. I've been the same with my girls,' she adds. 'But they've always been really good kids.'

Jan has a boyfriend, a Dearne man, now in Scotland, whom

she sees every few months. Her daughters like him, but she says she doesn't want a permanent relationship. 'This way, I can live how I want to, and look after my own money. We might not have much but it's mine,' she says.

What she and her two daughters live on is around £120 a week including a disability allowance, as Jan is arthritic in both hips. (She is too young yet to have hip replacements.) She explains what she thinks she would lose if she took a low-paid job (most of the work on offer is part-time and casualised, and women now have to compete with men for occupations they once thought were all their own, such as supermarket cashier and shelf-filler). She would have to pay all the poll tax (instead of 20 per cent), all the water bill, her rent, prescription dental and optician charges, and make a contribution to Carla's student grant. 'No job around here pays like that.

'What happens when you're poor,' she says, 'is that you look to the family next door and see that they're having to manage and so you just get on with it, too. That's why there's no anger about. But the limitations on your life, the energy you need to get by, just wears some people away – and if you slip up, if you get into a bit of debt that you didn't mean to do, it very quickly becomes catastrophic. I deal with cases like it all the time and financially, there's no one there to help anyone out – only themselves.'

In Goldthorpe High Street, the pressure to buy is as intense as everywhere else – T-shirts, trainers, shell suits, baseball caps, CDs, videos, cheap jewellery: the accessories which teenagers regard as the currency of having a good time. When Jan needs extra money, she goes – like many in the area – to the Shopacheque. 'You borrow £100 and pay back £140 over twenty weeks, at £7 a week. It's mad but what else is there? We've got no banks, no savings, and the social don't want to know.'

In Britain, between 1980 and 1985, poverty rose faster than in any other EC state, according to a study by the European Commission.[1] The period saw a 30.4 per cent increase in people living on less than 50 per cent of the average wage. No other country in the EC but Britain, in the past ten years, has also inhibited the incomes of the bottom 10 per cent in its population in order to finance tax cuts to the rich.[2]

In the years since 1979, that bottom 10 per cent has lost a massive £4,800 million pounds in tax and benefits, while the top 5 per cent has benefited by several hundred pounds a week: income redistribution *Alice in Wonderland*-style. The pain behind these figures is relatively easily concealed: by fixing the figures and having no official poverty line in the first place. As Mrs Thatcher said in the 1980s, when asked about the breadline, 'It all depends what you mean by the breadline.'

'Poverty', said the Church of England's 1985 report, *Faith in the City*, 'is not only about shortage of money. It is about rights and relationships; about how people are treated and how they regard themselves; about powerlessness, exclusion and loss of dignity. Yet the lack of an adequate income is at its heart.'

More prosaically, in Britain, in the absence of any official yardstick, poverty is measured by either absolute or relative standards. In 1886 Charles Booth, a Liverpool shipowner, read in the Pall Mall Gazette that one in four of London's population was 'in distress'. This, he decided, was left-wing propaganda, unscientific and emotive, and intended to obscure the truth and service socialism.[3] He decided to carry out his own survey and found the degree of distress even higher – a third of the population were in dire straits and particularly vulnerable were the equivalent of today's lone parent: 'widows and deserted women'.

Poverty had already been established fifty years before as an absolute condition. The Poor Law Amendment Act (1834) made it a crime to be ill or unemployed; the 'sin' was to be without resources. The punishment was the workhouse. In Britain, unlike much of the rest of the EC, shame and a low income have always traditionally been fused. And women have always proportionately suffered most.

In the nineteenth century, one woman, a labourer's wife, when asked how she could keep her large family on next to nothing, replied: 'Sir, we don't live, we only linger . . .' One hundred and fifty years on, poverty is now more usually considered relative (unless the rhetoric is in the hands of politicians). One of the most common measures is to assess that anyone living on an income below half the average is 'poor'. But even with a video recorder along with income support, there is still the sense of only lingering rather than living in a society which, for the majority, has got better and better.

One mother, for instance, quoted in *Hardship Britain*,[4] says: 'The children are always asking for things, they say their friends have this and this . . . we have to say no, so the children get upset and we get upset.' Another explains how her fourteen-year-old daughter reproaches her: 'Since daddy went you've been more and more like this. Since he's gone you've been doing this too much, saying we haven't got the money.'

In July 1992, the government finally published a report it had held over since before the April general election. It showed that its theory that if the rich are left to prosper, wealth will trickle down has gone horrifically wrong. In 1988, twelve million people were living on 50 per cent below the average income. In 1979, the figure was five million. A quarter of all children now live below this line compared to 10 per cent in 1979.[5]

One of the fastest-growing groups to be affected by poverty is lone mothers and their children One in seven families in Britain is now headed by a lone parent, over 90 per cent are female and 70 per cent are on income support. The Bradshaw and Millar study revealed that the range of income is pitifully narrow. A woman with two children surviving entirely on income support and other benefits receives around £73 a week; a woman in part-time work also in receipt of benefits receives an average of £89, while full-time workers receive an appallingly low £114 a week. This is in comparison to £340, the net average weekly income of a couple with two children in work.

A woman on income support has £14.55 a week – a couple of pounds a day – as a personal allowance to keep a child under eleven. The minimum basic weekly allowance for foster care of a child aged eight to ten is £60–£69. Research shows that the average length of time for a lone parent to depend upon income support is 2.6 years; for some, though, it is much longer, and the cumulative effect of being without money and often in poor housing in rotting neighbourhoods is obvious (although not always inevitable). It hits the children hardest. Low birth weight, infant mortality, recurring illness, dental decay, low growth rates, poor nutrition, academic difficulties and plain old-fashioned unhappiness are all on the list.

Authoritative research which proves the effects of poverty has a long history of being ignored, shelved or suppressed. Sir Douglas Black's 1980 report into the nation's health – or lack of it – for instance, appeared only after a struggle. 'Present social inequalities in a country like Britain are unacceptable and deserve to be so declared,' he said, by way of an obituary on his own efforts.

Ten years on, in 1990, in the *British Medical Journal*, a piece of research affirmed that the gap between the health of rich and poor is widening. 'The notion of the dispossessed and feckless "underclass" that imposes costs on the rest of society and is to blame for most social ills is becoming popular,' the authors wrote. 'Such an idea has obvious consequences for social policy, yet it sits uneasily with the evidence from the studies of differential mortality which reiterate the fact that British society is stratified to a fine grain from top to bottom.'[6]

In *Modern Conservatism*, David Willetts MP, consultant director of the Conservative Research Department, explains how the welfare system is not a favour extended to the poor, but an essential part of a capitalist society. It permits fresh labour to be recruited (by providing retirement pensions and unemployment benefits) and it is founded on the concept of mutuality: at some point every individual may have need of it. And there is a third factor:

> There comes a point when we really have to confront a simple moral obligation towards fellow members of our community. Regardless of whether people in need have been reckless or feckless or unlucky and unfortunate there comes a point when the exact explanation of how they became destitute ceases to matter. They have a claim on us simply by virtue of being compatriots. The welfare state is an expression of solidarity with our fellow citizens.

Except, as he goes on to explain, when there is a risk of 'moral hazard':

> Moral hazard occurs when the very fact that an adversity is insured against makes us more irresponsible and thus more likely to get into adversity . . . [the welfare state] wreaks this damage by giving short-term financial rewards to behaviour which is in the long term destructive both of the individuals involved and of the society at large.

Those on the right have unravelled this coded message to read that the lone parent, amongst the poor, is unique. She constitutes a threat to how orthodox society is supposed to behave because she has substituted the state for a partner. At the same time, the right implies, the attractions of income support are so great that she actually opts for it (pregnancy as a passport to the welfare state) and has no inclination to 'better herself' by moving out of the poverty trap. How can her values not be suspect? Respectable society is not only right, it has a duty to feel mad about these women.

Female lone parents may be divorced, separated or widowed (as four-fifths are); they may be single, they may be teenagers or middle-aged. They may be highly skilled or without a single qualification. No matter – as far as the right is concerned

135

what brings them together as a tribe and makes them both a threat and a drain on the nation's resources is the antisocial habit that they all allegedly hold in common: a dependency on the welfare culture.

'Increasingly, low incomes are associated with behaviour such as irresponsible sexual habits and unstable family formation,' wrote the right-winger, Digby Anderson in *The Sunday Times* in 1990, 'lack of commitment to work or training and failure to save or spend prudently . . . It is time to bring back the notions of deserving and undeserving poor, to restore moral discrimination to social policy.'

The single-parent mother, however varied her circumstance, is now, mainly through propoganda and confused and contradictory social security rules, a prime target for government.

First, through the Child Support Agency, the government aims to coerce women into giving information they might prefer, for sound reasons, to withhold. Second – and most cynical of all – this government seeks to create in lone parents a scapegoat, a 'cause' for the fact that parts of society appear to be in danger of disintegration. (The problem is not a lack of morals but the absence of investment in a number of areas that might give young people a sense of worth, and therefore of purpose.)

'I was brought up among people who had little,' John Major said in a speech at the Adam Smith Institute in June 1992, 'yet they – we – were no different from the next man or woman . . . Just because you have little money it does not follow that you need little choice . . . People in these circumstances long to have choices. They want to be independent, not dependent on town hall or benefit office. They want a share in this country, a hand-up not a hand-out.'

Mr Major's policies do not match his words. Instead they are sinking the hopes of so many lone mothers and their children. And worse is yet to come. The preparations were being laid almost a decade ago.

In 1984 the American polemicist Charles Murray, the

godfather of 'the underclass', published the influential book *Losing Ground*. In it he argued, as David Willetts was to imply later, that welfare payments had become so attractive that the incentive to work, for some in society, had evaporated. Murray's critics – and he has many – pointed out that in the States in the 1980s welfare had in fact been drastically cut back, and still the numbers of the poor grew. Charles Murray was unswayed.

In 1989, he adapted his views to Britain. Mr Murray is highly appreciated by Andrew Neil, editor of *The Sunday Times*, who, several times since, has given him copious amounts of space to elaborate on his views. Mr Murray believes that Britain, too, has an 'underclass' in the making. Its best predictor is 'illegitimacy'. In short, Mr Murray's target are women like Jan Gardner, never married, mother of 'illegitimate' children, a woman who has no intention of taking a husband and has been on income support for years. Mr Murray sees her situation as a decision dictated by her lack of moral fibre.[7]

In practice, Jan Gardner, like many hundreds of thousands of women, has moral fibre by the bucketload. What she doesn't have is Mr Major's 'hand-up' or choice. What traps her is not dependency on income support but a slavery enforced by the state: a slavery which pays her too little to survive with dignity on welfare, yet offers her jobs which often pay still less.

Rita Busby, forty-seven, a full-time welfare rights officer for Bradford Gingerbread (and another single parent, a mother of three, who also defies the stereotype, having spent the last several years getting A levels and a university degree), says that she often has to advise women that if they take a job, their income will drop and what they will have forfeited, in addition to time with their children, is money.

'Social Security is low but because pay is also low and there is too little flexibility in the system, it's almost impossible for a woman to break away. It's not that the social is too soft,'

Rita Busby adds, 'but that the system seems built to hinder and punish, not help.'

A single parent in work with two children, for instance, earning £4 an hour, is initially likely to emerge around £20 a week better off as a result of working – but from that extra money must come childcare costs (£1.50 an hour for child-minding), school meals (£8) and travelling expenses. In the school holidays, of course, childminding costs rise rapidly. She ends up no better off.

The government has also devised a new way of further penalising the lone-parent mother who tries to enter employment. Family credit is designed to subsidise low pay. If a woman receives it, she is no longer given income support. Income support has virtually a 100 per cent take-up among lone parents, according to the Bradshaw and Millar study; family credit, in contrast has a low take-up rate – possibly only 50 per cent. In addition, in April 1992, the rules were changed.

A woman previously had to work twenty-four hours a week to receive family credit; now it is only sixteen hours. The Bradshaw and Millar study revealed that only a third of lone parents knew what family credit is or how to become eligible, so some women are bound to find themselves now without either benefit; coincidentally, of course, saving the government money . . .

Another factor is that family credit is calculated for six months at a time. If, for example, a maintenance payment fails to arrive for several weeks, there is nothing a woman can do to adapt the amount she receives (income support is much more easily adjusted).

Family credit also does not cover mortgage interest repayments (income support does). One woman wrote to the Child Poverty Action Group to say that she would like to take up paid employment now that her children were older but she would find this financially impossible, because 'My mortgage interest is about £640 a month.'

'Some lone parents . . . may be tempted either to reduce

their hours of work or to give up work altogether when they realise they will be worse off as a result of the change in rules,' Fran Bennett and Vicki Chapman point out in *The Poverty of Maintenance*.

Details of ill thought out measures such as these are not the concern of Charles Murray. What he has decided is that in Britain we have 'a type of poverty' which is 'growing rapidly' and whose values are 'contaminating the life of entire neighbourhoods' – one of the most insidious aspects of the phenomenon is that 'neighbours who don't share those values cannot isolate themselves'. In other words, we are all in danger of yob rule. The cause? The lone parent.

Charles Murray says that in addition to illegitimacy, the other identifying tattoos of 'the underclass' are violent crime and dropping out from the labour force. (Lone mothers are in a catch-22 situation. In practice, many of them, far from 'dropping out' of the job market, do work constantly, as mentioned before, on the black economy, and for very little. If they are open about what they do, they may regain some credibility but they also acquire a criminal record – while their overall income, minus a court fine, is worse than it was originally. That route out of 'the underclass' comes at too high a price.)

In communities without fathers, Charles Murray lectures, 'The kids tend to run wild'. (As a result of his observation – elevated into 'fact' by repetition – now every time a housing estate erupts into riots, the popular mythology concludes that it is a rash of lone parent-itis again when the evidence may prove quite the contrary: another example of ignorance feeding prejudice.) Charles Murray is not yet done: 'Single young women get pregnant because sex is fun and babies are endearing,' he writes . . . And single-parent women, in avoiding marriage, are ignoring the duty they have to the rest of society: to tame testosterone.

'Supporting a family is a central means of a man to prove to himself that he is a mensch,' he explained. 'Men who do not

139

support families find other ways to prove they are men, which tend to take destructive forms . . . Young men are essentially barbarians for whom marriage . . . the act of taking responsibility for a wife and children, is an indispensable civilising force . . .'

In the States, the underclass is now identified not only by its moral 'looseness' but also by its genes. Forget the idea that fate or circumstances may catapult a woman from security to insecurity; now if she's at the bottom of society's pile, it's because she and her offspring are literally born to fail. In May 1990, Charles Murray appeared with Professor Richard Hernstein at a conference on crime culture in London. Kenneth Baker, then Home Secretary, also attended and seemed much taken with the argument Professor Hernstein made that 60 to 70 per cent of criminal behaviour comes from boys with 'genetic propensities'. The rate in the UK is less, the professor argued, but 'not negligible'.[8]

What is convenient in all this, of course, is that it absolves government policies from all responsibility – and, if anything, justifies an even more punitive approach for the mother's 'own good'.

In *The Making of an English 'Underclass'?*, Kirk Mann efficiently exposes the Murray argument for the dangerous cant it is:

> What is most remarkable about Murray's version of the underclass is how easily he has been able to disseminate his ideas . . . In this respect, he represents a long tradition of commentators . . . who have observed a stratum of hopeless degenerates . . . What Murray does illustrate is the fact that it is all too easy to slide from the identification of a social group who suffer problems into the position where the victims are regarded as *the* social problem.

Kirk Mann argues that the poor may be the most visible recipients of welfare, and therefore an easy target, but they are by far the least greedy of its consumers. Benefits may have doubled to £4 billion since the early 1980s, he argues, but tax relief on mortgages costs a hefty £7 billion. The middle classes also benefit, for instance, from tax exemptions on occupational pensions, tax subsidies on unit trusts, and company cars. If welfare corrupts the single mother, why not the male married corporate executive? 'There is no consideration', Kirk Mann says of Murray's argument, 'of how fiscal welfare or occupational welfare promote dependency and mendacity among the middle classes.'

Charles Murray also fails to acknowledge that while every period has had its 'underclass' allegedly damned by genetics, – 'the idle poor', 'the dilutees', 'the unemployables' – Kirk Mann says:

> Each period has also witnessed the rehabilitation of that stratum. The Victorian residuum appears to have evaporated in the heat of the First World War. Likewise, the class of unemployables of the interwar period failed to survive the Second World War. Why, we must ask, have these disappeared if the values of the underclass are transmuted across the generations?

The answer in part, of course, is that when reasonably paid work becomes available, the 'problem' is solved. History, however, has never been held in much regard by polemicists and policy-makers.

Before the radical reforms of the social security system in 1988, Professor Patrick Minford of Liverpool University, an influential voice on government, again applied the Murray/Willetts/*Alice in Wonderland* approach. The cause of unemployment, he decided, was that the gap between income support and low pay was too narrow. It was too easy to stay out of work. The government as one of its aims, decided not to impose a decent minimum wage but to squeeze social security even further, pursue 'scroungers' and introduce a variety of measures, including the Social Fund, to inculcate a sense of 'obligation' in the nation's poor. These changes – in the short term, at least – have saved the government a great deal of money.

The Social Fund is a system which replaced emergency non-repayable grants with repayable loans and cash-limited grants for items such as furniture, bedding and domestic equipment. In 1989–90 the Social Fund spent £60 million in grants; this compares with the £335 million handed out in single payments in 1985–6; a massive cut in help to the poor.[9]

The need has not gone away: it has simply been rendered invisible. The government was warned that the Fund could only deepen poverty, not encourage self-reliance, but John Major, then junior Social Security Minister, who bears a lot of responsibility for the Fund, was adamant. 'The intellectual case for the Social Fund is compelling,' he said.

In Goldthorpe, Jan Gardner takes me to visit Marie, who lives, ironically, in Welfare View. Marie, a powerful, exuberant woman, is a recipient of the Social Fund. She used to be a lifeguard before she married. 'It was good money, £186 a week.' Now she has three children: Jessica, four, and the twins, Keighran and Kristopher, two. 'We've had no twins in the family for sixty-six years,' she says, smiling. 'And I'm the one who has to drop 'em.'

Marie has been married for six years and recently separated from her husband, Colin. 'I keep my purse down my T-shirt now so no bugger could get it for a drink.' Her husband was 'brilliant' with the kids when he was around and helped when he was unemployed. (It is one of the idiocies of the system that it gives couples on the verge of separating a financial incentive to take that step. A man and woman apart receive just over £42 each; for a married couple, it comes down to £66.)

Alone now, Marie, thirty-three, has £100 a week in total – and £25 of that goes to pay her monthly bills: £40 gas, £20 electricity, £20 telly and video and £10 for the callers (hire purchase and catalogue repayments). Out of the £75 a week she has left, she is also repaying a loan of £5.5p a week to the Social Fund. The family has no telephone, no car and, Marie says, 'I'd rather buy a decent pair of shoes for my kiddies – they must be Clark's – than spend owt money on myself.'

The story behind her Social Fund loan illustrates how much individuals often save the state by their efforts, yet are still penalised: the dilemma at the heart of community care. Until a few months before, Marie says, she had had her Aunt Martha living with her for years. She was in her nineties and suffered from Alzheimer's disease. Marie received £33 invalid care allowance. 'That were gone in a flash but I didn't mind, I loved her to pieces and Colin was ever so good with her too. I knew it were Alzheimer's,' Marie says, 'when I found her one day washing the dishes. She was ever so houseproud. I said to her, "Pet, you can't do it with that." She were trying to wash up with a tea bag, and crying like a baby. Me and Martha, we were like Siamese twins. I loved that woman, bless her cotton socks. I'd do it all again.'

Marie explains the connection with Martha: 'I had a daddy in a million. He was as fit as arseholes, then one day, when he was thirty-six, he went down the mine and that was it. His head was smashed in. My mum was left with six kiddies; the Coal Board gave her £50 compensation for each one of us. The £300 paid for me daddy's funeral and that was it.' Marie, aged three, eventually went to live with Martha.

In January Martha died, and Marie applied to the Social Fund. Martha had been incontinent and she had a habit, because of her illness, of chewing her food and spitting it out. The sitting-room where she spent much of her last few months was urine-sodden and covered in food stains. Marie needed to buy a three-piece suite, a bed and a carpet, and she needed money to redecorate.

'We reckoned we could do it second-hand for about £1,800,' Marie says. The Social Fund has given her £150 and the effect is felt in the £5 she is docked every week and the state of the house, now carpetless. 'My house may be a tip but my cups are clean and my kids are loved and I've always got a fresh blouse, and they're fed,' Marie says. 'But it's still a bugger.'

In March 1992, a report by the all-party Social Security Advisory Committee of the House of Commons damned the Fund as 'an appalling lottery'. Did the caring Mr Major spring into action? Certainly not. Instead, four months later, in July, his government tried to manipulate public response to a second equally critical report on the same subject.

This report on the workings of the Social Fund, commissioned three years earlier by the Department of Social Security from the Social Policy Research Unit at York University was published on the same day (8 July 1992) as the White Paper on the 'Health of the Nation' (which itself managed not to mention poverty as a causal factor even once) and the annual Regional Trends survey. The aim was to ensure a distraction.

The report used virtually the same language as the earlier one. The Fund has turned life for poor people 'into a degrading lottery where emergency help . . . has been reduced to chance'.[10] 'We cannot show that those who got awards were in greater need than those who did not,' the York University team said in *The Guardian*.[11] 'Nor can we conclude that the social fund is meeting its objective "to concentrate attention and help on those applicants facing greatest difficulties in managing on their income".'

The only patterns the researchers could find to decisions as to who should and who should not receive loans and grants were 'similar to those which would be obtained if awards and refusals occurred at random'.

The report quoted one woman docked £4.41 out of £41.43 each week. She said: 'You're going down to £37, aren't you? And I mean that one payment alone would turn me around and give me the benefit of paying my electricity each and every week.'

The 'lucky' timing of the publication of the report, just before the House of Commons' recess, meant that MPs had the opportunity to forget all about it over the summer break – a privilege not extended to those who still have to battle with the effects of the fund.

'It is only so far as poverty is abolished that freedom is increased,' wrote Harold Macmillan in *The Middle Way*. British public opinion appears to agree. The 1990–91 British Social Attitudes Survey shows that three-quarters of people believe that income differences are too large; two-thirds support action to reduce income differences and 82 per cent think the government should spend more on benefits for the poor.

Where Mr Murray may have succeeded – and this should be a warning for the 1990s – is in the public's attitudes to single-parent benefits. Single parents are bottom of the list of candidates for increased benefits – only 21 per cent felt that they were entitled to an improvement in 1983, but an even *lower* percentage – 17 per cent – felt the same way in 1989.[12]

'He had never felt poor, and he had no power of imagining the part which the want of money plays in determining the actions of men,' wrote George Eliot in *Middlemarch*. Mr Major claims, of course, that as a Brixton boy he has known poverty, he has known what it's like to be on the bottom rung. Perhaps he therefore needs to reacquaint himself with the experience and visit the many and varied 'types' of lone mothers whom his policies are not only denying independence but also labelling as the wastage of this otherwise affluent society.

Strategies for change have been presented to this government and to Labour governments, time and time again – not just to 'cure' poverty but to prevent it as well. Any new proposals need to begin by abandoning the belief, held by Beveridge, that a woman's place is in the home: an appendage to her husband.

'The great majority of married women must be regarded as occupied in work which is vital though unpaid, without which their husbands could not do their paid work,' the Beveridge Report, the basis of the current welfare state, said in 1942. 'The attitude of the housewife to gainful employment outside the home is not and should not be the same as that of the single woman. She has other duties . . . taken as a whole the Plan for Social Security puts a premium on marriage in place of penalising it.'

In *The Making of an English 'Underclass'?*, Kirk Mann details how the trade-union representatives on the Beveridge committee were as contemptuous of the needs of women as the employers. The union men were equally disrespectful of the needs of other subdivisions within the poor, such as the 'very poor' and 'the type of person who will not join a Friendly Society'. They were also in favour of withdrawing of public assistance from the wives and children of strikers.

'Whether or not it was due to the TUC's evidence,' Kirk Mann writes,

the Beveridge Report removed any proposal to assist single parents, through the [national] insurance scheme . . . Few voices were raised in opposition, despite the fact that the report was laying the basis for millions of women to be dependent on a male 'breadwinner' . . . or on means-tested public welfare. It is remarkable that women who were asked to make such tremendous sacrifices during the war, were so poorly rewarded for their efforts.

Times have changed (although not the way many women are rewarded), but the social security system hasn't. 'Once they are forced to stop treating women as the financial responsibility of their partners, governments can decide whether to acknowledge and reward these women as workers or as carers,' Lynda Bransbury, legal and parliamentary officer of the Local Government Information Unit, has said.[13] Instead, the government finds itself in the ridiculous position of attempting to force individuals off welfare without providing childcare and adequate financial incentives while also proclaiming itself as the Party of the family, in favour of keeping mothers at home: again, without adequate financial help – the ideology of *Alice in Wonderland* once more.

Examples of how a more equitable (and in the long run for the Treasury, far cheaper) system might be organised are readily available, but it would mean the government abandoning its role of moraliser and rejecting its fear that, in essence, we all want something for nothing.

In Sweden in the 1980s for instance, according to Australian academic Gisela Kaplan,[14] legislation and welfare were based on the principle that every adult ought to be responsible for his or her own support, independent of marital status; that no form of cohabitation, including marriage, was superior to another; and that the child's needs ought to be met irrespective of the circumstances into which he or she is born. (Sweden too, in the 1990s, is now undergoing cuts in welfare spending.)

In addition, Mr Major's concept of citizenship has traditionally been extended in Sweden to welfare recipients too. John Logue explains how the aim of the Swedish welfare state is not to punish but to create equality, 'beyond equality of opportunity to economic equality and equality in control of one's own destiny'.

'[Sweden] has raised the standard of living of the worst off markedly above the subsistence level, abolishing the material deprivation and obvious penury that continues to characterise life for substantial numbers in other industrial societies,' John Logue writes. 'The mesh of the welfare net is very fine indeed; to fall through virtually requires that you cut a hole first . . . Moreover, the net is cast widely . . . Perhaps this is the reason for the breadth of political support that the Scandinavian welfare states have enjoyed; if you do not benefit today, you are likely to tomorrow.'[15]

What is needed in Britain as we move to the turn of the century, is an official minimum standard of living; a minimum wage; income support at realistic levels (so that a mother can afford not to work and stay at home if she so chooses); the end of the Social Fund and the restoration of entitlement to non-repayable grants; child benefit paid at an adequate level; a woman's right to keep maintenance without forfeiting benefit; the removal of penalties on women who refuse to disclose the name of their child's father; and a woman's right to earn much more before her level of income and benefit support is affected.

We also need a flexibility in the system so that what is gained is not immediately lost elsewhere; truly independent taxation for men and women; an end to the game of hunt-the-victim; and the publication of regular and accurate research. Instead of less information, we need more. And much more action.

Very few of the 200-plus recommendations of the Finer Committee on Single Parents (1974) have subsequently been implemented. Too much of what the Court Report (1976) suggested on the subject of child health services received the same treatment. 'We have come to realise the extent to which experiences in childhood determine the adult outcome,' the report said.

Lone parents have that information; their children live out the evidence. In the next few years, as more men taste the experience of lone parenthood – particularly when, because of a lack of affordable childcare, they are forced to give up work – perhaps some of the more ridiculous barriers placed by the state in the way of lone mothers and fathers achieving financial independence, may be dismantled. (Just one lone parent in Cabinet with guts might be an even more effective spur.) Until that happens, the government stands damned by the evidence.

'The continuance of social evils is not due to the fact that we do not know what is right but that we prefer to continue doing what is wrong,' R. H. Tawney argued eighty years ago. 'Those who have the power to remove them do not have the will, and those who have the will do not, as yet, have the power.'

CHAPTER SIX

A bit of a domestic

A regimental sergeant major in the war, Vic was big: 6 foot 2 inches, sixteen stone, the man who defeated Hitler single-handed, a tremendous figure in the force. Gary Haigh, only nineteen, a new recruit to the police, thought Vic was C-in-C to God.

One Friday night, Vic told Gary: 'We're off to do a domestic lad, hop in the van.' It was Gary's first. The house was in Crossland Moor, and the two could hear the yelling and shouting from down the garden path. Vic walked into the house and went up to the sobbing, distraught woman.

'Who do you think I call, love, when there's a bit of trouble at home?' he asked her. She stopped crying and looked puzzled.

Vic turned to the man standing in the room. 'And who do you think I call?' The man shook his head. 'Well, I'll tell you both who I bloody call and it isn't the bloody police.' And then Vic left.

The couple were never heard from again. A little domestic difficulty resolved? Or another licence to batter issued? Gary Haigh is now forty-three, an approachable and direct, detective chief inspector. He has been an operational detective for twenty-one years, serving in a variety of CID posts, including the Regional Crime Squad. For the past three years, he has been head of a team of fifty-one detectives, two-thirds women, who run West Yorkshire's eight Domestic Violence and Child Sexual Abuse Units. He says he never forgets Vic.

'I was young, impressionable and with no experience. I

thought, well, that must be how you deal with a domestic. We're finding out now that it's tough, really tough, trying to change practices and attitudes which have been unchallenged for years, but it's got to be done. I like to think officers are changing because there's a need for it but if, at times, we have to use the stick instead of the carrot, then so be it.'

On the issue of domestic violence, Gary Haigh is a convert. The chain of events which prompted his conversion began in Bradford and Wakefield in the mid 1980s with Peter Sutcliffe, the Yorkshire Ripper – and feminist research.

'We did badly on the Ripper case and, alongside other forces, we began to realise that we weren't addressing the needs of women. Jalna Hanmer's work in *Well Founded Fear* helped us to focus on where we were going wrong.'

Well Founded Fear, a community study of violence to women, was published in 1984 and based on research, unique in Britain at the time, by Jalna Hanmer and Sheila Saunders. Jalna Hanmer was a lecturer at the London School of Economics, helping to train social workers, in the early 1970s. It was then that the issue of domestic violence, disregarded for fifty years since the suffragette movement took it up, began to re-emerge.

At that time, the Goldhawk Road Women's Liberation Group in West London had been allowed, by the local authority, to turn a run-down house due for slum clearance into a meeting place. 'They had women coming to them with horrendous stories of their domestic lives, and there wasn't much anybody could do,' Jalna Hanmer recalls. 'Finally, one woman came in with such a terrible story that the group decided, "Oh to hell with it, we'll let her stay." Of course, the moment she moved in, how could they stop other women with equally bad situations doing the same?'

Later, in 1972, Chiswick Family Rescue, the first refuge for battered women in the world, opened. It was eventually run by Erin Pizzey. Jalna Hanmer was drawn into it because one of her LSE students asked if she could arrange a placement.

In 1974, Jalna Hanmer became one of the founder members of the National Women's Aid Federation, which now has 160 refuges in Britain. By the early 1980s she was also co-convenor of the Violence, Abuse and Gender Relations Research Unit, Bradford (where she still is). For *Well Founded Fear*, she and her colleague, Sheila Saunders, decided to focus on several streets in a single area, chosen at random, in Leeds. A hundred and twenty-nine women were asked about their experiences of physical and sexual abuse in the previous year, whether they had reported any crimes to the police, and what kind of response they had received.

The women suffered ten major crimes: one robbery, three rapes, two indecent assaults, three offences of grievous bodily harm and one instance of aggravated bodily harm. In addition there were 116 'minor' crimes involving indecent exposure, obscene phone calls, breach of the peace and insulting or threatening behaviour. A fifth of all offences happened in their own homes.

What struck a chord with the West Yorkshire police was how few of the women had turned to them. 'We conclude that the vast majority of women interviewed do not think the police in practice either able or willing to protect them,' Jalna Hanmer and Sheila Saunders wrote. 'The police do not interfere in any serious way with male violence to women.'

Colin Sampson, then chief constable of West Yorkshire police, agreed that Jalna Hanmer and Sheila Saunders could conduct further research into police handling of sexual violence. *Women, Violence and Crime Prevention 1985–87* was the start of a major overhaul in police practice on domestic violence.

'Everyone in the force knows the tricks when it comes to a domestic,' Gary Haigh says. 'The officer records: "No reply to repeated knocking" – that's always a good one. "All quiet on the western front," when it patently wasn't but the officer didn't want to get involved. Or the officer tells the woman: "You go and see a solicitor, love, and get an injunction, then we can do something about it . . ." but of course, it's just fobbing them off . . .'

It was decided that domestic violence had to be given some status; hence Gary Haigh's appointment in 1989. A massive training and re-education programme was also launched, but the bottom line had to be that no matter whether a police officer approved or disapproved of a man beating 'his' partner in the privacy of his own home (or hers), a domestic violence call would elicit a serious police response.

To test what attitudes and practices already prevailed, each policeman or woman on a domestic violence call had to complete a highly detailed special report for a three-month period in 1990, 1991 and 1992. This information was monitored and analysed and has been used, year on year, to change policy further.

For the first time, the police also began to make contact with local women's groups, refuges and rape crisis centres. A couple of years after the trial of Peter Sutcliffe, a series of rapes occurred in the Leeds area. I was then writing news features for the London *Standard*. At a press conference I attended, I asked the detective in charge of the investigation if he was liaising with Leeds Rape Crisis Centre. 'No,' he said. 'We don't look for that kind of help.' Today, through the Leeds Inter-Agency Forum, the Centre works in close liaison with social services and the police, and Gary Haigh is on the management board.

'The first meeting I went to it was sandbags, flak jackets and mortar. Whatever I said was sexist, wrong, misinformed,' Gary Haigh says. 'I think that was an understandable reaction. I came with the best intentions, but of course, I wasn't trusted. Now the police have started to deliver, it's an entirely different attitude. We all work as a team.'

In *No More Sex War*, Neil Lyndon questions this new-found enthusiasm of some police forces for tackling domestic violence. 'Their "clear-up" rate in that seam of crime is the only badge of efficiency they can don, the only medal of achievement they can sport . . .' he writes. But so what? If the police have belatedly been fired into action on behalf of battered women, does it really matter what has prompted that enthusiasm?

In 1985 the Women's National Commission, an advisory group to the government, made specific recommendations on domestic violence in a report on violence against women. It included better police training, better police liaison with other agencies, including Women's Aid, and greater use of injunctions with powers of arrest attached. The following year the Home Office duly issued a circular (circulars are counterfeit money in that they do not buy real commitment to change) to all Chief Officers of Police. It emphasised that domestic violence must be treated seriously and suggested that Chief Officers might consider 'how best to ensure that the victims could be informed of the sources of assistance available to them'.

In practice, however, while almost all forty-three forces have since made token gestures, only a minority, have made attempts at much more radical and uncomfortable change, among them South Wales, Northumbria, the Metropolitan Police as well as West Yorkshire. In most of those cases, too, it has not come as a result of a sudden awareness that the easiest way to improve your clear-up rate is to bag the batterer in his front room, as Neil Lyndon suggests; it has more often been the result of one police officer, influenced by research and with some power, acting as a catalyst.

In the Metropolitan Police, for instance, it was the then Commissioner, Sir Kenneth Newman, who in the mid 1980s had become familiar with the Canadian policy of domestic violence units. London now has several dozen units attached to individual stations. (This approach, because it does not tackle methods head-on, as West Yorkshire has tried to do, can mean that the units are seen as peripheral to 'real' police work. They are also not monitored – a major flaw. But at least they represent a break from tradition.)

In the South Wales police, also in the 1980s, Assistant Chief Constable Alan Bourlet, who had completed a PhD thesis on marital violence, also encouraged more liaison with women's groups as well as instituting a number of other policies. He argued at the time: 'If ever we are to get it across to men that violence is not part of the matrimonial contract, then we have to show them in all circumstances that we will prosecute. Among the police it will be a matter of evolution, not revolution.'

In West Yorkshire, 'evolution' has now been put on fast-forward. The detailed report each detective had to file on every case of domestic violence included: detailed time of call; how long it took to respond; gender of officers; advice given; physical injury noted; action taken; if an injunction was in force (to prevent a man coming near a women) and if it carried with it powers of arrest (not all do); was it enforced? And what happened after an arrest was made. The police role was defined as protecting the victim from further attack, eliminating any further risk to the victim or her children, and 'taking firm and positive action against the assailant and to investigate any offences that have been committed'.

The results reveal something about police attitudes (and the West Yorkshire force is as representative as any other), but they also show how quickly practice can alter, within the space of a year, if a new regime is instantly institutionalised. In that way, personal prejudices and assumptions which have traditionally dominated police reaction to domestic violence do not have to be changed; they are simply rendered impotent.

In West Yorkshire (covering Leeds, Wakefield, Kirklees, Calderdale, Bradford South and Aire Valley) in 1991 there were 2,380 reported incidents of domestic violence – a quarter of all violent crimes (2,700 in the previous year). Forty-two per cent involved physical injury; 88 per cent were against females (85 per cent in 1990), but the proportion of Asian and Afro-Caribbean women was smaller than might be expected. (This, Gary Haigh says, backs up other research which indicates that black women are even less willing to come to the police than white.)

Arrests in 1990 were made in only 39 per cent of the cases where an injunction (with powers of arrest) was in force. In 1991, after criticism, this percentage rose to 61 per cent. 'This welcome increase must not be taken complacently,' says the 1991 Domestic Violence survey. 'There were still 38.9% of cases when the police did not enforce powers incurred by the injunction.'

The West Yorkshire Police made arrests in 28.5 per cent of all cases in 1990, but sometimes they held the man for only a matter of hours. In 1991, this percentage rose to 37 per cent, with the arrested, in the main, being held in custody until the court hearing their case sat. In addition, many more serious charges were brought. For instance, grievous bodily harm increased from 56 cases in 1990 to 80 in the following year. In both years, two women were murdered by their partners within a three-month period.

'We still get our horror stories where police haven't delivered the goods,' Gary Haigh says. 'Women still aren't sufficiently protected, but we are very slowly beginning to get there.'

In a discussion on 'Woman's Hour' early in 1992, Neil Lyndon first revealed his theory that the issue of domestic violence was a matter of the emperor's clothes. He announced: 'A largely wilful magnification has gone on . . . of the extent and the influence of this phenomenon.' In *No More Sex War*, he returns to his theme:

Domestic violence . . . has been the focus of a moral panic, fired by sociologists, criminologists and propagandists of the sisterhood fuelled by the police and by ministers of state. The sisterhood stoked up this panic because, as they have claimed for 20 years, incidents of violence in the home illustrate the power relations of all women and show us how far men will go to exert and keep control.

In practice, domestic violence has not been a 'focus of moral panic' – if that has existed anywhere in the women's movement it has been located in the efforts of those who see the core of feminism as the issue of pornography; sexual, not physical abuse. Most of those involved in domestic violence have been too preoccupied with meeting the need to do much in the way of propaganda.

Matters of polemics aside, Neil Lyndon has not arrived at the decision that partner-battering is the crime that never was by any normal journalistic practice: interviewing battered women, visiting refuges, talking to men who are allegedly violent in the home, and the police who are supposed to deal with them. On the contrary, ironically, he has gone for the sixties feminist approach which he criticises heavily elsewhere for its essential ineffectiveness. He has decided that it is his personal experience which counts most. 'My experience is no more universal than any other individual's,' he tells the reader, 'but it is very likely to have been broader than yours . . .'

And he, for one, has never laid a finger on a woman – except, of course, when provoked.

'I want to draw on my own experience . . .' he writes.

In cohabitations with four women over the last 25 years, including two marriages, I have four times been involved in rows which ended in blows. I have twice slapped a woman's face with my open hand . . .

Pains and injuries were inflicted both ways . . . The women were, beyond question, doing their utmost to hurt me. I can say, with absolute truthfulness, that I did not – never have – used more than a fraction of my strength or my power to injure; and, in two of the four scenes, I was using my strength to diminish injury.

This may well be the general mêlée of the intimate lives of many – but it has nothing to do with domestic violence. In *Wife-torture in England*, published in 1878, Frances Power

Cobbe explained the difference succinctly: 'There are two kinds of Wife-beating which I am anxious the reader should keep clearly apart in his mind . . .' she wrote.

The first, she explained, was 'wife-beating by combat', in which

> both parties have an equal share . . . Bad words are exchanged, then blows . . . If the woman generally gets much the worst of it, it is simply because cats are weaker than dogs. The man cannot so justly be said to have 'beaten' his wife as to have vanquished her in a boxing match . . . It is nearly exclusively, I think, that the hateful virago gets beaten at all. As a general rule she commands too much fear and is so ready to give back curse for curse and blow for blow, that in cold blood, nobody meddles with her.

The second kind of wife-beating Frances Power Cobbe describes is one in which the husband attacks the wife:

> sometimes without any provocation at all . . . to drag her out of her bed when she is asleep . . . Sometimes, there is a preliminary altercation . . . in either case, the wife is passive so far as blows are concerned, unless at the last, in self-defence, she lays her hand on some weapon to protect her life – a fact that is always cited against her as a terrible delinquency.

Modern-day parallels are not hard to find; the issue is not a mutual muddle of rage and alcohol, but the control of one person over another: control which is exercised by means of sustained physical and/or emotional abuse. Traditionally, this was seen not as a form of deviant behaviour but as a male 'right' established in English common law.

To be a wife meant becoming the property of a husband, taking a secondary position in a marital hierarchy of power and worth, being legally and morally bound to obey the will and wishes of one's husband, and thus, quite logically, subject to his control even to the point of physical chastisement and murder,

explain R. Emerson Dobash and Russell Dobash in *Violence Against Wives*, one of the seminal books on domestic violence.

They point out that until the nineteenth century, so long as a man stayed within certain limits, force was allowed. In 1895, the Married Woman's Property Act made conviction for an assault grounds for divorce, but the difficulties of obtaining proof rendered it almost useless.

In *Power and the State*, published in 1978, Jalna Hanmer explained the importance of control:

It may be necessary to kill, mutilate, maim or temporarily reduce a woman's ability to carry out services . . . in order to be in control. Prestige, self-esteem, a sense of personal self-worth is gained, expressed and made public by the acquiescence of others.

'It was that I wanted to make her think the way I was thinking no matter what it took,' explains Howard Marks, thirty-three, who beat his wife, Ann, for twelve years. 'Once it happens, it's not hard to do the next time.'[1]

Charlotte, aged thirty-five, has been at Chiswick Family Rescue (now three West London houses with fifty women, and 120 children) for two months. She has two daughters – Emily, four, and Rachel, eighteen months – and has decided that after a six-year marriage, she is not going back.

'Mike is four years younger than me, a mechanic. I've got my own home, a lovely home, but it became a prison. He was fine for the first year we were courting. Everyone said how nice and quiet and reserved he was. It was fine when I had my job as a secretary, but then I got pregnant and suddenly, money became a big issue.

'The first time he hit me, I was carrying Emily and I thought he'd made me miscarry. After she was born, and I gave up work, it very quickly escalated. He would pay all the big bills and give me £25 for housekeeping. I couldn't cope, nappies alone took a lot of it, but I'd hide the bills out of fear.

'Some days he'd come home and he would be OK. Other days, he'd come in and I'd see the look in his eye and I'd know. It was the unpredictability. I never knew what would trigger it or when. But suddenly, he'd explode. It might be the food on the table, or the kitchen not clean enough or the way I looked. He'd just suddenly rain blows down on me, anywhere he could hit. It was a mess. Towards the end, I didn't even bother to run. All I could do was curl up as some kind of protection. It was all so *undignified*. He never hit the children but he terrified them. Emily won't leave my side.

'I come from a loving family who now can't even begin to fathom how or why I got into it. They thought he was such a pleasant man. I was in his total power and there was nothing I could do. I'd lost touch with my friends, I wasn't allowed out except to go shopping, I didn't tell my mother because I was too ashamed. If he hit me, he'd say later that it was the only way I'd learn, it was for my own good.'

In the few months before she left, after over five years of violence, Charlotte says her husband's behaviour grew worse and he began to turn on the children. 'He knew that was how he could get at me. I'd become so passive, he needed a fresh reaction. One night after a beating, it just came to me that if I stayed, one or other of us would die. I wasn't sleeping, I wasn't eating. Even then, I didn't go. He'd taken away my will.'

A few days later, Mike went into a rage again and, for the first time, took his temper out on the house: he tried to break up the furniture in the kitchen. A neighbour called the police. Charlotte barricaded herself in the bedroom.

'The police drove Mike away and he was back within the hour. 'He told me I would never get away. I was his wife and that was that. I used to think perhaps it was my fault? Perhaps I was spending too much? Perhaps if I could be nicer? This time, I decided I'd just had enough.'

The next morning, when Mike left for work, Charlotte contacted her health visitor (who had never noticed anything untoward). She gave her the number of Chiswick Family Rescue, and Charlotte left with a handful of clothes, no money, and the children.

'When I look back, I think: "What happened to me?" I used to be pretty strong and I turned into a mouse. Now, I'm more myself, I'm in control again. I even feel enthusiastic about life. I'm not too old, I want to go back to college. And I want to make my two little girls happy.'

Neil Lyndon not only misunderstands the characteristics of domestic violence, he misinterprets its consequences, particularly in the way it affects the flow of women in and out of refuges. 'The killer blow with which the sisters and their followers ... always try to finish and to extinguish an argument on domestic violence is to say that every woman's refuge in this country is filled to overflowing,' he writes in martial fashion in *No More Sex War*. 'If you can get off the floor and look into the numbers, you discover another view.'

He calculates that as there are 160 refuges in England, offering 1,280 places – half to women – only 640 women are in need of help in England each year. He pits these 640 women against the 2,000 to 3,000 people sleeping rough in London:

What the hell has happened to us as a generation, a nation, a people that – in our damnable fixation with the proposition that the personal is political – the plight of 650 women should be treated with so very much more sympathy and political energy than a million people who have, or may have, no home?

Every social injustice is as valid as the next to those who experience it, and to establish a hierarchy of need is an invidious route to take. In any case, many among those homeless may be women and children who have been forced to abandon their homes because of violence. But Neil Lyndon's faultiness with figures should be corrected though because it provides excuses for present funding to be curtailed and future resources to be put in jeopardy. It also entirely removes from the national picture the way in which distorted male–female relations can ruin so many lives.

Neil Lyndon's first error is to assume that the population in and out of refuges is stable: it isn't. Women may stay for a few days – or increasingly now, as rehousing becomes more and more difficult, remain for several months. So in England, 30,000, not 640, women passed through refuges in 1990, and a further 45,000 were given information and/or counselling. In London, refuges could accept only 40 per cent of those who applied for help. They were forced to redirect other women outside the London area.

In Scotland, where there are thirty-four refuges, in 1989–90 1,880 women and 3,002 children were helped, 3,396 had to be turned away and over 10,000 were given advice. (Compare this with the 846 women and 1,500 children helped ten years earlier.)

In Wales, there are thirty-two refuges and twelve information centres. Again, the numbers have risen. In 1978, the year Welsh Women's Aid was established, 432 women and 600 children were helped; in 1990, 1,379 women and 2,104 children. Again, another 1,500 women and just over 3,000 children had to be referred on because of a lack of facilities. Northern Ireland repeats the pattern: nine refuges, 1,156 women and 2,003 children helped, 498 women and 1,021 children refused accommodation. In brief around 34,000 women were helped in 1991 – but the proportion who turn to a refuge may be only a small minority of those in need.[2]

The fact that we don't know, that we can only guess at the

extent of the problem, is not a feminist conspiracy. On the contrary, Jalna Hanmer, among others, called for a national incidence study as far back as the 1970s. The criminologist Susan Edwards has conducted one of the major pieces of research into policing practice on domestic violence with the co-operation of the Metropolitan Police. She is a feminist so she is impugned by Neil Lyndon: 'we know where she is coming from . . .' as if the task of marshalling the hard and, in themselves, neutral statistics is somehow invalidated by her beliefs. Susan Edwards has also pointed out that domestic violence is 'the biggest blind spot in official statistics'.[3]

Florynce Kennedy has an irreverent view of polemicists like Neil Lyndon, who play their own games with figures. She is the black lawyer who represented Billie Holliday in the 1950s and splendidly helped to lead the charge of the feminists' rights brigade in the 1960s. At seventy-six she still demonstrates, organises, lectures and battles, now from a wheelchair, in her apartment on East 48th Street in New York (a sign over her headboard reads 'Flo's deathbed', but she never lies down long enough for it to happen).

'You always have those', Flo Kennedy says laconically, 'who, when the shit is hitting the fan real hard, get busy measuring the size of the turds to make sure you don't overstate the oppression.'

The question, however, remains: why should we know so little about the extent of domestic violence since, as Neil Lyndon says, it is one of the easiest crimes to detect?

In part, the answer lies in the familiar story, it is politically dangerous to reveal a demand that you are reluctant to satisfy. In 1975, the House of Commons Select Committee on violence in marriage advised against a series of national conferences on the issue, as this 'might well create new and greater demands for resources than could be met'. But there are other difficulties too.

The first, as Jalna Hanmer uncovered, is that women are reluctant to go for help – because they believe they won't be taken seriously, because they are ashamed, or because they are too terrified. Or because they are in love; at times it might be a combination of all four factors. In the highly influential Home Office research study *Domestic Violence*, written by Lorna J. F. Smith and published in 1989 (which also took into account many of the feminist arguments and research of the previous years), the author explains how varied are the assessments on the proportion of women who do report that they have been battered.

The range begins with only 2 per cent suggested by the Dobashes in 1979 to 71 per cent in a study in 1985 which concentrated entirely on women in refuges. In the same year, in *Woman* magazine, one in four in a readers' survey on domestic violence said they had told *no one*; of those who *had*, only a quarter named the police.

Second, even when women do go for assistance, as Gary Haigh learned twenty years ago, what they may have repeatedly experienced – and what would immediately be classed as an assault if it was carried out only once by a stranger – may be dismissed as a 'little domestic difficulty'. The progress is the 'may be'. Practice now can vary not just from force to force but from policeman to policeman. And in that change, feminism has played no small part.

Kate is twenty-five and has three children aged six, four, and eighteen months. She met her boyfriend, Paul, when they were both fifteen. 'I'd recently lost my dad and I think I wanted someone to lean on.' Paul's father had been a violent man, beating his wife and children. 'As we got older, I realise, looking back, that Paul was always watching me, pulling me down a peg or two if I got uppity. He was jealous and possessive, but I was too young to know anything else. I was flattered.'

Their first child, Karen, was an accident. 'I was eighteen and that's when the bashing took off. He never hit me with his fists. Instead, he would pick me up and throw me against the wall. Or pull my hair; once he put me into a scalding bath.

And he was always trying to make me feel small. If I saw the signs, I'd lock myself and the kids in the bedroom – although he never laid a finger on them.

'Right from the beginning, his sister warned me. She kept on trying to persuade me to leave. I didn't know where to go or what to do. I had no money and when Paul was good, he was great. I kept telling myself that it would get better. If I could just do this or that, it would be OK. The kids loved him, in spite of it all – they still do.'

A few weeks before Christmas 1991, Paul lost his job as a toolmaker. Kate had found part-time work as a packer in a warehouse. 'Paul had begun to follow me to work. He was convinced I was having an affair. He'd spend hours trying to force me to confess. This time he threatened one of the men I worked with and locked me in the kitchen overnight as "punishment".'

On Christmas Day, the punishment was repeated. A week later, Paul broke four small bones in his hand, aiming for Kate and hitting the wall. He threatened her with a knife. 'That was it, I went to the police station with the children. I could see it was getting worse. I had five interviews. Two policemen were lovely. One looked as if he was twelve. I thought how am I going to explain so he'll understand. "I've had a bit of a domestic with my husband and he got happy with a knife"? The other policeman was an obnoxious git. He said, "Had a little tiff, have you . . .?"'

Two policemen drove her back to the flat. Paul was outside in his car. The policeman Kate decided was 'obnoxious' had a chat to Paul and Kate. 'You two have been together for years, you need your heads banging together.' He left. Kate discovered that Paul had the same knife under the driver's seat. He threatened her again. Kate grovelled, the children cried, her son, aged four, wet himself in fright.

Two days later, on a Friday, Paul abducted her from work. 'He'd flipped. He tried to attack me sexually in the front seat. He dragged me out of the car and hit my head on the pavement. People stopped. "It's my wife and I'm going to do what I like," he kept shouting. Nobody could get near but thank God several phoned the police with his car registration number.

'He finally dumped me at home. I rushed to get the kids from school and from my sister's. I wanted to get away. People at work, who were brilliant, had also contacted the police. I'd tried the police once, so this time I hid in a bed-and-breakfast place over the weekend.

'The CID man contacted me on the Monday because I'd told my mother where I was. I couldn't go to her because Paul would know. The CID man said there was nothing he could do unless I took out an injunction.'

Kate moved in with her mother and successfully obtained an injunction with powers of arrest. Five days later, Paul broke the injunction. He grabbed Kate in the street and bashed her head against a telephone box. On the third occasion the injunction was broken, the police still failed to take action. 'They walked him around the block and told him to be a good boy. Half an hour later, Paul was back and broke the door down. I didn't have a copy of the injunction on me, it was still at my mum's, so the police said they couldn't arrest him.'

By this time, Kate says, she was an emotional wreck. 'The door knob only had to turn, and I could feel the fear sweep over me. It was horrendous for the children.' Kate decided to leave job, friends and family and move across London. She came to Chiswick Family Rescue. 'He found me not here, but in the area. I was driving with the kids and saw him. I was so frightened, I drove right across the roundabout and up the wrong side of the road. Now, I carry the injunction and all the papers on me all the time, so the police here finally arrested him. I think they've got much more sympathy in the first place.'

In court, two months before Kate saw me, Paul was given a year's suspended sentence and warned to stay away from his ex-partner and children. Kate says now she would like the children to see their father – 'They miss him, he was a good father. I even said that in court' – but she daren't, because the children will lead Paul to her. 'They are all disturbed. Ben, the middle one, keeps drawing pictures of his daddy behind bars, even though I try to explain. Karen is like me, she's very controlled and then suddenly, she'll break down.'

Kate, in the refuge, says she feels safe, but she plans to move with her mother to the North of England. 'I have to hide from him and get some peace to make it up to the children. But wherever I am, I feel as if sooner or later, he'll find me. It's what drives him on.' Her optimism about how much help she will receive from the police next time Paul appears on the doorstep is not high.

In 1984 and 1985, Susan Edwards and colleagues at the Polytechnic of Central London conducted research into police response at two London police stations, Hounslow and Holloway. Researchers found that stations received around two and a half calls a day concerning domestic violence. From this information, a figure has been extrapolated – and often quoted, that in London the police receive a thousand calls a week about domestic violence – an approach which Neil Lyndon rightly criticises as far from accurate. The problem, though, is not, as he implies, a wilful desire to exaggerate; instead it lies in the absence of funding to provide more accurate information.

In trying to get at least some measure of the problem, Susan Edwards looked at 449 incidents from Holloway and 324 from Hounslow in more detail. She discovered that only 12 per cent of the domestic incidents reported were recorded as crimes (a habit called 'no-criming') and men were charged in only sixteen of those cases, or 2 per cent. She also reported that police tried to downgrade injuries.[4]

In two-thirds of the cases in which a report had been made, the injury was detailed as 'common assault' (a charge for which a man is not usually arrested) – despite the fact that there was bruising, cuts and swelling, and in some cases weapons had been used.

Injunctions too, Susan Edwards discovered, were regarded by the police as 'useless' and 'a waste of time, not worth the paper they are written on'. (They certainly didn't do Mary Khelifati much good. In 1984, she was stabbed to death by her husband, Mohammed – an event she had predicted would happen for several months before, since the police had failed to give her protection in spite of the injunctions with powers of arrest which she had obtained.)

'Police attitude' is clearly no longer monolithic – younger policemen may not be as chauvinist as older ones; more progressive forces hold to a different ethos – but tradition remains. Some police believe certain women 'ask for it'; other policemen are, by the law of averages, batterers themselves; some may see domestic violence as a 'normal' part of private, married life. In 1983, in *The Times*, an Assistant Commissioner of the Metropolitan Police suggested categorising 'domestic disputes' along with 'stranded people, lost property and stray animals' so that the police could get on with 'real crime work'.[5]

Another serious inhibitor to domestic violence being taken seriously is the police belief that some women refuse to make a complaint (or withdraw, having done so). In 1989, Judge James Pickles jailed Michele Renshaw, aged twenty-four, for a week for contempt of court (it was quashed on appeal), because she was too frightened to give evidence against her boyfriend. Judge Pickles said she should have had courage; Michele Renshaw said that his reaction would further deter women from seeking help.

Again, the extent to which women do back out is not known (the Dobashes put it at 6 per cent; Susan Edwards's work suggests 96 per cent; enough of a discrepancy to suggest that other factors may be at work such as police pressure to withdraw charges). Nevertheless the view that many women do withdraw has passed into mythology, so the damage is done; the police attitude 'Why bother?' has strong roots.

If a contemporary picture of domestic violence is to be drawn – and more of its subtleties detailed – then clearly, new and more widespread research of the kind Susan Edwards and the Dobashes conducted over a decade ago is required. It needs to include not only patterns of violence as they affect women and children and police attitudes, but also how the courts behave in sentencing and what type of man raises his hand in the first place.

Jim Wilson is thirty-four, a lorry driver and, for a number of years in his twenties, a wife-batterer. He is now one of the prime organisers of Move, a self-help group in Bolton (which works in co-operation with local women's refuges) that tries to help men who wish to stop being violent. In 1991, Move received 1,625 calls for help. 'Most of the men are finally pushed into doing something for selfish reasons. They finally realise, if they don't, they will lose their partners altogether. This time she will really go,' Jim Wilson says.

The programme lasts for fourteen weeks and can be carried out by the man at home. In addition, there is a weekly support group to which men come from all over England: 'the out-of-work; surgeons; judges; salesmen; middle-class and working-class'. 'We're not interested in people's childhood or what justification they can drag up for doing what they've done. Investigating your past', Jim Wilson says, 'we regard as a hobby.'

(Jim Wilson's past, none the less, includes a violent father. What little research there is indicates that adult behaviour may be affected more by observing violence as a child than by experiencing it themselves. Jim Wilson's father is now in a wheelchair, dependent on the woman he battered. He is also father of a dozen children; only one, Jim, has managed to maintain a stable relationship. 'My mother has my father now where she wants him,' Jim Wilson says. 'It's not an easy marriage.')

The Move programme attempts to instruct men how to take responsibility for their behaviour, and not to blame others.

'We teach that assertiveness is better than anger. Quite often, no matter how well-educated, these men are emotional cripples. They can't identify how they feel and they can't communicate it except through rage.'

WASP – Wait, Assess And Slowly Proceed – is taught to break the chain of aggression. How successful is it? Nobody knows. What rouses the suspicion of some battered women is that men are placed on such programmes in the States as an alternative to prison. It is seen as a soft option; once the course is completed, the man goes back to his more familiar ways.

In the States, such self-help groups have been active since the 1970s. Emerge, the first programme, was founded in Boston in 1977. RAVEN, Rape and Violence End Now, set up in St Louis, followed later. Both shun the idea of family therapy or couple counselling (which Move does offer) since this, they argue, shifts the blame from the man to the interactions within relationships. And in domestic violence, almost all 'normal' interaction has ceased because of the intrusion of fear.

Jim Wilson says that the counselling for couples deals with a unique problem. Previously, women may have left violent men, but there is little experience of women who find the man they have become accustomed to knowing mainly through violence undergoing change. 'Women have to adapt their expectations too. They may have become institutionalised and ground down into believing that is how real men behave.'

Emerge challenges the idea of the 'value' of macho behaviour. It says that men 'brought up with a belief in male dominance and inclined to violent activities as a means of proving their own masculinity do not necessarily see anything wrong with their actions. Rather, such violence is sanctioned among men.'

In *The Rites of Man*, Rosalind Miles endorses this view: 'To explain violence is to explain the male: the reverse is also true.' But as I argue in Chapter Four, in this attitude lies a weakness in feminist thinking, one which denies it the success it's had in adapting traditional masculinity. Clearly, there has been a change in attitudes to domestic violence: masculinity can alter; peer pressure can be employed to alter concepts of how 'real' men behave. It is perhaps more accurate to say: 'To explain violence is to explain certain types of male.' The key question then becomes not simply why these 'types' strike out but – equally importantly – why other men subject to the same conditioning and in identical circumstances, do not.

The issue for women, then, is not how to live in a world in which all men are a potential threat – this is a self-imposed tyranny – but how best to isolate and immobilise those who are a danger. To do that we have to separate them from other men; we must clearly emphasise their differences, not their similarities, and in doing so label their habits as hostile to the interests of the whole community. As Rosalind Miles puts it in a different context, we need to ask: 'How does a man get to be an ordinary regular guy?' – at least as decent, non-violent women understand the term.

Research, however, costs money, and already some American feminists believe that practical help for men who batter is taking priority over their victims' needs. (Chiswick Family Rescue, for instance, is in dire need of more resources.) Jim Wilson recently asked the Home Office for a grant of £672,000 over three years to set up two dozen groups around the country (a fraction of the sum, he argues, that the government has to spend on children in care, delinquent behaviour and legal aid in divorce, products of violence in the home). The grant was refused. Move runs on no funding at present.

Ask Jim Wilson what rewards a man receives for giving up his capacity to dominate and terrorise, and he replies: 'What he gets is respect. He's happier within himself, he's still in control, but this time over his own emotions. He finds a way out of a place which he basically hasn't ever wanted to be in.'

The apparent lack of curiosity into what prevents men battering women has not been applied to the issue of what makes women stay in an abusive relationship – or why they return, once they have made a break. In part, this is because, as Fernando Mederos of Emerge says, 'Victim blaming becomes the compromise to radical social restructuring.' The practical reasons why a woman endures a violent relationship are perhaps more readily understood today than they were twenty years ago: no money, no housing, no skills, no confidence.

For Asian women, in traditional communities, all these factors are multiplied many times over. In the early 1980s, Krishna Sharma decided the only way out was suicide. When her body was discovered, it was covered in bruises. Her death prompted the opening of the first Asian women's refuge; now there are over a dozen. Kiranjit-Ahluwalia, thirty-six, also tried to take her own life twice in 1989. She failed, and finally murdered her husband. At the time of writing, she is awaiting a retrial.

Even when women do take the decision to leave, they have to be extremely strong (not the usual state for a woman to find herself in after years of abuse) to withstand the new pressures. 'Women, if they're rehoused, often find themselves on run-down estates with high crime rates; they have difficulty in getting money from the Social Fund; they usually leave everything they possess behind,' says Sandra Horley, director of Chiswick Family Rescue. 'The children may miss their father, he promises to change, and the woman lives in hope that he will because she has little else. Until we provide a proper network of decent housing, adequate income and back-up support, of course women will go back.'

Many battered women also suffer from 'learned helplessness', a mix of shame, humiliation, depression and low self-esteem, which – as Paula J. Kaplan explains in *The Myth of Women's Masochism* – clouds ability to take stock of their life and make rational decisions. So even if a woman does have a job and an income and a history of independence, she too may continue to be shackled to an abusive man.

In Britain in January 1992, for the first time in court, Sandra

Horley, who has helped over 3,000 women, was allowed to testify as an 'expert witness' on this condition. The case involved a young woman who had been battered by her partner and whose child had died as a result of its injuries inflicted by one of the parents (each in court, blamed the other). The woman, Sally Emery, was convicted for failure to protect her child, and sentenced to four years. The judge did, however, take note of the characteristics which may affect a battered woman's behaviour.

This notion of 'victimhood' is a tool to help achieve justice for some women, but American feminists have already learnt that it is one to be used with care. In the 1970s, Elizabeth Schneider, a professor at Brooklyn Law School, helped to develop the theory – now used in the courts – that a battered woman who kills her husband is a victim, not an aggressor. In a recent interview with the *New York Times*, she raised doubts about what has become part of feminist philosophy:

> It's a two-edged sword. Many battered women lose custody
> of their children because judges see them as helpless,
> paralysed victims who can't manage daily life. And if a
> woman seems too capable, too much in charge of her life to
> fit the victim image, she may not be believed.[6]

'Woman as victim is a cultural script which evokes sympathy without challenging the hierarchical structure,' adds Nan Hunter, also a Professor of Law at Brooklyn who handles abortion and gay rights cases. 'It's a kind of melodrama that doesn't lead to any changes in the condition that causes the victimisation.'[7]

In the courts now, feminists are attempting to change the legal definition of provocation and self-defence, but also to avoid these, the dangers of victimhood. Sandra Horley says that the legal definitions of provocative and self-defence, the two main defences to murder, are not applicable to battered women who eventually kill because they see no other escape.

'Their defence must not be diminished responsibility because that implies deviance or abnormality. Instead, I would argue that they are reacting rationally and justifiably in order to defend themselves from events which threaten their lives,' she argues.

'The defences of self-defence and provocation need to be amended in order to address the needs of this particular group; reducing sentences or abolishing the mandatory life sentence is not the answer.'

Not only does victimhood slow or even stop change, it can deny reality. What is impressive about many battered women – and I have been in contact with refuges for fourteen years or so – is not how much they suffer but how well, ultimately, many of them survive. Many, eventually, either build a life for themselves and their children without a partner, or move into normal relationships in which violence plays no part.

Jo was with her partner Tom for eight years; the abuse was mental as well as physical. She was an art teacher, he was a computer programmer. 'He was obsessively jealous of personal relationships and my work. In the end, I never told him if anything good happened in my job, because he would either sulk for days, belittle me for hours or suddenly lash out – and convince me it was my fault,' she says.

Jo left 'at least a dozen times' and went back. She made a final break only by changing her whole life. She resigned from her job, left her house, and moved from the Midlands to Wales, to a rented cottage, with her eight-year-old daughter. 'I was thirty-nine, I felt that if I didn't do it by the time I was forty, my life would be written off. I'd be stuck for good. It's taken two years, I have a new relationship about which I'm very cautious, but what helps is this overwhelming feeling that if I can survive what I've experienced, there's nothing else I can't do.'

Perhaps where fresh research is required is in analysing at what point a woman decides that she has had enough. Does it vary from class to class? Does economic independence play as large a part as is assumed? At what point can outside help best intervene? How do women who do not enter a refuge manage? Anecdotal evidence again says that women are leaving abusive relationships much more quickly when they are young enough to begin again. 'And before their spirit has been broken,' says Sandra Horley.

The major shift now taking place in attitudes to domestic violence which is beginning to promote it from a private issue between a man and 'his' woman to a serious crime is, I believe, one of the main achievements of feminism in the last twenty years. But the job is still only half done – and further progress could be threatened by a backlash, now under way.

In September 1992, a House of Commons Home Affairs committee, inquiring into violence in the home, is to hear evidence from battered men. Domestic violence, always too general a term when applied very precisely to men abusing women, is now finally proving to be more appropriate as violence by teenagers against parents, parents against grand-parents, lesbian violence, and cases of women who attack their male partners is beginning to emerge.

Without research, it is impossible to say how extensive the problem of battered men in particular is. Very early surveys suggest that it makes up 2 per cent of domestic violence cases.[8] Numbers are irrelevant. If men are abused, then that should clearly be investigated and the need met. (A women's refuge in Swindon, for instance, already offers a help line.) Yet, in a bizarre way, the emergence of this problem has been used against feminism, as if it were evidence that as females are clearly less than perfect, the women's movement should call off the whole campaign against domestic violence.

In truth, the fact that the issue of battered men is slowly being recognised is a tribute to the principles that feminism has laid down – chief amongst them is that the home should never be so private that those who dominate it with pain and abuse of power are deemed to be exercising privilege, not breaking the law.

Instead of acknowledgement, however, abuse of males by their female partners is being used to condemn all women (ironically, as some women have charged *all* men with violence) and to perpetuate a myth that when it comes to dealing with domestic violence, the law is 'on the woman's side'. The law, on the contrary, is highly inconsistent – a fact which is to the satisfaction of neither men nor women.

In the *Daily Mail*, Dr Malcolm George, a neurophysiologist, is quoted as saying: 'It is socially unacceptable that women can be violent. I know of men who have been stabbed by their wives but have never reported it. They are totally demoralised and have lost all confidence. The law is always on the side of women, whatever the circumstances.'

In 1989, according to the Home Office, 234 women were murdered – half by their partners, 17 per cent by family (most often a parent), 12 per cent by strangers, the remainder by associates. In the same year, 342 men were murdered – only one in ten by their partners, 16 per cent by family, 32 per cent by strangers and 32 per cent by a friend or associate. Murder in the home remains predominantly a masculine solution; the courts frequently dispense mercy – suspended sentences or probation. As in the case of Rajinder Bisla, who strangled Abnash, his 'nagging' wife, watched by his teenage children. He walked away from court a free man after he claimed he had been severely provoked in his eighteen-year marriage. In January 1992, Judge Neil Denison, giving him an eighteen month suspended prison sentence for manslaughter, told him: 'You have suffered through no fault of your own a terrible existence for a very long time.'

If justice is to be seen to be fair and consistent, we need to know more about the circumstances of domestic murders. Is it simply that a woman forgets to put the mustard on the table or loses radio reception of 'Desert Island Discs'? Is it that a man is truly 'nagged' to the point where he loses all control? (The evidence of men killing women shows that many are prompted by the knowledge that they can no longer 'own' a former partner.) Is it that a woman, in claiming abuse, now has a ready-made excuse for violence? To pose the questions is not to suggest that women (or men) 'ask for it' or that murder is never self-defence but to propose that without such knowlege, sentencing can only grow more erratic and the backlash grow more vindictive in the absence of knowledge.

In the meantime, resources for and methods of dealing with domestic violence – despite all the improvements – are still largely inadequate. The English, Welsh, Scottish and Irish Women's Aid Federations all say they are in extreme difficulties. In 1975, the Select Committee on Violence in Marriage suggested one refuge per 10,000 of the population – we now only have a third of that target figure.

Funding is a hotchpotch, dependent upon trusts, charity, urban aid and local authorities – so while some refuges are impoverished, others only just get by. Lliw Valley, in Wales, for instance, a three-bedroom house, survives on £21,000 a year, while Cardiff (two houses, ten paid workers and an information centre) runs on £147,000. Money is also unreliable because of the frequently late arrival of government grants, the constant time-consuming search for fresh resources and the changes to housing benefit rules. If a local authority is generous, then, as in the case of Turriff District Council in Scotland, they will offer to provide a purpose-built house and lease it to the refuge (the present refuge is due for demolition). In contrast, in the Surrey area, women tried and failed for twelve years to persuade the local authority to help fund a safe house. It was finally acquired through a private legacy. The same variations are found in rehousing. Some women in London refuges, for example, have to stay for two years, living in one room, often shared with a second family, before they are provided with accommodation . . .

The network of refuges only continues to operate – because workers are underpaid and overworked or overworked and not paid at all. At the same time, vital areas of need have to be ignored – outreach work, counselling women in distress, aftercare and perhaps, most important of all, offering help to disturbed children.

'I've seen kids that pull out their own hair by the handful, very, very aggressive, very clingy, disturbance at school, not reading or writing, nightmares, bedwetting,' the refuge worker in Bangor told Nickie Charles of Welsh Women's Aid. 'When Mum's language isn't bad, their language is bad; bad language is almost an abuse . . . and then we see some very nice ones, nothing wrong with them at all, who are taking the whole thing very well and very supportive of their mums . . . but you don't know what's going on underneath. You've got to be careful you don't ignore those children . . . sometimes they can just crack and do something totally out of character . . .'

Centrally, too, English Women's Aid is in difficulties. At the time of writing, there are no funds for the help line; the Home Office has refused a grant, as has the Department of the Environment; funding from the Department of Health which allowed for the appointment of a national children's resources co-ordinator and a national housing officer has come to an end. The staff of five deal with inquiries from 170 refuges, conduct research, co-ordinate services, prepare publications, lobby and submit evidence to government organisations, monitor legislation and try to fund-raise. The reason why they take on such an impossible task is perhaps seen in a 'thank you' letter published in the 1991 English Women's Aid Federation report:

> My life was totally shattered. I had no money, nowhere to go. I didn't know what to do, it was totally degrading. The refuge was not just a safe place. The support I got from the other women and the workers gave me the confidence I needed to piece my life back together. When you're out there, you think you're the only one. They gave me back my self-respect.

Women's Aid needs reliable and sufficient resources (without affecting its independence, an important part of its organisation) to provide enough refuge places and proper back-up services to help women and children (and refuge workers). It also needs better access to housing and more co-ordination (of the kind now seen in West Yorkshire) between all the agencies involved: social services, housing, the police, education authorities and women's groups.

In July 1992, a report by Victim Support was launched by the Princess Royal. She went to great lengths to explain that she did not want men to feel that they were being 'got at'. There was little fear of that, since after a staggering two years of effort, the report's recommendations were mainly toothless. Instead of piecemeal measures, critics say, a strategy such as the one implemented in Ontario, Canada, in the 1970s should be brought into force.

In Ontario, arrest and prosecution are automatic. Women are relieved of bringing charges because the police do it instead (one of the few tough recommendations suggested in the Victim Support group). In the first few months of the new policy, in 1981, thirty-eight common assault charges were laid by the police. Two years later, there had been a staggering 2,500 per cent increase. Researchers found that the change of policy increased the co-operation between women and police and appeared to deter further acts of violence (although not entirely).[9]

Lorna J. F. Smith, in the Home Office Research Study on domestic violence, said the Canadian police initially felt that they were not getting the back-up of the courts for the new policy. Special training for crown attorneys was subsequently established. Also part of this co-ordinated approach are counsellors who work as liaison officers, a permanent civilian branch of the police force, taking over from an officer once the crisis in the home has been defused. In court, a woman is also provided with an advocate who offers emotional support and practical information. In addition, in Ontario, an information card is given to all victims, a community education programme aimed at professionals and the public is under way, and group counselling through the family court clinic is given to children who have been exposed to domestic violence.

The success of the Canadian approach, Lorna J. F. Smith says, indicates that a lack of intervention on the part of the courts is not the way forward. 'On the contrary, its basic premiss was that the criminal justice system was the most appropriate system but that solutions would have to go wider than mere invocation of criminal law processes; victims' needs extended beyond that and the machinery of the criminal law would be ineffective if not backed by a host of other measures. In short, an integrated response by the whole community was needed.'

Neil Lyndon argues that domestic violence is a mirage; in contrast one researcher, M. D. A. Freeman, suggests that it affects half a million married women in Britain each year (he gives no figures for girlfriends and cohabitees). Until we have research, until domestic violence is listed as a separate offence along with the gender of the victim in the Home Office's criminal statistics (instead of being absorbed into different types of assault and murder), who knows where the exact balance lies? All we can do is be guided by the clues – and, as Lorna J. F. Smith argues, focus on prevention – to move to a society in which violence in the home is simply not tolerated.

'There is increasing recognition in the research literature . . . that any policies designed to prevent domestic violence have to look to the norms, attitudes, beliefs and the structural conditions which both give rise to it and support it,' she writes.

This involves confronting how as a society we construct and define behaviour termed 'masculine' and 'feminine'; how we ascribe roles within marriage and how those processes regulate the position of women. These have important implications for how, as a society, we socialise children. The educational system has a potentially important part to play in the furtherance of long-term prevention. Not only is it important that gender stereotypes are questioned, but it is also important that the message is conveyed that violence is not a legitimate response to problems. In Ontario, Canada this has been taken on board in the development of schools' curricula.

Lorna Smith goes on to argue that the economic independence of women has to be enhanced and job discrimination tackled: 'None of this is likely to be achieved easily or quickly. Arguably, however, it is through the promotion of greater equality between men and women – and the promotion of greater respect for that equality – . . . that real progress in the prevention of domestic violence will be made.'

CHAPTER SEVEN

Who's the boss's darling?

> I never cherished any illusions about changing women's
> condition, it depends upon the future of labour in the
> world. It will change significantly only at the price of a
> revolution in production.
>
> *Simone de Beauvoir*, Force of Circumstance, *1965*

When I registered at the Employment Exchange, and
obtained a job as a railway porter, my friends all said I
could never manage the heavy work. Not only do I handle
trunks and all other packages, but I deliver them within a
radius of a mile on a wheelbarrow. My hubby is a POW
and doesn't know I hold this job. I also have a girl of three:
it can be done.

So wrote a young woman in World War II to *Woman's Own*
on 20 March 1942. A year later, *Woman's Own* was reporting
again:

Job experts said that no woman could do boring, screwing
a breech ring for the barrel of a six pounder tank gun in a
giant lathe, but Miss Megan Lewis, 22, from Wales, ex-
clerk at a London Hospital, has been doing it at the Home
Counties ordinance factory where 80% of machine
operatives are women. 'I learned by watching the setter at
work on the machine'. Officials were astounded.[1]

In the Second World War in Britain, 80 per cent of married women were in work and 95 per cent of single women; within a couple of years of the outbreak of hostilities, 100,000 children had been found nursery places. 'Joan's doing a real job . . . that's what I like about her. She's not playing at war work . . .' said the dashing RAF pilot in a government recruitment ad.

> Swift to do Britannia's bidding
> Never asking why, nor when;
> They will feed her fighting men;
> In machine shops, in munitions,
> Toiling hard for Britain's sake;
> Nothing – nothing – British women
> Cannot – will not – undertake.[2]

Even with Britannia's bidding and the certainty that there were no suitable male hands around to do the job, and that women doing exactly the same tasks were being paid half or less of the male going rate, men hated the idea of women in the workplace. And in spite of the gung-ho tone of the media at the time, there were good reasons why a woman might not want a factory job.

'There was often resentment on the part of men workers, who felt that their skills were belittled if women could acquire them; and a predominantly male trade union leadership showed little sympathy for the problems of women,' Jane Waller and Michael Vaughan-Rees explain in *Women in Wartime*.

Men hated women as work colleagues in World War II, and they had hated them in World War I. 'Working class women became stokers, tool setters, painters, carpenters, bus conductors . . .' writes Angela Holdsworth in *Out of the Doll's House*.

Intransigent trade unionists opposed women joining the workforce with every argument they could muster from the inadequacy of the lavatories in factories and shipyards to women's physical unsuitability for heavy work. All the unions' carefully constructed safeguards to protect men's jobs appeared under threat from the new source of unskilled, cheap labour.

The government persuaded them to relax their rules to allow women to do semi-skilled work or assist men in skilled jobs but promised that this would only be for the duration of the war. Managers were delighted. Not only was a woman cheaper . . . but she adapted instantly to the new assembly lines. 'Men will not stand the monotony of a fast repetition job like women, they will not stand by a machine pressing buttons all their lives, but a woman will.'

Men had hated it in the 1840s, too, when the working class had begun to establish its own hierarchy and a 'decent' man kept his wife at home. But it wasn't just decency that made him wish to deny a woman her right to economic independence. When a Bill was passing through Parliament to ban women from working down the mines, the *Northern Star* said: 'Keep them at home to look after their families; decrease the pressure on the labour market and there is some chance of a higher rate of wages being enforced.'

In the 1990s, the hostility of many men towards sharing the workplace with women has, if anything, intensified. In July 1992, James Buchan wrote an article in the *Daily Mail* with the headline 'The Redundant Male: how women are destroying the British working man'.[3] In this feature, originally published in *The Spectator*, James Buchan nags away at the traditional theme: 'In the past 20 years, the British labour force has grown by 3.2 million. Of these 90% were women. What this means is that women took many of the new jobs and displaced about 1.3 million men from work.' (What this actually means is that women took the work they have always been offered: low-paid and repetitive. 'Men's work' has been lost, in part, by male Ministers of State, the gambles of the predominantly male City, and mediocre male managers.)

The Buchan argument does, however, have a 1990s nuance which is totally in keeping with the backlash. Women in their millions are not *forced* into the sewage end of the labour market where there is risible pay; part-time employment with no rights; short-term contracts; no pension schemes; no holiday pay; no in-house training; no bonus schemes; no career plans; too little union involvement, and no status. According to Mr Buchan, women have *chosen* to occupy this special little niche:

> In effect, British women have made a Faustian bargain with British business. To feed their families or escape the hysterical boredom of the British household, many married women or single mothers have offered their ill-paid, part-time and unprotected labour to business people desperate to reduce fixed costs in the face of slumping product markets.

Mr Buchan fails to realise that 'these women who often have had to put children out in the care of strangers' faced exactly the same terms of employment when Britain allegedly 'never had it so good' in the fifties and in the Swinging Sixties. Employers have never needed the excuse of recession to hold a good 'girl' down; what they have always sought is a reserve army of labour which they can pick up and drop in tune with their profit margins.

Mr Buchan is not done yet: he ends his 'analysis' with this implicit message: if only women had stayed at home, doing what they know best. 'Theoretically, if the labour market works properly, male wages will fall and ex-dustmen will be taken on as trainee beauticians at £60 a week. The labour market will have achieved flexibility,' he writes.

> It will be a market dominated by short-term, unprotected, un-unionised, insecure, low-paid and unmotivated labour

184

without employment rights where, as Winston Churchill once said, 'the good employer is undercut by the bad, and the bad employer by the worst,' and children will see little of their mothers [and what about their fathers?]. Wages and prices will presumably be in free fall. Devaluation, except of an entire society, will have been avoided.

The British workplace is, of course, sodden with bad practice not because of women's treachery but because for years and years it has suited trade unions, governments and employers to treat women as those whom they could most easily exploit. Now female 'standards' are, for some, becoming universal – and men have no one to blame but themselves. As the Spanish artist Juan Frances has said, 'Man is trampled by the same forces he has created.'

The warfare not only continues, it grows apace. Open any tabloid or many of the so-called 'quality' newspapers, on any day of the week, and the implicit message of the headlines is identical: women in work cause enormous damage to men but even more to themselves, allegedly forfeiting the chance of children, sex and love while ratting on any concept of sisterhood.

The chief utiliser of this newspeak whose underlying theme is, again: 'Woman: get back home or at least to the bottom ranks of the corporate ladder where you belong', is of course, the *Daily Mail*. And the journalists most eager to produce the copy are the very women whose aspirations as a group the male section heads on the paper, not to say the editor (first Sir David English and now Paul Dacre) seek, with enormous efficiency, to undermine. It is a long tradition in Fleet Street that the part of the newspaper which is 'only' for women is, in fact, 'merely' for women – and the quickest way out for a 'girl' who wants to become one of the boys is to dump on her own sex.

To give an example of some of the headlines: 'The Mothering Wars' (allegedly between working and non-working

mothers); 'Can a Good Mother Ever Make a First-Rate Boss?'
(the answer, of course, is no); 'Downfall of the Woman Boss
Who "Frightened" Top Men at British Gas' (Hilary Williams
subsequently went on to win her case of sex discrimination);
'The Woman at War – now gran could be a working mother's
biggest enemy' (a survey showing that four-fifths of women
under twenty-four thought it was not a woman's responsibility
to look after home and family – 54 per cent of women over
sixty-five insist that it is – hardly a landslide); 'The New
Spinsters – why do so many successful career women find love
eludes them?'; 'Tyranny of the Woman Boss'; 'Beware the
Single Girl – I invited a career woman to dinner. Now she is
living with my husband' (the spurned wife, it transpires, is
also no mean shakes at turning a few pounds in business) –
and so it goes on and on.[4]

Why do women continue to buy the *Daily Mail* in such high
numbers? Because the propaganda is part of a larger package
which they find attractive. Do they absorb its viewpoint? It
depends, I suspect, on age, class and marital status. The prime
issue is not so much the impact of the *Daily Mail*'s views as
what they reveal about the male attitude to that allegedly
monstrous creature of the 1990s: the woman with aspirations
and a building society account. (Ironically, it is precisely to
reach her that the advertisers opt for the *Mail*.)

Given the paper's readership, a campaign for good childcare
or equal pay or improved conditions for returners or a change
in the Sex Discrimination Act might be appreciated – but such
issues are omitted. This isn't just politics; in part it's what
inevitably happens when, at executive level, the female perspective is as rare as a *Daily Mail* employee who can claim to
feel at ease at work.

Many other newspapers are as avid in their hunt of the
working women as prey (or, in the case of the *Sun*, any woman
as prey), but they don't call the pack out quite as often. 'Why
Don't Daughters of Working Mothers Want Children?' asked
The Standard on the testament of one daughter, Carol

Thatcher.[5] '900,000 new career girls but one in three will live alone,' said the headline in *Today*.[6] This was a conflation of a Social Trends report which actually said that one in three households would hold a person living alone (but not necessarily a 'career girl'). *The Guardian* (not usually so remiss) published a story about the Midland Bank which estimated that lack of childcare facilities meant that it lost 70 per cent of trained women at a cost of £14 million. The headline? 'Motherhood Costs Employers Dear'. A more accurate phrasing might have read 'Lack of childcare costs employers dear'.[7] And virtually all the media, of course, devoured the story of Diane Cornish, a highly successful director of the Brook Street Bureau, a recruitment company, who decided to call it a day.

'Woman gives up £100,000 job for her family', said the not untypical headline in the *Daily Telegraph* in January 1992. Only *The Times* discovered a month later that it was a more complex story. Ms Cornish, in her late forties, had given up the job as managing director to spend more time with her newly retired husband and her daughter, now twenty-five. 'Of course I will miss the money, but I won't miss the rat race, office politics, traffic jams and twelve-hour days,' Ms Cornish told Anne Steele.[8] But what the earlier coverage had failed to mention is that Diane Cornish hasn't opted out altogether.

Instead, she and her husband are developing the stables they own, along with an indoor riding arena and seventy horses. Ms Cornish is also considering joining the lecture circuit. Twenty years ago, when she was divorced from her first husband, she had employed an *au pair* to care for her four-year-old daughter, Pennie, and taken a job. 'I was the only woman in the street who went out to work,' she is quoted as saying. 'People around were very critical and very nasty.' Many still are.

Neil Lyndon sees it as a failure of feminism that it has pushed so hard to get women into the workplace. What he does not also acknowledge is that paid work is necessary because it is the only route to independence, however limited, in a capitalist society. Give individuals £1,000 a month simply for being female, and no doubt many would hand in their cards instantly. A paid job for the majority of women is not a badge of emancipation, it is a means to an end. That end is money and companionship.

At the same time, this society – in the name of what Neil Lyndon, in *No More Sex War*, rightly calls 'the god of profit' – has hijacked emotions such as pride, a sense of achievement and the need to be publicly valued (none of which society accords to full-time motherhood) and associated them almost exclusively with work. That's why 'And what do you do for a living?' is such an automatic introductory question.

To rise to the top in a career is the mark of a 'successful' human being in the eyes of the male Establishment. Ambitious women, rightly or wrongly, will respond to those messages just as enthusiastically as any receptive man. The issue for feminism, then, in a work-orientated society, is to negotiate the best possible deal – one which makes the workplace more humane, the work ethic less dictatorial, the rewards fairer, the personal sacrifices less damaging, and the neglect of children, minimal.

Simultaneously, if feminism succeeds in these areas, it will also begin to subvert the very values which underpin the consumer society. It may demonstrate that 'worth' is not associated only with what you make and how much you spend, but with who you are and how you balance your time – and what importance you give to seeking an identity which is not dictated entirely by an annual career assessment or the 'need' for a mobile CD player and an avocado bidet in the otherwise solidly British bathroom. As the American Margaret Case Harriman put it: 'Money is what you'd get on beautifully without, if only other people weren't so crazy about it.'

As it is now, in the 1990s, the workplace threatens to become the bloodiest war zone yet in the battle between the sexes – unless change is introduced quickly. This is because while some men may feel angry at the female intrusion into 'their' territory, some women are equally enraged that so much of what was promised twenty years ago has yet to be delivered.

Younger women who allegedly made up the post-feminist generation in the yuppy 1980s are beginning to realise that the 'sense of entitlement' they felt to gains hard-won by the previous generation is insufficient protection once the backlash takes hold. In April 1992, for instance, Cheri Rippon was awarded £8,000 compensation after her complaint of unfair dismissal against Executive Contracts, a cleaning firm in North London, of which she was a director, was upheld. Ms Rippon was dismissed while she was pregnant. She told the industrial tribunal that her business partner, Maxwell Hampshire, had taken the news of her pregnancy well at first. 'Everything started to go rapidly wrong after that . . . He was making my life unbearable because he said how could I do this to the company . . .'⁹ She took a wage cut from £460 to £150, but then false allegations were made against her and she was dismissed. She told the tribunal that she was now a lone parent (having split up with her boyfriend), living on £54 a week supplementary benefit with a six-month-old baby. She was unable to afford a childminder while she tried to put the pieces of her career together again.

In 1991, the Equal Opportunities Commission received 951 complaints about unfair dismissal during pregnancy – an increase of 289 on the previous year. Forty per cent of women in work, in any case, do not qualify for maternity leave, and 20 per cent receive no pay even if they are allowed the time off.

For older women, women of my generation, experience has cleared the head. At first, the pattern of being marginalised, passed over and excluded from the old boys' network is often attributed to a woman's own failings in commerce or industry or advertising or education. With patience, hard work and determination, she tells herself, her time will come. It doesn't. Common sense tells her, as the years pass by, that those men who have come up from behind and overtaken her are frequently no better material than she is, and often a lot worse.

My generation is also getting a second wind for another and perhaps more important reason: our daughters. And our sons.

'Learning to live in the world meant seeing the glass half full,' writes the *New York Times* Pulitzer Prize-winning columnist Anna Quindlen, who is in her thirties.

> . . . And then I had a daughter and suddenly I saw the glass half empty. And all the rage I thought had cooled, all those how-dare-you-treat-us-like-that days, all of it comes back.
>
> Every time a woman looks at her daughter and thinks, 'She can be anything', she knows in her heart, from experience, that it's a lie . . . My little girl deserves better. She has given me my anger back, and I intend to use it well.[10]

And so do I.

In the States, in January 1992, a woman who had recently read Susan Faludi's book *Backlash: The War Against Women* wrote to *Mother Jones*, a monthly magazine. She said: 'Ms Faludi puts eloquently what I have been feeling for the past ten years as a woman in the workplace: angry, pissed off, chagrined, subjugated, ignored, put down, left out, devalued and insulted. I also feel exhausted.'

Britain now has almost ten million women at work – two million have joined since 1983 (making up 42.9 per cent of the total). Eighty-three per cent of child-free women and 56 per cent of mothers have a job. Women in work also share a threefold problem.

First, over four million women are part-timers (800,000 men), and according to the Equal Opportunities Commission, 70 per cent want to stay that way. The EOC also says that by the year 2000 another 1.5 million part-time jobs will be created, most of them going to women. Yet in the 1990s, a career and job-share or part-time work is regarded as mutually incompatible while employment rights are, as James Buchan has said, a luxury.

The second problem is the growing army of women (and men) forced to work full-time for too little money and with almost no employment protection – victims of casualisation. As Lynne Segal has warned, if work is supposed to be the vital step towards female independence, then on these terms all we are doing is 'liberating' women into a different kind of poverty.

Third, the limitations on the choices facing those women who seek a career and full-time work. The EOC says that management jobs will become available in the next decade, but the glass ceiling will also be reinforced, 'moving jobs further up the hierarchy still beyond the reach of most'. More women in work, more women angry?

Neil Lyndon thinks this anger is misplaced. In an article in *The Spectator* whose modest aims were encapsulated in its title: 'The Wrongs of Women: how civilised society is being corrupted by feminists and their mad doctrines', he suggested:

> If there genuinely exists a seriously profit-minded group of male employers and executives whose members are averse to the hiring and promotion of women, I should genuinely like to meet them: they are such rare and antique specimens that they ought to be preserved as a national treasure.[11]

He explained:

> Even the roly-poly Rotarians, trenchering and troughing at their monthly luncheons in the market town near my village, congratulate themselves and each other that, in their bank, in their building firm, in their small factory, in their legal firm, any woman can take any job for which she is fitted by ability and application.

The progressive attitudes which may prevail among the more porcine members of Suffolk clearly have not travelled. Women are desperately underrepresented in the top ranks. Gillian Shephard, the Employment Minister and the Minister responsible for women's issues (surely they should be the responsibility of each and every Minister?), expressed 'shock' at the extent to which the system allows women into middle management, but not to rise further.[12]

Only 16 out of 108 Chief Education Officers are female; in five years 49 male Recorders have become circuit judges, but only 2 women; women make up 2 per cent of chartered engineers, and only 7 per cent of the top three grades in Whitehall are female. According to the National Economic Development Office, only 4 per cent of senior managers are female. In addition, men are 50 per cent more likely to have had job-related training.

The labour market is littered with conundrums. Why, for instance, if 80 per cent of teachers are female, are men four times more likely to become heads in secondary schools? And if 17 per cent of academic staff are female, why do women account for only 3 per cent of the jobs as university and polytechnic professors and senior lecturers? Women could, of course, have 'only themselves to blame'. They may be unwilling to take on responsibility, they may be indifferent to ambition. And there is nothing wrong in that – large sections of the male population have expressed such healthy attitudes for generations, but without the whole of their gender being held back.

It may also be true that inequality itself becomes a depressant. A report in the late 1980s by Staffordshire Polytechnic looked at graduates three years after they began work. The women tended to earn less, have lower-status jobs and more limited career prospects than men. In five years, the men expected to be earning £16,000 plus; a third of the women expected to be earning under £10,000.[13] But other forces are at work too.

In 1968, at Michigan University, Matina Horner conducted an experiment. She gave her male and female students a short story which began: 'Anne ended her first year medical school top of her class.' The students were asked to complete the tale. Ninety per cent of the men accepted Anne's success; 65 per cent of the women dwelt on the negative aspect. 'Anne is an acne faced bookworm,' wrote one woman. Another gave Anne the words 'I'll be the best doctor alive', and added: 'Yet a twinge of sadness comes through, she wonders what she really has.'

If some women *do* expect less for themselves and *are* ambivalent about success – as the American writer Letty Cottin Pogrebin remarked, 'Boys don't make passes at female smart-asses' – those attitudes are in transition, and may be destined to change further. A survey conducted on 389 parents with children aged eleven to fourteen, published in March 1992,[14] showed that 76 per cent of mothers who have a career expect their children to leave school at eighteen (compared with 59 per cent of non-working mothers). Eighty per cent of working-mother families believe their children will attend university or college. (What is heartening is that even among non-working mothers, the figure is 70 per cent.)

Some women may act as a brake on their own aspirations, some may be deterred by what society places in their way – but research also indicates that given the right circumstances and encouragement, the change is dramatic.

As Valerie Hammond and Viki Holton prove again and again in *A Balanced Workforce?*, an excellent research project conducted on behalf of the Ashridge Management Research Group, into companies where efforts *have* been made to give women a fair shake, the results are often immediate and clearly of value to the employer. (No company has yet switched to an equal opportunities policy out of altruism.)

'IBM's policy of equal opportunity is founded on sound business judgement and our basic belief in respect for the individual,' John Akers, IBM chairman, is quoted as saying in the Ashridge report. In the last ten years, IBM in the USA has doubled the number of women it employs; tailored policies have also increased the percentage of women managers from 9 to 20 per cent.

British Rail has increased the number of women managers and executives by 70 per cent in four years. Career breaks at ICI have trebled the number of women managers. In 1985, only 4 per cent of managers were female; six years later, the proportion had reached 11 per cent. The Littlewoods Organisation, a large UK retail, mail-order and football lottery group, has 36,000 employees, two-thirds female. Between 1986 and 1991 the proportion of women store managers has increased from 22 to 40 per cent and the proportion of general managers has increased from 0 to 10 per cent.

Valerie Hammond and Viki Holton quote Bjorn Sprangare, managing director of a Swedish company, Trygg-Hansa, to show that the message has international ramifications: 'Developing capable managers is one of the most important tasks a company has. Capable managers are in short supply and if we want to be able to cover this shortage, women must be involved.'

These (very few) companies have recognised that what inhibits women's progress may be assumptions, practices and procedures – problems which, in time of an acute skill shortage in certain areas, now have to be tackled. Male attitudes also play a part. In New South Wales, Australia, in the 1970s, when ABC, the public broadcasting network, decided to appraise its policies on hiring women and minority groups, it called in Eva Cox.

If it expected that one appointment and a couple of publicity handouts would just about handle the issue (a not untypical view of equal opportunities), it was wrong. Eva Cox organised a survey which exposed the logjams, hurdles and poor management practices which impeded female talent. She also asked the male staff to fill in a seemingly innocuous multiple-choice questionnaire. (A tactic yet to be tried by the BBC – which still values workaholism so highly, it automatically excludes all the women of ability who prefer a balanced life.) Of course, many of the prejudices were revealed: mothers are not dependable, single women only get married and go off and have babies, etc., etc.

Neil Lyndon asserts: 'Political, social and commercial institutions in a modern society come into being and take their shape, character and purpose in response to the contemporary needs of that society. The social and economic forces which shape them are impersonal, genderless, neutral.' But even if this is true – and I doubt it – the conduits through which such needs pass, the filter which decides what has a higher priority and what doesn't, are almost entirely man-made.

In Britain in the last ten years, many more women have gone into higher education (two in three females between the ages of twenty-five and twenty-nine have an educational qualification compared with only one in three women in their fifties). Forty per cent of those taking a full-time business degree are female; 50 per cent of new lawyers are female; 30 per cent of those about to qualify as chartered accountants are female; as are 50 per cent of medical students.

One choice new female recruits have is to enter the labour market – and accept it as it is. When they bear sons and daughters, they can become macho mothers, rendering their children's needs invisible, as many fathers have done before them. A woman's capacity to 'take it like a man' can become part of the proof of her metal. And so the traditional workplace remains *virgo intacta*.

In *No More Sex War*, Neil Lyndon views this 'adoption of male mannerisms in male institutions' as 'one of the more postulant lines of piss in the crock of cant which is modern feminism. It is so unintelligent and insensitive, so feeble as an account of the origins and purposes of political institutions,' he says, 'that we wouldn't, in any time other than our own, give it the time of day it emerged from the drooling mouth of a drunk at a bar . . .'

Dagmar Woodward, aged thirty-nine, 1992 Hotelier of the Year and the only woman manager of the five-star hotel, the May Fair Intercontinental in Mayfair, London, runs a staff of 280 and a budget of millions. *The Standard* tells us that she achieved her goal by 'a relentless round of sweat and hard work'. Her marriage has ended and she has no children. 'It would have been much more difficult for me to do the job if I'd had kids,' she is quoted as saying.[15]

In *The Independent*, Angela Lambert interviews Janet Cohen, fifty-one, corporate finance director of a merchant bank, mother of three teenage children and a novelist. 'The thing to be in this world is a man,' Janet Cohen says. 'Or at least assimilated into a male world – and goodness, how I tried to be a high-powered man.'[16]

In the States, this path taken by so many women reveals a glimpse of hell. In Britain, we should be warned. In 1987, a team of British company managers, organised by Ashridge Management College, visited New Orleans and New York to exchange information on management practice.[17] 'One woman told us that she had been made redundant by a manufacturing company early in her career because she had been too forceful and aggressive,' the team's report records.

> These qualities, whilst they would have been prized in a male employee, were seen as threatening when manifested by a woman . . .
>
> The key to success seems to be to . . . learn to manipulate the system to one's advantage within a very narrow band of accepted female behaviour . . . Overall a woman has to accept male values, systems and structures if she is to succeed and having accepted these, many women then demonstrate little interest in or sympathy with other women rising up through the same organisation . . . Many of these women deny that they manage in any way differently from their male colleagues – one vice-president told us that it was wrong to think about such differences,

which simply did not exist; the attributes of male managers were the qualities which women needed.

As things stand, women have to 'play the game'. But it is a game where all the rules are made by men and where the stakes are very high, requiring a total subordination of self and the sacrifice of family and private life . . . Even if a woman does all she can, she may still not reach the top. Many women find they hit the glass ceiling when they are barred by invisible but rigid barriers and practices . . . Years of pressure to enhance the acceptance of women in organisations has 'simply moved the ghetto upwards'.

Perhaps this camouflaging of the female executive helps to explain Neil Lyndon's personal experience:

'Having frequently retained or consulted women doctors or lawyers, estate agents, literary agents or business advisers, having had regular and constant dealings with women educators and administrators, having met and done business with or interviewed hundreds of women in business or politics, having frequently worked with and for women as colleagues, what impresses me most vividly is not the qualitative differences in performance or attitude between men and women in those professions but the extent to which those elements are indistinguishable,' he writes in *No More Sex War*.

Women, of course, are as varied in their political views as men, and just because they 'get on', that does not mean they suddenly owe allegiance to the principles of the women's movement. Indeed, assumptions should not even be made of those paid up sisters who 'succeed'. 'How can we trust the feminists when, as employers, they treat us so badly?' asks Mary Castro, leader of a domestic workers' association in Brazil.[18] My argument is that those women who do move on and upwards, without feeling any obligation to alter the terms under which the workplace operates, not only damage prospects for future generations, they also damage themselves.

The second 'choice' which faces a woman who enters the traditional labour market with aspirations and high hopes is to drop out as soon as the first fence comes into sight. Better still, she drops out blaming not the system for failing to yield to the demands of parenthood, but herself. It is she who has been at fault for not realising the power of her biological instinct. She is, after all, different from men, but special: she is a mother.

In 1909, Vatican doctrine confirmed that woman's contribution to the world was in this, her main role. As Gisela Kaplan points out in *Contemporary Western European Feminism*, 'employment outside the home was seen as a severe corruption'. She explains how Mussolini decided, in the 1920s and 1930s, to take that religious orthodoxy to its less than logical conclusion.

In Italy, among the laws he passed were the banning of women from the position of school principal; he made any form of birth control punishable by law; abortion resulted in severe penalties (unless, of course, the woman had been ordered to have an abortion by her husband); taxes were levied against 'unjustified celibacy'; and women were not allowed to refuse intercourse with their husbands. He also established the National Foundation for Mother and Child and slashed women's wages in the menial jobs still left open to them. (Women did not take this lying down. Under Mussolini the birth rate dropped and in 1929, Gisela Kaplan writes, abortion may have been as high as 30 per cent – although given the penalties, it is hard to see how such a statistic could be obtained.)

In the 1990s, of course, the restrictions on mothers entering the workplace are much more insidious; the net effect is often *mea culpa*. In the autumn of 1991, for instance, journalist Minette Marin appeared on BBC-2's personal opinion slot, 'Fifth Column', to explain how, twenty years earlier, she had succumbed to the arguments of Women's Lib. Now, she told the viewers, she realised that, after all, women aren't biologically attuned to the competitiveness and aggression of the working world. What women are best at is mothering.

'It seems that the disillusionment and disappointments of some women have created a spiritual void and a need to find something to believe in, about themselves and about their futures,' Gisela Kaplan writes. 'It is at such vulnerable psychohistorical moments that we see the rise of ideologies which revert to concepts and beliefs that have been tried before and failed . . .' She goes on to argue that these 'feminine virtues' to do with mothering and nurturing are not biological but 'long fostered in socialisation processes'. 'To date,' she adds, 'I have found it difficult to believe that such traits . . . should be vested in only half of humanity and that they could not be developed and allowed to surface and be supported in men.'

The price for buying the line that women have a 'special feminine value' is well known: 'It has usually been employed as a lever to rationalise why women are unable to take part in active politics and to justify women's relegation to the private domain,' Gisela Kaplan writes. In other words, it has been used to keep women out of the workplace when they choose to compete within it.

A third option available to women who wish for a career is to argue that equality means the right for each individual to develop their potential to the full. If a woman or a man is not only an employee but also a carer of children and/or an elderly relative, then since this is also part of a contribution to society, the labour market has to adjust and accommodate, not penalise. That means the need not only to institute career breaks, CVs which may be considered unorthodox (some companies in the USA will take on board a woman's 'career' as a voluntary worker) and a career structure for part-time work, but to give a genuine commitment so that these changes become an integrated part of company policy.

Jane Wiltshire is forty. In 1973, she was one of only two

women to graduate in chemical engineering from Imperial College London. She joined BP fifteen years ago and has more recently benefited from the company's 'cultural change' policy encapsulated in the acronym OPEN: Open thinking; Personal impact; Empowering; Networking. The Americanese translates, in theory, into more flexible career patterns. In practice, it is still not without its problems.

Jane Wiltshire was originally a chemical engineer. Her background includes refinery investment planning and business development, production control and supply. Most of her work has been in the business development of refining from a commercial and technical point of view, working with engineers and planners. Her current job is competitor analysis. In 1983, she was put on the Individual Development Programme (IDP), the corporate fast-track programme. Her manager asked her if she would like her name to be put forward, or did she want a baby, because there were other candidates who were male.

Jane's response was that she had every intention of becoming pregnant, but why should that stop her selection? Two years later, she had Thomas and four years ago, Jonathan. In 1985, she said she wanted to work from her home in Sussex. 'If I'd continued to work full-time and commute to London, it would have meant leaving at 7 a.m. and getting back at 7 p.m. I wanted to see my sons.'

She was the first – and there are still very few – executive homeworkers. BP installed a high-tech office and negotiated a contract: twenty-two hours a week (three days); pension scheme; eligibility for bonus, shares and company car plus maternity leave intact.

'Initially, they kept seeing it as a temporary arrangement,' she says. 'And I kept saying: this is how I want it to be permanently. The result is major problems in terms of my career development. I'm already quite a senior manager and it means I can go so far and no further. I've lost out on the fast track, spent six years on a plateau which wouldn't have happened before because BP couldn't yet think in terms of career development for part-timers. However, recently, I've been promoted and am now doing a different job. I've lost out – but at least I've exercised choice.'

Jane Wiltshire has an annual contract of hours which, as long as the work gets done, she can organise as she chooses – taking time off, for instance, during half-term and in the school holidays. A home-based part-timer, she says, has to have discipline. 'The difficulty is not that you do too little but you feel guilty, so you do too much. I've learnt to manage it now but a couple of years ago, stress was creeping in. I was working at weekends and in the evenings after the children had gone to bed. I realised that I wasn't giving enough time to my husband, home and family.'

Other difficulties involve quelling the feelings that ambition feeds: others have moved on, why not me? And isolation: 'I've never really felt the need to be visible in the office in order to prove I'm doing a good job. But now I go in every Monday because people think if you're not there, you're not available. I have to remind them that I am.'

She is helped by the fact that BP is interested now in flat planning: small teams led by managers which take the place of the traditional vast pyramid structure. She reports directly to the financial director of BP Oil. 'I choose my junior staff very carefully to avoid them taking advantage of the fact that I'm not in the office.' She has also found that while women are very supportive, some men have been resentful.

'I dealt with it head-on and asked one colleague if he had a problem. The truth is, men could work full-time on the same sort of deal but they don't want to. The culture of the workplace for a lot of them means much more than earning a salary. People always say how lucky I am. But they see it as working shorter hours and then doing nothing. They forget that when I'm not working, I'm involved in childcare and running a home.' (A nursery, school and friends help out with the two boys).

'Guilt still operates,' she says. 'You never feel that you've got it quite right between work and family. But I don't regret working from home and I know that I couldn't give up work altogether. It's difficult, but it does offer some sort of compromise.'

In autumn 1991, a plainly nervous John Major launched Opportunity 2000. It wasn't Mr Major's idea; he merely stitched himself on to the endeavour like a small grey logo. The Women's Economic Development Target Team, part of a Business in the Community venture, thought up the original concept. 'The aim is to encourage employers to increase women's potential in the workforce by publicly committing themselves to action,' campaign director Liz Bargh told *Cosmopolitan*.

It is not the fault of her team that Opportunity 2000 is a sham. A handful of companies without carrots or – even more important – a large stick wielded by the government are celebrated because they declare that they intend to amble along to some unfocused point in the future when they may have a few more women in company cars. In terms of initiating radical change, it's like using a toy spade to dig the Channel Tunnel.

Even Paul Johnson, writing in *The Spectator* at the time, was appalled. What he wants is women in the workplace, but not as feminists – much too subversive. He belongs to the 'You can join my game in the playground but don't you dare change it' school of thought. 'The waste of women's brainpower, ideas and energy in this country is tragic,' he wrote. 'At present, half [our human resources] are squandered, discriminated against, sneered at and suppressed. We must unleash them.'

In some companies – mainly because it makes money – some women have already been unleashed, as Valerie Hammond's research has demonstrated. Her work has provided the raw material from which Opportunity 2000 evolved. 'We started out with the basic question: we've had equal opportunities in theory for fifteen years. Not very much has changed – why?

'We looked at companies in the UK, the USA, Europe and Japan. What we discovered is that when a company is involved in a takeover or a merger or decides on a philosophical change of direction, as BA did when it inaugurated its theme of putting people first, that change involves a much more profound turnaround than implementing equal opportunities. So we looked for the business reasons which can make equal opportunities attractive. There is *always* a business reason.'

The most obvious reason is a skill shortage and the need to retain what staff you already have. In the States, 500 employees – many of them female lone parents – at Nyloncraft, a factory supplying plastic mouldings in Mishawaka, Indiana, in 1989, were given a staff of 26 people to provide 180 children, aged between two and twelve, with childcare around the clock. In the 1970s, James Wylie, then chief executive, had a high staff turnover. In one year he recruited 900, at a training cost for some of $2,000 each, to fill 250 jobs. Since childcare has been provided, the turnover has gone down from 300 per cent to 3 per cent.[19]

In Britain, provision for the under-fives is among the worst in Europe. (We are beaten only by Portugal. In France, to give just one example, there is suitable childcare provision for 90 per cent of children aged three to five.) We have no real tax relief on childcare, no government-funded childcare centres, no system of subsidised childminding. On the contrary, the effects of government cuts on local authorities have meant that much of the provision for childminders (themselves an outrageously exploited group, earning around £1.50 an hour), such as in-house training and toy libraries, has been severely reduced, while local authority inspection of individual childminders (necessary to re-register under the Children Act) is hampered by lack of nursery and sufficient staff. This forces some women to place their children with illegal minders – or not at all.

In an unctuous interview with Sally O'Sullivan, editor-in-chief of *Good Housekeeping*, published in June 1992, John Major is asked about childcare. 'There is a wide variety of childcare provision available in this country,' he says, and quotes the exemption of employees from paying income tax on the benefit of workplace nurseries. As John Major must know, 'variety' is not the same as 'quantity' – and Britain has 3,000 workplace nurseries for several million women with children under five.

Virginia Bottomley, when she had responsibility for women's issues, played the same game as her boss. When, early in 1992 the Labour Party published its document *Women Today*, promising improved childcare, she is reported to have said: 'The diversity of childcare provision and choice in this country is unparalleled in Europe. Over 90 per cent of three-to-four-year-olds are involved in some organised group activity.' How long does 'organised group activity' last? Half an hour? Two hours? Long enough to write a company report or clock in and out of a factory shift? Ms Bottomley is the diva of the disingenuous.

A report by Heather Joshi and Hugh Davies of the Centre for Economic Policy Research, published in February 1992, assesses that motherhood costs the average British woman £224,000 in lost earnings. This sum is calculated on a woman with two children earning £9,000 a year, who stops when the children are born and returns to work when they reach school age. Not only does a woman lose out because her career path has been interrupted (as does the company), she is also worse off in pay, pension rights, bonus schemes, lack of overtime and the consequences of sporadic payment of National Insurance contributions.

'It is quite likely that better childcare would pay for itself over fifteen years because of tax gains, especially for lone mothers, for whom the state is paying an income,' Heather Joshi said when the report was published.[20]

Even George Bush, in his time, has considered a tax credit

of up to $1,000 a child for low-income families to spend on childcare, while the so-called ABC Bill (Act for Better Childcare Services) was proposed to provide federal funds to subsidise daycare centres. 'We have made real progress on the issues concerning women,' John Major told Sally O'Sullivan. She failed to ask the crucial question: 'Where?'

(Valerie Hammond also presents a second economic argument for subsidised childcare. By the year 2015, she says, the working population will have diminished and the elderly dependent population will have grown larger. 'We need to make sure women can work *and* have children because we need both women's abilities and their offspring, to balance the population in the future.')

In Valerie Hammond's research, she discovered that some individual companies have already acknowledged the business sense in equal opportunities. Rover, the car firm, knows that four out of five jobs will be filled by women, so it has introduced a career break scheme and a maternity package which offers 100 per cent pay.

Bradford City Council discovered that 42 per cent of the staff using its kindergarten would leave if the nursery was closed. It costs between £5,000 and £17,500 to replace an employee; it's cheaper to run the nursery.

The National Savings Bank in Glasgow created a Christmas holiday scheme offering childcare facilities. The company saved £4,000 a week because staffing levels were maintained throughout the holiday period. Boots the Chemist offers termtime contracts so that women can have all the school holidays at home – an offer also made by Littlewoods which, in any survey of good company practice, emerges with all the Brownie points for good behaviour.[21]

The policy changes at Littlewoods began in 1965, with a code of practice, a training programme for all line managers, and a five-year action plan with targets to improve the performance of women, the disabled, and ethnic groups. This has evolved over time, so there is also now an Equal Opportunities

Unit, rolling targets, career grooming and maternity provision, which includes part-timers and a paternal leave scheme. John Moores, director of Littlewoods, who initiated the changes after working in the USA in the 1960s, explains: 'We attach a great deal of importance to our equal opportunities programme. It helps us to meet both our legal and moral obligations; utilise people's abilities to the full by removing artificial and irrelevant barriers to recruitment and promotion; draw from the widest possible pool of talent and implement good management practice.' And he adds: 'It is also good business.'

In addition to concern for profit, companies may also feel that in the 'caring nineties' (yet to live up to their hype) a corporate identity is improved by a balanced workforce – while others argue in the more mystical realms of women having 'special' management skills (a point of view that makes me nervous, since women have always paid so highly in the past as a result of accepting the male definition of their 'specialness').

Almost every major British company intends to employ fewer people in the next three to five years according to Charles Handy, visiting professor at the London Business School. He says that the hierarchical 'I'm boss, you're not' structures will flatten out; there will be more freelance contracts, individuals will organise their own 'work portfolios' from home. The net result will be to 'de-skill' men (and presumably anger them still further) and – in theory, at least – to hand the advantage to women.

'Men will have to bring out the feminine side of their characters,' Professor Handy says (whatever that may mean).

The skills of negotiation, persuasion, relating to the customer and building up trust are [aspects] which women are instinctively better at than men because they've had to be. Men must realise the sort of feminine side of their nature which has been suppressed by our culture and schooling because they will not be able to rely on power.[22]

In *Shaping the Corporate Future*, Kevin Barham and Clive Rassam interview 'leading executives' who 'share their vision and stategies'. What emerges is a view that change will be fast and competition tough; management structure will have more bends, loops and redesigns than a pot of Playdough. The language is of 'intrapreneurship' (entrepreneurs within the firm) and quality circles and managerial autonomy . . . 'The main thing . . . will be to get things right first . . .' one executive tells the writers. 'To innovate to order', says Sir John Harvey Jones. A manager of ICI says of the new manager material the company requires: 'It is no longer Passchendaele leadership. We need a different kind of leadership, one in which the leader can generate a sense of vision of purpose.'

A senior manager at Accor, a France-based company that owns the ninth-largest chain of hotels in the world, operating in sixty-eight countries, also says: 'In Europe, we are habit bound. It's virtually impossible to get people to change. To bring about change, you really have to do astounding things to shake people up.'[23]

In many of the companies, Valerie Hammond discovered, one man is often the key to this shake-up (or a woman, in the rare situation when one is in charge). He has the vision and drives along the changes in the face of opposition: John Moores of Littlewoods; John Harvey Jones when he was at ICI: Lord Alexander of National Westminster Bank.

A government too, of course, can do 'astounding things', and the advantage a government has over an individual entrepreneur is that instead of a few thousand people being positively affected, the whole country benefits. A government can use laws, incentives and penalties to create an ambience which swamps traditional conditioning. The tough legislation in the USA in the 1960s and early 1970s (now overturned by a highly conservative Supreme Court) helped to achieve that for women and ethnic minorities with a series of class actions. What was decided in court for one woman applied to all women in the same area of employment. (In Britain, 'victory' is acquired on a case-by-case basis, which should mean the end of discrimination by the year 3020.) Companies in the States were not only fined millions of dollars, they had to produce programmes of action and monitor results.

Critics complained that this 'quota' policy was diluting talent – it was said that women were being appointed because of their gender, not their abilities. Whether or not that is true, the penalties helped to focus the minds of many companies wonderfully well. In 1970, for instance, only 0.6 per cent of General Motors' students of engineering were female; seven years later, the proportion had risen to 32 per cent.

In Britain, the legislation of the 1960s, the Sex Discrimination Act (pushed through by Barbara Castle when she was Labour's Employment Minister) and the 1970 Equal Pay Act (the work of Baroness Nancy Sear) need to be replaced. They were never more than a child's first footfall on the road to equality. The Equal Opportunities Commission has individuals of calibre working for it, but it too has proved itself so gummy, it needs a new set of dentures to give it fresh bite.

The EOC has proposed a new Equal Treatment Act with the hint of a suggestion of class action. Gillian Shephard, who behaves as if she is the fairy godmother who needs only to wave her magic wand of 'persuasion' for it all to get better, has said she will do 'whatever is necessary' – except, of course, whatever is necessary.

On 4 June 1990, Alison Halford attended an industrial tribunal. She alleged that the chief constable of Merseyside, the Home Secretary, Northamptonshire Police Authority and the Inspector of Constabulary had repeatedly passed her over for promotion to the post of deputy chief constable. Two years and a million pounds later, Alison Halford is taking early retirement; the ridiculous chauvinist rituals of police life, including numerous 'liquidacious' lunches, have – usefully – once more been exposed to the public gaze, but blame has not been apportioned and police practices theoretically remain untouched (although if that is really so, the police are even more in the mire than they appear to be).

The EOC says that since 1990, complaints about sex discrimination from policewomen have increased fourfold. In 1991, the EOC received 9,060 complaints in total about sex discrimination in the workplace, a rise of 2,500 on the year before. Today, anyone who decides to prove a case of sex discrimination is a martyr to her own cause – even if she helps to change the system for others . . .

At present, it takes two years for a case to come before a tribunal – during which time a woman's job is on hold. No legal aid is available; the EOC provides backing (but much of its legal budget has now been spent on the Halford case). The maximum compensation is £10,000, and a tribunal has no power to order a woman's reinstatement or promotion. Vera Chadwick is one of the many less well publicised women who 'won' her sex discrimination case.

In 1985, Vera Chadwick was the deputy headmistress of a Lancashire comprehensive school. She applied for a headship and was told that she needed more qualifications. She proceeded to acquire a degree in education and an MA. At the time, 50 per cent of Lancashire's teaching staff were female, but 98 out of 100 of its secondary-school heads were male. Vera Chadwick took her case against Lancashire Education Authority to a tribunal. She won. She was given £600 compensation; the pay for a head at the time, she says, was £27,000.[24] Vera Chadwick has now requalified as a chiropodist, and teaching has lost a talent. The good news is that since then Lancashire Education Authority has adopted a written equal opportunities policy, it has an EO officer and it has career break and re-entry schemes for teachers – and several more women have been appointed to headships.

The onus, however, should be not on individuals to prove that they have been mistreated but on employers to prove that they are *not* practising discrimination. A strengthened EOC should be able to kick the Establishment hard – and in a way that hurts. It should have a team of inspectors who can make unannounced calls on companies to conduct a social audit: to ask what targets there are for females, ethnic minorities, and the disabled? To ask what methods are employed in interviewing, and on promotion panels? And when a company is seen to be failing, to impose tough penalties.

The EOC should abandon the production of research reports – there are organisations by the hundredfold in Britain and in Europe, duplicating such work. It requires only one goal: to work itself out of a job because the climate in society has changed sufficiently to regard discrimination on the grounds of race, gender or physical ability as unthinkable.

What Britain lacks is a foundation of fair play in the workplace. This may have to be instituted initially by the fear of the law, but subsequently endorsed as normal practice because it makes sense – and it makes money. Instead, now, for a female employee in the 1990s, much depends upon chance. Is she 'lucky' enough to choose a company where one chief executive has woken early to what competition in the 1990s means? Is she 'fortunate' enough to be employed by the small number of companies who accept that equal opportunities, childcare arrangements and a redesigned workforce are not simply *ethical* considerations but hard *commercial* necessities too? (The National Economic Development Office assesses that only 3 per cent of companies provide childcare facilities.)

'Progress' is relative, of course: even in an ideal world in which government does begin to take a lead, where childcare provision is automatic and the demands of having a family are integrated into companies' policies – even then, workaholism, the last retreat of the John Waynes of industry, will remain the dominant ethos. Unless, that is, women are prepared to take responsibility for themselves and stand against the crowd.

What is depressing about the 'vision' of many leading executives is that far from being freed by their success, they appear hooked on it. More depressing still is the fact that they want employees to share in the addiction. The chief executive of Norsk Data, a computer and software multinational corporation with branches in Britain, says: 'We demand from our employees that they work forty-three hours a week. A lot of people work every Saturday because they like to.'

The Burton Group (menswear and clothes) is reported as having an ethos of 'hard work regardless of cost'. At Electrolux, a manager says there is a workaholic culture: 'which is fine, "so long as it was working for you"' (what does this mean? Outliving all your equally overstressed rivals for the next management post?)[25]

In the States, women are expected to work horrifically long hours. Male colleagues are too – except, as the American journalist Gail Sheehy revealed in a massive survey in the 1970s, that many are now opting out of the burn-out track, having learned from the very mistakes which women now seem all too willing to repeat. The Ashridge management study tour of the States indicated that women in management were often at their desks by 7.30 a.m., leaving eleven or twelve hours later. They rarely take holidays, or if they do, they restrict them to a week. They are also prepared to uproot themselves frequently, since mobility means promotion.

'One female vice-president told us that she herself would not consider having children, and moreover, she would not be prepared to have working for her a woman with children because her commitment to the organisation would be affected,' a member of the British management team reported.

Valerie Hammond is married and child-free, but she is a carer, looking after an elderly mother. She admits that she is a workaholic. 'I have a predisposition to output,' she says dryly. She also argues that as a work ethic it does more damage than good. '"Balance" is the new model in the nineties in the States but the British thought of it first in the eighties,' she says. 'Work should not be all-pervasive. The progressive managers are talking about the holistic approach. Eventually, it could be possible to view workaholics not as those who win extra points but as those who are managing badly. In any case, as we become much more pluralistic in work patterns – working from home, for instance – the workaholic won't be *seen* to be working hard – so some of the motivation will disappear.' Even so, someone soon has to start saying 'No' as the workload grows heavier.

Women in better-paid jobs, some with career structures, have a choice – albeit limited – before them. The choice involves the terms on which they decide to join the workforce – whether as token men or as their own women – and how much they are prepared to sacrifice for the sake of that executive bathroom and a company car (or, for that matter, the kudos in the 1990s of appearing on 'Question Time', proving that women do know that G7 is not a device for removing cellulite).

Inevitably, some women will argue that there is a fourth choice: to stay at home. To be a full-time mother is as honourable an option as any other, but in a society in which two out of three marriages fail, it holds a high-risk factor. The mother at home is now the exception, not the rule. But still, industry, business, commerce and the government prefer to pretend otherwise. The continuing dominance of this stereotype, even though it now applies to a minority, sanctifies the government's inertia – and neither the woman at home nor the woman in paid labour benefits.

In the last twenty years, men in the workplace have been buffeted too. They have had to swallow their prejudices, accept – as many men see it – 'special' treatment for women, bow down to new entrants to the labour market who only increase the competition; and, at times, they have been forced to change practices 'which have worked all right for years'. Some may have even found themselves facing charges of sexual harassment for activities which, although thoroughly unwelcome to its recipients, they have always viewed as their 'bit of fun'.

It's tough for men; it's tough for women too. What is

needed now is a national strategy – one in which the government sets the boundaries of good practice, the goals and the rewards (bring back contract compliance, all is forgiven). The government should also monitor efforts to ensure an acceleration of pace, and provide cost-effective childcare to oil the system.

What we shall get instead, however, is a government which prefers to leave it to the 'free' market, imprisoning talent the country desperately needs as a result. Some women, of course, do have an individual salvation; the market will value them highly enough to pay whatever price they dictate. For the majority, however, an alternative solution has to be found.

Perhaps the search begins with the male labour force at the lower end of the market recognising that the animosity it has traditionally expressed towards females may have to be put on one side. 'Power is what it's perceived to be,' writes the American journalist Marilyn Berger. And power – in the 1990s, as it has been throughout history – is more likely to be perceived when working men and women stand side by side.

CHAPTER EIGHT

Sleeptime, worktime, overtime, rock

Sleeptime, worktime, overtime, rock.
Sleeptime, worktime, overtime, rock.
What about playtime? Ain't no play, jus'
Sleeptime, worktime, overtime, rock.
'Overtime Staggers Rock': Australian in origin

On 10 November 1959, Violet Dawson, aged twenty-nine, a married woman with two daughters of nine and five, clocked in at 7.30 a.m. at Ford in Dagenham to take up a job as a sewing machinist. Previously, she had earned poor money for 'work indoors' (homeworking). Now, she earned £8 a week for sewing a daily quota of car seats made of cloth, hide, and later, PVC. Women were not allowed to do shift work, so the day ended at 4.30 p.m.

Every Friday and Saturday night, Violet would work in the local fish and chip shop. On Saturday and Sunday mornings, she was up at 5 a.m. to work overtime at Ford. 'My husband is one of those old-fashioned men, he was dead against me working. He wouldn't even pick up a cup. I'd come in shattered from Ford and start the cooking and the ironing. But my husband was good in other ways. He was anti-union too. But I'm the kind of person who, if they have something to say or do, won't be downtrodden,' Violet says.

Violet Dawson's father-in-law lived with her and helped with her older daughter; her sister looked after the younger one. The extra money meant that Violet could give her retired parents 'a few bob for coal'. 'I also went with my mum and the girls to a holiday camp – and holiday camps weren't cheap. My money bought us all the extras. And it was *my* money.'

Seventeen years after she joined Ford, in 1968, Violet came out on strike and found herself part of the history of the women's movement. A new grading system was introduced which placed the machinists on the same level as unskilled men – except that, unlike the men, the women had taken a proficiency test, and been put on a month's trial on the machines.

'We didn't want equal pay because if we'd got that, we would have had to have done shift work and we didn't have the cover for the kids. But the men came out with us, and if they hadn't, we never would have got what we got,' Violet says.

'We had big meetings up and down the country and we were picketing. I was out from seven in the morning until midnight. My husband was really good. He said, "She'll come home when she's ready." Women from all over the country sent us letters of support and money but we had a terrible time from the press. We were supposed to be all sorts of things that we weren't. I was lucky my husband was in work the whole time, but some of the women with me went through terrible hardship. In the end, it was all a disappointment, but we did what we could.'

Within days of the women coming out, the whole plant shut down. A delegation went to see Barbara Castle, then Minister of Employment and Productivity, who allegedly shed tears. She promised equal pay legislation and more money – but not the B grading (from C) that the women sought. Violet says the union officials wanted the strike to be settled and pushed for the women to accept, so they did – for 95 per cent of the male semi-skilled rate.

Unintentionally, however, the women at Ford had also won a second reward: they put equal pay on the national agenda. (The more cynical would say that once Britain signed the Treaty of Rome, with its reference to 'equal pay for equal work', its aim was to see how cheaply it could enforce it. The 1970 Equal Pay Act was a perfect cut-price solution.)

In 1984 the Ford machinists, then four hundred in number, came out again. This time, they had the particular support of one of the convenors, Joe Gordon. The women used the newly passed equal pay for equal value clause (again forced on the British government by the European Court of Justice). Finally, after a two-month strike, the women were awarded a B grade.

'My mother worked in Ford during World War II,' Violet says. 'She was a panel beater and she had eight of us at home. Dad worked there too. As soon as the war was over, she said: "That's it, let a man have my job". And she went home. But it was different for most of us, we had to work. We needed the money. We needed the extra money that came with the grade, too.'

Violet retired from Ford in 1991 after twenty-seven years. She says her grandchildren have had 'terrible difficulties' finding jobs. 'My granddaughter's a lovely girl, a bright girl, and all she can get is restaurant work on the motorway working unsocial hours, 3 a.m. to 11 p.m. for pennies. First thing they ask you now is "Have you got kiddies?" If you say "Yes", they don't want to know. Women still have to fight harder than men. We won't ever go back, but I don't think we'll ever be equal either. They won't let us.'

Dora Challingsworth, who is in her fifties, joined Ford the week before the 1971 strike. 'They must have seen me coming,' she says. Her husband, a self-employed carpenter, gave her a lot of support. 'But I always came home at teatime to cook his dinner before I went to a meeting. I still do.'

Seven years ago Dora was elected a shop steward, and for a time she was the only woman among sixty. Now she has two female colleagues. 'I feel the situation is getting much, much tougher for women because no matter what the union says [the Transport and General], they look after the men first. You get individual shop stewards who are very supportive but that's not the general mood. The men didn't like it, for instance, when we finally got upgraded. But we were doing the job, so why not?'

Today in Ford, the Print Trim and Assembly plant (PTA) employs around 5,000 and the H building around 250 – 50 of them women machinists. Historically, H building has been represented by the PTA's convenor. 'It means that we women haven't got representation. I'm supposed to be invited to meetings of the Joint Working Committee when company policy decisions are discussed, but it doesn't happen much in practice,' Dora says.

Women at Ford, she says, have been short-changed again and again – a story not atypical of that told on many factory floors. When the company took over the payment of sickness benefit from the union four years ago, for instance, it was agreed that anyone who was ill should receive 100 per cent pay – except pregnant women, who receive half-pay for eighteen weeks.

Recently, too, new retirement ages were decided. Women previously retired at fifty; now it is fifty-five in line with men. 'I've always argued you shouldn't lose what you've got. I fought hard to avoid the change; I organised a petition but the union here didn't really want to know,' Dora says. As a result of the women's complaints at Ford, the legal department of the T & G at national level are now fighting their case.

Until seven years ago, Dora Challingsworth used to work on quality control. The section was disbanded, and only one post was left. Although she had worked there the longest and had the highest seniority, the job was given to a man. 'They said it was because in law I couldn't do shifts. But I found out later there was no law – and anyway he's only ever done one night shift since.'

At about the same time, she had a hysterectomy. 'I came back after three months and I was put on the end of the conveyor belt. It's the hardest job of all. I was dripping blood but they wouldn't change the job. The union said, "You wanted heavy work, you wanted equality, well this is it."

That's when I stood for shop steward. I knew what had happened to me and I didn't want it to happen to other women.'

In 1975, Dora developed what is now known as repetitive strain injury in her left hand (she is right-handed); she was awarded £3,500 compensation. In 1992 RSI returned, but this time to her right hand. 'The sewing, especially with tough material, has damaged the hands. It's like having one of the wires loose inside a plug. Some days it's OK, other days the pain is terrible and I can't so much as unscrew a bottle.' This time, the compensation was £3,000 – £500 less for a hand which she uses all the time. 'It makes you smile, doesn't it?' she says wrily.

Pay for women in Ford is £207 a week, compared to £263.70 for a male counterpart; women earn 78 per cent of the male wage. (In Denmark women earn 84 per cent, in Italy 83 per cent and in France 81 per cent).[1] Wage costs in 1990 in the UK were among the lowest of all the world's leading auto-mobile-producing countries.[2]

The motor industry in Britain in 1992 employs 30,600 women out of a total of 242,000. Nearly one in ten women are part-timers, employed for under thirty hours a week. The part-timers (who have rights proportional to full-time workers) are frequently brought in at Ford on Mondays and Fridays to cover for acute absenteeism. Sixty per cent of the workforce in Ford are semi-skilled; 45 per cent are Asian or Afro-Carib-bean. The recession means that staff turnover is low.

Steve Hart, the full-time T & G official at the plant, says that 'there are strong arguments for a crèche', but it has yet to materialise; Ford has an equal opportunities policy and a policy on sexual harassment. A man or woman found guilty may be suspended from work or sacked if the offence is serious enough, but according to Dora Challingsworth, that happens very rarely.

'Changes *have* been made since the seventies,' Steve Hart says, 'but in the end this is still an assembly-line, clocking-in, bell-to-bell car factory with no flexibility of hours and twenty-seven days' holiday a year. The absenteeism runs at 11 to 15 per cent. It was, and is, hard graft.'

Dora Challingsworth has two daughters and a son, now in their thirties. Each is married and none has a factory job. One daughter is a dealer with Allied Dunbar and earns £40,000-plus a year; one daughter works for Barclays Bank; and her son is a painter and decorator.

In 1991, twenty-five years after Dora helped the women to win their grading at Ford, the T & G recorded that it had lodged equal pay for equal value claims for 250 sewing machinists in Jaguar (Coventry), 130 sewing machinists in Vauxhall Motors (Luton) and five sewing machinists at Aston Martin Lagonda. Upgrading would add between 40p and £3 a week to the women's wages.

In July 1992, the sewing machinists at Ford were told that the efforts of 1968 and 1984, for them, are to come to naught. From August 1995, the work will be contracted out to the newly 'liberated' Poland. The rate for Polish women is £3 an hour, half what the women and men of Ford fought together to achieve. 'Progress' holds many ironies.

Between 1970 and 1979, female membership of trade unions increased by a staggering 41.7 per cent while male membership rose by only 6 per cent. In the period since 1979, according to Anna Coote and Polly Pattullo in *Power and Prejudice*, male membership has fallen by over three million while female recruitment has continued to rise . . . slowly. Unemployment has had an effect on male membership, while the entry of women into the labour market and the shift from manual to non-manual work has drawn them, mainly unenthusiastically, into the unions.

A report by the Policies Studies Institute in 1984 indicated that Afro-Caribbean and Asian women were more inclined to join unions but less likely to hold positions of power. (Asian women were the driving force, of course, in long-running disputes at Trico and Grunwick in the 1970s). Thirty-four per cent of white women belonged to unions compared with 57 per cent of what the report called West Indian women and 38 per cent of Asian women. Nine per cent of white women had attended a union meeting in the previous six months compared with 19 per cent of West Indian and 10 per cent of Asian women – but only 2 per cent of all three groups held an elected post. (This enthusiasm on the part of Afro-Caribbean and Asian women who are first-generation immigrants, according to Anna Coote and Polly Pattullo, did not appear to transfer to their daughters.)

A TUC report in 1987 said:

Racism not only prevents black and ethnic minority women and men gaining employment in the first place, it also militates against union activity to improve their position in employment and within the union.

Additionally, often, racism and sexism go hand in hand: black women therefore face the sex discrimination faced by white women together with the racism faced by all black people.

The report recommended changes such as the collection of statistics on gender and ethnic origin, positive action, special training and the need to address the issue of why women appeared to lack confidence – perhaps more accurately, it should have said 'lack confidence in an entirely male environment'.

In 1991, the T & G published the results of qualitative research conducted by public affairs consultants Gould Mattinson Associates (in itself a sign, since it was the first time a British union had used such research methods to inform recruitment and bargaining strategy).

Only a quarter (28 per cent) of part-timers belong to a union compared with 44 per cent of full-time workers. The research showed that women found unions too 'male dominated and insensitive to women's needs and problems'. Where problems existed, unions were not seen as powerful enough to help. 'There was often a resignation to problems at work – a feeling that nothing could be done.'

The report committed the T & G to taking on board the concerns of local government part-time workers: the unpredictability of hours; pay; pensions (employees who work fewer than fifteen hours a week cannot join the local government superannuation scheme); job security and the effects of privatisation. The report realistically concluded: 'The research, and two years listening to women in local government, also demonstrated, however, that cosmetic changes or simple propaganda are not enough. The union must change not only its image but also its bargaining agenda to make it equally relevant to both men and part-time women workers.'

Unions, such as the T & G are being forced to change at branch level; some – such as NUPE and COHSE, representing shop, factory, service, office and health service workers (where female labour is traditionally clustered) – have bent to that change more gracefully. These unions now have meetings at times convenient to women, special training courses, quotas on committees, women's officers and women's committees; they also take up issues such as cancer screening and sexual harassment as well as childcare. But still these measures, too, often, cling like shiny new stickers, to the bumper of what amounts to the same old banger. The macho trade-union culture prevails.

Even when a woman does have support and is confident, other inequalities may impede her union activities. In 1990 a bulletin of the T & G's national women's advisory committee[3] told the story of Anthea Grover.

Anthea went to work part-time in a factory. The women were expected to work machines making carrier bags out of hot plastic without any protection. 'Very often we got bad burns . . . also we used to get a lot of painful shocks off the machines. The place itself was a mess, there was oil and water running out of the bottom of some machines that were never cleared up, and there were wires sticking up everywhere.'

She decided that the only way to improve the situation was to contact a union; she chose the T & G by chance. Anthea Grover organised a meeting at her home, attended by a union official, and leafleted the factory. In return, she received a letter from management saying that some women were complaining of being harassed to join a union. She was called before a disciplinary hearing and won. At the same time, the non-unionised factory was given a pay rise: 17 per cent for men, 7 per cent for women.

'I was really surprised how the majority of people I spoke to there didn't really know what a union was about,' Anthea Grover says. 'They thought Arthur Scargill was going to come in and take them out on strike . . . there's a lot of bad propaganda about unions.

'One of the supervisor-setters . . . was going around saying, "Why are you in this union, it'll never take off, you don't need one". It was like a power thing for him because he had power over all his shift . . .

'I found the women are their own worst enemies,' she adds. 'They still have the attitude that they're not worthy to stand up for their rights. That was my experience in that particular firm.'

Anthea Grover attended a shop stewards' course, but then she had to leave her factory job. She separated from her husband and the part-time income was insufficient to pay for childcare. Once her son starts school full-time, she says, she will return to union work.

'I . . . really believe in working-class rights and justice. It might sound a bit like self-martyrdom, but it isn't. I just hate the fact that they treat you like that.'

Apart from alienation from male union organisation, a lack of confidence, and a belief that it is all a hard-Left plot, some women also feel a deeper mistrust of unions. As early as the eighteenth century women set up their own work-based organisations. By the late 1880s, several dozen had been established. At the turn of the century, the men began to organise women, allowing them to join male unions or setting up allied women's societies.

'Their . . . object was not entirely disinterested,' says Barbara Drake, author of a classic history, *Women in Trade Unions*, first published in 1920. 'The men's object was not so much to exclude women entirely from employment – an aim generally viewed as impracticable – as to confine them to certain branches of the trade and certain districts. Under the circumstances, some degree of sex antagonism was almost inevitable, and did not tend to make organisation any easier.'[4]

In *The Making of the English 'Underclass'?* Kirk Mann describes how, in the 1940s, the Amalgamated Engineering Union allowed women to join, but they were confined to a 'women's section' with lower subscription rates and benefits than even the lowest-grade male worker. The AEU also pursued equal pay – not out of consideration for its female members, but because 'they were looking to the post-war period when they anticipated – correctly in the main – that employers would dismiss women workers in favour of men where "a rate for the job" applied'. Fifty years on, 'a rate for the job' can still have perverse twists.

The factory on an industrial estate just outside Stockport is small, thirty-nine employees, although it is part of a large multinational concern. The factory is a tribute to Mrs Thatcher's dream of turning Britain into a giant service sector. Whereas before in this area, men and women served apprenticeships and learned to weave and make and manufacture, and sometimes even had a pride in their individual tasks, now the order of the day is flexible working. Men and women in this factory don't make, they redistribute. They handle over 30,000 different electronic components (mainly made, of course, in the Third World) and repackage them for different mail orders. They also sell directly to the public. In 1984, management arrived with a proposal to hasten equal pay. The men, it announced, would take a wage cut to come down to the level of the women. In addition, to sweeten the change, the men would receive a lump sum of £600.

'The management said we had three options. We could take what they offered; we could all lose our jobs; or third, some of us would lose our jobs in reorganisation,' says Moira McDonald, the shop steward in the factory from 1983 until 1988 (she is now the health and safety representative). 'The men with one exception voted for it because they were frightened of getting the sack. Ian said to the women, "It's all right for you, I've got a mortgage and kids to looks after." Pauline wiped the floor with him and said, "What do you mean? I'm on my own, I've got a mortgage and three bleeding kids. How do you think I feel? The management have taken money out of our pocket."'

Julie Walton, who is twenty-eight, shows her wage slip. She and her brother workers now have a take-home pay for a thirty-seven-and-a-half-hour week of £143. Julie spends £80 a week on the mortgage and £60 on the childminder; the family lives on her partner's wage. 'And God help us when he has a short week.'

No single person with a mortgage can afford to live on what the factory pays. Pauline, for instance, in her fifties, divorced and with two daughters at home, works in a pub three evening and helps to prepare buffets for caterers at weekends.

Moira McDonald says she is better off than most because her mortgage is only £20 a week and she shares that with her partner, Henry, who has succeeded her as shop steward. (Henry fights as hard for women's rights as men's in the workplace, she says, but domestic duties are still being negotiated. 'It's one of Henry's favourite phrases, "I've cleaned the kitchen." I say, "Henry, you haven't cleaned the kitchen, you've washed the dishes. Cleaning the kitchen is mopping the floor, putting the rubbish out, tidying the place up." And he says, "Don't get at me, I do enough," and I tell myself, "Oh God."')

Moira is forty-four, divorced, with a twenty-seven-year-old son who is reading development studies at university. ('He has', Moira says affectionately, 'a passion for clean water in the Third World. And he's been studying long enough to bloody know about it.') Moira represents the good news about the trade-union movement. She did well academically at school, she says, but left art college at seventeen when she became pregnant: 'I wouldn't even consider an abortion.' She married the father, Jim.

'My husband was a builder. He made quite a bit of money and I eventually gave up work and stayed at home until the baby was three, but I didn't like having to wait for his money every week. I felt tied.

'Everyone thought we were the perfect couple. He did too, but that's how blind men are. I left after twenty years. It was a drawing apart, there was no sex life left, nothing. It wasn't anybody's fault. But I thought: if I don't make the break I'm going to be stuck in this situation for ever and I want to do something more with my life. On the day I left, I felt this enormous sense of relief.'

That was almost ten years ago. Moira had already (in 1980) got a job in the factory and joined USDAW (the Union of Shop, Distributive and Allied Workers) – a union which was also at the time having a midlife crisis. 'I think it was the debate on abortion that first got the women galvanized,' Bernadette Hillon, the union's first women's officer, told Anna Coote and Polly Pattullo in *Power and Prejudice*. 'In 1980, USDAW was a fairly conservative and Catholic union and it was saying abortion was a bad thing. The women began to say – "We're browned off with the union telling us what we should think and feel, and we're not having it any more".'

In the mid 1980s, USDAW, the union with the fourth-largest female trade-union membership in the country, not only appointed a woman's officer, it now has a female president and more women than men on the national executive. It also set up a network of divisional women's committees, of which Moira

225

McDonald has chaired one. She has also, as a shop steward, attended numerous USDAW courses and conferences.

'A while ago, the union would have been ashamed to admit it organised the lowest-paid workers in Britain,' Moira says. 'Now all the unions are doing it because we are the only area of growth; the only people who are getting the jobs. So what does that say about the state of women in work?'

Moira has no problem at all with confidence – but she recognises that other women may. Julie, for instance, is on a TUC assertiveness course, with Moira's encouragement.

'I've argued for a long time to get women active, they've got to feel competent first,' Moira says. 'They've got to feel confident approaching members and management. The TUC were initially wary of the word "assertive", so we got round that by packaging it along with employees' rights.

'I think it will be a great day, if it ever comes, that a factory doesn't need a shop steward because people are competent enough to work their own problems out and feel strong enough to say, standing together, "We know our rights, you can't do that."'

Ask Moira about feminism and she says she is a socialist first (she is a member of the Labour Party), then a feminist. She also illustrates one of the problems of the 1990s: while we have feminism alive and well in the attitudes of some trade unionists, we don't have trade unionists alive and well and visibly active in large numbers in the women's movement. It is, she says, too white, too middle-class.

'The problem', Moira explains – accurately, in my opinion – 'is that feminism alone doesn't change anything. It doesn't change law, it doesn't give you a minimum wage, it doesn't give you rights at work. It has to make alliances and work through what already exists. It has to build on what's already been achieved.

'If men ask me if I'm a feminist, it's usually more of an accusation. I say that I'm not a feminist, I'm a socialist who believes in equality for all. But it's hard for them to believe

226

that feminism is about equality for all when you see how it's portrayed in the media.

'For the last five or ten years, it seems to have been all about power dressing and women managers. Well, how many working-class people do you know who are managers – male and female? How many working-class people do you even know who are managers in any great numbers?

'The issues feminism has to address is what is happening to so many women. They are being pushed right down the line. In our factory, even the cleaning jobs which were once women's work are being given to lads of sixteen and seventeen. What the women are left with is temporary work, the lowest of the low, a couple of pounds an hour. And childminding, which is needed but is also bloody awful pay.

'Feminism', she says, 'is nice to have, but it's got to look as if it's more to do with how life's really lived.'

In the period immediatly after the Tories were returned to power for a fourth term in April 1992, the trade-union movement suffered from acute post-election depression. It had banked on a Labour win, and for women, among other gains, a minimum wage (although some of the female electorate had traditional reservations that this would harm the male income), better childcare and improved training facilities. 'Now,' says Margaret Prosser, 'we have to sit down and think again. It's as good a time as any to start afresh.'

Margaret Prosser, in her fifties, is one of the most senior women in the trade-union movement. She is the women's national secretary of the T & G, a member of the TUC General Council, an EOC commissioner and a member of the Labour Party's national executive women's committee. She also comes from the kind of background which many women in Britain would recognise.

Her dad was a builder in South London; she was one of a family of four children. When she was in her late twenties her husband, a coalman, became paralysed by an undetected abscess on his spine. Margaret Prosser had three small children, so she couldn't take a job. 'We had eight hard years on benefit. I joined a local Child Poverty Action Group (CPAG) group and the experience taught me how the state operates – and what some women have to face, always up against the odds.'

Eventually, her husband (who is now dead) was placed in a home, and in 1977 Margaret began working in Southwark Law Centre as a welfare rights adviser. She trained as a legal executive, became involved in the T & G and eventually took a job as a full-time official. 'It was clear when I started that there was nothing at all on offer for women.'

The T & G now has a relatively small staff. So, in addition to so-called women's issues, Margaret Prosser is also responsible for campaigns and training. 'The Labour Party always acts as if the unions are a drag anchor but I think in many ways, because our future in part depends upon it, we've woken up to the need for a female perspective far more quickly than it has.'

If feminism is not as visible as it should be in the trade-union movement, it is still, nevertheless, a strong current – and could become stronger. The trade-union movement, if it is to appeal to women, has to forge for itself a more populist female image – instead of accepting the face of male villainy with which the media have saddled it. When, for instance, was a female trade unionist a regular on an afternoon TV chat show? Or a radio consumer programme? Or had a regular column in a mass-circulation women's magazine? Or, to be realistic, when was a female trade unionist asked to contribute to any of the above?

Margaret Prosser welcomes such approaches, she says. In the 'new' thinking for the 1990s, the government will probably be sidestepped because it has chosen to offer so little. 'We have to work with companies who have business reasons for attracting and keeping women. Until the election, the unions had all their eggs in one basket and that belonged to the Labour Party; now we have to diversify.

'We have to make new partnerships, we have to become more modern and negotiate change. At Ford now we have an equality audit under way because it suits management, too, to learn how to keep female staff.

'Women have to accept, though, that if what the men are doing on their behalf isn't helpful, they have to get in there and do it themselves,' she adds. 'It's hard when you have a family at home as well as a job – but in the end, there's no other way.'

If the unions have belatedly recognised that they need to fashion a new model army with women as the main recruits, women, in turn, need assurances that some of their own agenda, as well as that which they share in common with men, is likely to be delivered – and, more importantly, what they will do when it is not.

NAWO (the National Alliance of Women's Organisations), set up in 1989, represents over two hundred eclectic organisations, among them the Mothers' Union, Business and Professional Women, the Older Feminists' Network, the Married Women's Association and the League of Jewish Women. Through these groups, it lays claim to five million members. A base so wide might mean that politics becomes diluted to a nonsense: a compromise in the name of unity. On the contrary, on one issue at least, before the 1992 budget and the general election, the women were as one, according to Jane Grant, NAWO's director. The issue was childcare – or lack of it. 'Women', she said at the time, 'are very angry.'

NAWO duly presented all the political parties with an agenda for women – it included improved education and training, action on violence, support for strategies to eliminate inequality internationally, an analysis of the budget in terms of its impact on women (a policy long adopted in Australia) and childcare. (The tone of the agenda for women alone is a tribute to the influences of feminism.)

Apart from NAWO's efforts, numerous surveys at the time of the election, too, indicated that women would vote for the party which took action on childcare. In *The Times* the day before the budget in 1992, for instance, a survey indicated that only one in four women wanted lower taxes. The rest preferred to see higher spending on public services, including childcare and the raising of benefits. Labour's private surveys also seemed to show that the majority of younger women favoured its policies on nursery provision, a minimum wage and higher taxes.

In the general election, of course, many women voted for the Conservatives. They not only voted for the Party which offered them nothing on the family except the continually postponed promise of imminent prosperity, they also voted for a government which has done more over thirteen years to erode women's rights than probably even the Labour Party would have managed, had it been in power.

If women want childcare, they have to vote for it – and take their vote away again, if the politicians fail to deliver. Women also need to make their anger and collective power much more manifest. 'Be reasonable,' said a slogan during the student rebellion of the sixties, 'ask for the impossible.' And if that fails, demand it. A consistent campaign of direct action not only reveals the depths of feeling (look at the poll tax campaign), it also rejuvenates those who take part. In Iceland in 1984, for instance, women organised a national day of action in which they invaded supermarkets across the country, did their weekly shop – and then paid only two-thirds of the cost, since they earned only three-quarters of the wage.

In Norway in 1971, a women's electoral lobby organised a strategy so that, using loopholes it had discovered in the electoral system, it could change the gender composition of Parliament and municipal councils virtually overnight. Norway had 450 municipalities – 78 then without any female representation. After the election, the number had dropped to 22 and nine of the largest municipalities had 40 to 50 per cent female membership; it was the feminisation of politics. Now (1992) Norway not only has a female Prime Minister, but eight out of eighteen Ministers are women. (In itself that does not guarantee radical policies, but at least it offers a different perspective from the traditional male outlook.)[5]

In Australia in the late 1960s and early 1970s, the Women's Electoral Lobby worked less spectacularly but more systematically to get women selected within the Labour Party and draw active female support to it. In 1972, the first Australian Labour government for twenty-three years came into office. Under Gough Whitlam, for a brief period, all manner of legislation of value to women and children, including a national health service, was implemented. A Women's Unit was attached to the Cabinet and all policies under consideration had to acknowledge their impact (or not) on women.

Direct action takes energy and imagination, as well as organisation and money. One-day strikes, public tribunals on low pay or the glass ceiling or child poverty; boycotts of newspapers, business or supermarkets which prove not to be friendly to the interests of individual groups of women and their children; full-page ads by prominent women (a strange term) which don't read 'I'm not a feminist but . . .' but do proclaim 'I am a feminist because . . .' would all help to make the media a tool of the women's movement instead of the other way round as has been the case for too many years.

In *Western European Feminism* Gisela Kaplan quotes a definition of feminism which appeared in 1977 in *De Bonte Was*, a Dutch feminist journal. It imposes an impossible standard, it may alienate some women, it may frighten some men, but it is a useful reminder of why it helps to 'maintain your rage':[6]

You are not a feminist, if you are merely a modern woman: a little more independent, a little more sexual, a little more critical.

You are not a feminist, if you participate in exploiting women sexually, erotically and economically even further.

You are not a feminist, if you do nothing to improve the status of all women . . . The personal means nothing

231

without other feminists. It is not enough for you to consider yourself emancipated.

At this stage of feminism nothing is enough. The set goals of feminism are nowhere realised. Oppression cannot be solved personally. Oppression is structurally determined. As long as there are women who are not free, there is no freedom. The oppression of your sister is your own oppression. The only fight is the fight for all of us . . .

CHAPTER NINE

Happy ever after?

'**M**odern capitalism beguiles with flickering lights, it mystifies with a giant kaleidoscope. We lose ourselves and one another in the reflected images of unrealisable desires,' wrote Sheila Rowbotham in *Women's Liberation and the New Politics*:

> We walk into a world of distorting mirrors. We smash the mirrors. Only pain convinces us we are there. But still there is more glass. Your nose is pressing against the glass, the object suddenly finds herself peeping at herself. There is a possibility of a moment of illumination.

There is still, for each individual, I believe, that possibility of a moment of illumination.

It is time for feminism to be less prescriptive: time, if you like, for a federalised feminism in which differences are accepted and consensus is found in specific causes: childcare, equal pay, an improved welfare system, a war on poverty, the environment. The one muscle which women have least used is their collective one.

We are saddled with a government which is unlikely to implement the kind of national strategy which is necessary to help women who work both inside and outside the home, or to battle against poverty, or to invest adequately in health, housing and education – all policies which are not only morally just but also cost-effective. So we have to make coalitions which, when required, cut across class, race and gender to lobby and campaign, to take direct action, to consider civil disobedience, to tap anger – and to recognise that it is possible, in some cases, at certain times, that the differences between women may be greater than that which they share in common with particular sections of men.

We need to recognise that in the past thirty years, both men and women have performed a somersault in terms of expectations, roles and relationships. If friendship between the sexes is to make new roots, then it will have to be on the basis of understanding, trust, respect – and the acceptance of risk. Men and women need to bow to the fact that we are all in a state of transition. We all have to take a gamble and, if the anger of men and women is not to grow, we all – until proven wrong – must expect the best.

Paradoxically, because women have gained so little, they have the least to lose.

If women can celebrate the *differences* between men, rather than caricature the similarities, not only will that help to reduce the tyranny of constant fear under which too many women live, it may draw new allies. At the same time, if men feel that they are victims of inequality in certain areas, then, they have to take their own initiatives, as women have been forced to do. 'A shadow or penumbra of neglect has fallen upon the realities of life for men,' Neil Lyndon says, 'and upon the social terms and conditions by which men's personal and family lives are extensively defined and limited.' But by whom? It has to be said that where neglect of men has occurred on an institutionalised level, it must have been as a result of the actions of other men. Change begins with an acknowledgement of that fact.

At the same time, for good and necessary reasons, feminism has, for many years, spoken to women alone. If men are to be 're-educated', perhaps feminism now needs to accept that it must be less exclusive.

Feminism must also, I believe, recognise that 'the personal is political' is only a starting point, not an end in itself. What happens outside the home to the structures of society, nationally and internationally, may be just as important as what happens within.

In work and at home, both men and women need to forfeit some control and recognise where our interests overlap. The rights of the child require attention, as does her or his need for parental time. It would be a backward step if, instead of one workaholic parent, a child now has to endure two. So-called 'quality time' is an adult comfort, but it's not always sufficient compensation for a child. Men and women need to negotiate so that each carries some of the weight of family duties – and neither feels more burdened than the other. It is hard holding down a job and running a home, very hard – and men might now begin to appreciate that fact more readily.

One of the easiest weapons that men can wield is to do nothing. Exhaustion then steals away a woman's anger and her conviction that she has a right to something more, if she so chooses, than the role of mother and wife. Feminism loses a supporter; chauvinism claims a victory.

In our private lives we also need to unravel the ambivalent messages that men and women seem to be sending each other. If men say they want a partner who is equal, do they behave that way? Likewise, does a woman express guilt, for example, if the housework isn't entirely her domain and then feel put upon if it's left for her to do? Feminism isn't about dictating one way to live, it's about widening the choices for *both* female and male.

Are we also prepared enough for relationships and marriage – when aspirations are impossibly high and the staying power, for some, is dangerously low? Men might begin to accept that becoming a born-again father, chef and domestic engineer two months after the divorce becomes final is several years too late, while if women feel discord, perhaps they should be more open about it, and sooner, in the development of the relationship?

In July 1992, John Patten, the Education Minister and a

committed Christian, announced that government will take a bigger hand in preparing children for society in the 1990s. The young will now be taught the difference between 'right' and 'wrong' in the classroom. (As if this didn't occur before.) 'Ministers believe if some children are not taught how to behave when they are at home, they must learn it in the classroom,' reported the *Daily Express* with glee.[1]

A return to 'old-style morality' is 'heralded', it announced. But whose morality? And according to what definitions of 'right' and 'wrong'? This is the kind of language which, in the past, has boded ill for women, many of whom now seek the right to act in ways which may not conform to the standards of thirty years ago but can carry very much more of a burden in terms of personal responsibility.

'All that's needed is for the woman to learn enough respect for herself to be unwilling to live with a man who treats her with contempt,' said Dana Densmore, a radical feminist, in the late 1960s, encapsulating the ethos of the women's movement.

Will that kind of self-respect be taught to girls and boys under Mr Patten's new regime? Already much of what was working within the education system, for instance, to correct the lack of equal opportunities has been cut back. Yet in example after example, Myriam Miedzian, in *Boys Will Be Boys*, shows how preparation in the education system can help young adults in their relationships and their aspirations.

To quote one: Educating for Parenting began in 1979 in Philadelphia. Its founder, Sally Scattergood, explained that 'she was disturbed by the fact that child rearing, which is probably the most important task that most human beings will undertake and one of vital importance to society, is ignored in the school curriculum' (the same is true in Britain).

The courses in nine schools begin in kindergarten and teach, through theory and practice, how to care for children and how parents relate to each other. It is of particular value, Myriam Miedzian says, in schools where there is a high proportion of boys from single-parent families (again an issue in education that we have yet to tackle here). The result has been a greater awareness of the dangers of teenage pregnancy and young marriage and the responsibilities involved in having a child – as well as the difficulties the pressures can bring to bear on a couple.

Sue Plant works for a local education authority as one of the country's few full-time Personal and Social Education (PSE) advisers. PSE, she says, is not mandatory in schools; resources have to be squeezed from a budget that is already stretched. Mr Patten's crusade, it appears, will not extend to financing what already exists – nor will the other 'crusade' launched by his fellow Minister, Virginia Bottomley.

'Drive Against Teenage Pregnancies' read the headline across the front page of *The Sunday Telegraph* on 5 July 1992. 'Bottomley into battle to prevent unsafe sex.' In battle maybe, but without the benefit of uniform, armour, equipment – or condom. This appears to be a 'battle' without funding.

In 1989, 117,500 women aged between fifteen and nineteen became pregnant, the sixth increase in as many years. A month before Ms Bottomley's press release was swallowed wholesale by the media and John Patten published his White Paper, a report was produced by the Sex Education Forum (an alliance of organisations such as the Family Planning Association, the Health Education Authority and the National Aids Trust) which detailed the reality of the situation.

It said that although governing bodies have been legally responsible for shaping policy on sex education in their schools for five years, nearly a third have failed to produce a policy or refuse to include sex education in the curriculum. The reasons why include a pressured timetable, lack of staff, teacher embarrassment and the complaint that sex education simply encourages promiscuity.

The Forum called for more resources and more direction and warned:

Provision of school based education on sexuality and relationships has never been so important. Not only are increasing proportions of youngsters becoming sexually active at a younger age, but they also face greater potential choices and danger than their parents' generation.[2]

'What we're talking about is family policy, which includes preparation for life,' Sue Plant says. 'What many young people in secondary education receive, if they are lucky, is three lessons a year. Perhaps fifteen hours over five years to gear them up for the highest divorce rate in Europe. PSE', she adds, 'is the poor relation.'

Sue Plant devises sex education courses which help children to deal with relationships, the family, and their bodies, and to nurture a sense of responsibility. She extends these workshops to include parents and school governors.

'I try and show the parents that we all face moral dilemmas and contradictions. For instance, in talking about families, we have to be sensitive to the feelings of parents and children who don't live in what was the traditional family situation.

'We also have a problem in that this society is all about competitiveness and being out for yourself, yet that operates against the collaborative family values which we also advocate as good.

'I believe you can only teach "values" by exploring the range of choices, considering the consequences of them, and by encouraging each individual to take responsibility for themselves and for others in exercising this choice,' she says. 'It's not a matter of "wrong" or "right", inculcated by fear of punishment.'

The left, including feminists, have had too little to say on the issue of family policy – and now the right hold sway. Education appears to be overshocked with born-again Christians (Lord Griffiths of Fforestffach, probably the man wielding the most influence in education today as part-time chair of the Schools Examinations and Assessment Council, is one, as is David Pascall, chair of the National Curriculum Council), while educational material is being designed by organisations such as Family Youth and Concern, a pressure group for the moral majority, run by Valerie Riches.

Valerie Riches, a charming woman in her fifties, was a social worker. She is the mother of two adult children and since the 1970s she has campaigned vigorously to keep the man at the head of the house, the woman in the home, and the feminists at bay.

Her educational video *The Three Rs of Family Life* (Respect yourself; Respect your partner; Respect life) sells enormously well, as do her numerous pamphlets and booklets. She is against sex education for the under-sixteens and against family planning, part of the 'hidden connivances, implications and activities of an interlocking power structure . . . sex education is a vehicle to spread an amoralism that is destructive of the family and of society,' she writes in *Sex and Social Engineering*.

Virginia Bottomley's tactic of announcing a campaign on sex education while making no provision for it must please Valerie Riches hugely.

It is easy for feminists and the left to mock much of the material of Family and Youth Concern, but at least it has recognised that without church or a consensus on 'good' and 'bad' a fast-changing society which undersells any kind of ethics and values and oversells the importance of self-fulfilment, no matter what the cost to others, may find itself lost. It may also find itself more attracted to the ideas which hark back to the so-called 'good old days', when the woman was in the home, and the man was the boss; the anthem of the backlash.

Richard Whitfield of the National Family Trust, set up in 1987, also has connections with the right, although he says he is careful to keep a distance, and he is also producing literature for schools. (One of his proposals, for instance, is that a mother should stay at home for the first two years of her child's life.)

'The issues are how can you change behaviour?' he explains.

'The right would try to preach or punish. But you can't mobilise people if your precepts are too rigid. Moral authority has to grow from the individual. We need to project a view that's ethically rooted without being moralistic. And which reinforces the right people have to feel they control their own lives.'

John Patten has said that, as part of his campaign, children will be taught to be 'good citizens'. Good citizenship begins with government. It is seen in policies which value individuals highly enough to give them enough to live on and an opportunity to earn more. It is seen in legislation which offers rights and protection in the workplace irrespective of whether the employee works for ten hours a week or a hundred.

It is seen in a government which will not tolerate poverty and discrimination. It is seen in a government which allows time in the national curriculum – and an adequate budget – to prepare children for the fast-changing society in which they will live, taking responsibilities for their own decisions.

For the future, Gisela Kaplan warns that the changes in what was the Soviet Union and Eastern Europe may not be good for women. The story has a familiar ring. She quotes Ruth Rosen, writing about Hungary:

Propaganda which seeks to send women home is pervasive. From the church, the media and pro-life groups comes the . . . chant that women's participation in the labour force and absence from home is responsible for the high divorce rate, juvenile delinquency, alcoholism – even men's rates of heart attacks . . .

As unemployment rises . . . economists plan to retire women and the elderly to ease the economic plight of working-age men. The calculation is simple: dismantling the crèches and bringing the women home with their children is cheaper than keeping women in the labour force and paying their childcare.

Still, Gisela Kaplan is undaunted. 'I fail to find grounds for pessimism,' she writes in *Contemporary Western European Feminism*.

> Both in terms of a change of women's role and in terms of the continuity of the knowledge of feminism. This time round in human history, the parameters have been set differently, the questions have been greater and political and legal processes . . . and development of feminist ideas have been more consistent and widespread, and they have been more entrenched overall than at any previous time.
>
> In all the feminist work so far accomplished, be this in the most abstract or grassroots work, one of the motivating forces was to exorcise the ghost of oppression from humanity.
>
> No one can doubt that important ground work has been laid so that women may never become invisible victims and silent majorities again.

I too believe that women will not slip back but the issue in the 1990s in Britain is how very much further there is still for them to go. And how much more hostile will be the opposition as the foundations of the male Establishment begin to rumble with the strain.

This opposition will come as many women are at their most tired, depleted by juggling home and job, confused perhaps by the claims of post-feminism that the battle has been won when their own experience plainly tells them that the contrary is true. The fight to win equality, decide priorities and achieve a balance between the many demands on their time, has barely begun.

The monumental shift to the right has also made many women and men all the more defensive. The recession has made equality appear, for some, a luxury. What we need to reclaim is the right to anger and passion and the conviction that the requirements of women and children and the family are not peripheral to society but at it's core, in bad times as well as good.

Inequality isn't somebody else's concern, it's mine and yours, male and female, because even if it doesn't effect us as individuals, it corrupts the community of which we are a part. For too long, in this so called post-modernist world, feminists and those who advocate social justice and the right to genuine, responsible choice, have had their voices of protest marginalised or silenced – or they have hushed themselves, fearful of ridicule and condemnation and smears. (I'm not a socialist, but . . .' has become almost as much of a cliché as its sister 'I'm not a feminist, but . . .'). We have to take up the fight again, not alone but collectively, without apologies, confident that the greater the reaction, the more effective are our arguments.

Even without the women's movement, men and society have experienced massive change. Profits dictate that women are needed in the workforce; demography demands that older women return to employment; marital breakdown means many wives have no choice but to fend for themselves. At the same time, men are charting emotional waters apparently unknown to their grandfathers while some appear as anxious to get back into the home as women are to leave it.

In these circumstances, we need fresh rules, greater understanding and new contracts so we can treat each other and our children with respect and consideration. Feminism for me provides a greater number of clues towards this, a more humane society, than I find in the privatised nightmare which passes for citizenship in the patriarchal society of John Major (or for that matter, in the apolitical society which is John Smith's 'vision'.)

In 1990, in *The Sunday Times*, Neil Lyndon wrote:

Something ruinous and evil has happened between men and women in the last 25 years. Something so wounding and sore that it's hard to see how the last generations of this century can come of age, unafflicted by the ills of the past.

Feminists, too, have an analysis which goes back much further than the past two decades and applies even more strongly today . . . It is, as Neil Lyndon and his supporters say, a time for rage.

NOTES

FOREWORD

1. Esther Oxford, 'What did you do in the Sex War, mummy?', *Elle/Guardian Supplement*, 9 July 1992.
2. ibid.
3. Neil Lyndon, *No More Sex War: The Failures of Feminism* (Sinclair-Stevenson, 1992).
4. Interview with Sean O'Hagan, *Esquire*, May 1992.
5. News section, *Achilles Heel*, Autumn 1991.

CHAPTER ONE: Tremble, tremble, the witches are back

1. 1970s Italian feminist slogan.
2. 'Demon texts': term used by feminist Ann Snitow to refer to seminal books of the women's movement, such as *Sexual Politics* or *The Female Eunuch*.
3. Marcia Cohen, *The Sisterhood: The Inside Story of the Women's Movement and the Leaders Who Made It Happen* (Fawcett, Columbia, 1988), p. 152.
4. Alice Echols, *Daring to be Bad: Radical Feminism in America 1967–1975* (University of Minnesota Press, 1989), p. 162.
5. Neil Lyndon, 'Badmouthing', the *Sunday Times Magazine*, 9 December 1990.
6. Neil Lyndon, 'The Wrongs of Women', the *Spectator*, 23 November 1991.
7. Andrea Dworkin, *Right-Wing Women: The Politics of Domesticated Females* (The Women's Press, 1983).
8. Mary Robinson, The Allen Lane Foundation Lecture, London, 25 February 1992.
9. *The Sisterhood*, p. 128.
10. The *Standard*, 19 June 1992.
11. Rebecca Fraser, *The Times*, 4 July 1992.
12. *Daring to be Bad*, p. 84.
13. Gisela Kaplan, *Contemporary Western European Feminism* (UCLA Press, 1992), p. 72.
14. *Daring to be Bad*, p. 234.
15. Cate Haste, *Sex in Britain: World War I to the Present* (Chatto & Windus, 1992), p. 205.

16. Jane Waller and Michael Vaughan-Rees, *Women in Wartime: The Role of Women's Magazines 1939–1945* (Optima, 1987), p. 68.

CHAPTER TWO: Come into my parlour, said the spider to the fly

1. Susan Ardill and Sue O'Sullivan, 'Dizzy Pace in Women's Publishing', *New Statesman*, 25 October 1985.
2. *Elle/Guardian Supplement*, 9 July 1992.
3. Home Office figures: notifiable sexual offences and robbery recorded by the police in 1990.
4. John Carlin, 'After Violation, there is only fear', the *Independent*, 30 May 1992.
5. Rosemary Carpenter, 'Are the laws of rape now out of date?', *Daily Express*, 13 December 1991.
6. 'Epidemic of Fear', *Today*, 12 June 1991.
7. See Lynne Segal and Mary McIntosh, *Sex Exposed* (Virago, 1992).
8. My interview with Lynne Segal, London, June 1992.
9. In Lynne Segal, *Slow Motion: Changing Masculinities, Changing Men* (Virago, 1990), p. 232.
10. Ellen Willis in Lynne Segal, *Slow Motion*.
11. My interview with Robin Morgan, New York, January 1992.
12. Reggie Nadelson, 'Foetuses: how did they get so big?', the *Independent*, 2 July 1992.
13. *Sunday New York Times*, 10 May 1992.
14. ibid.
15. Karen Houppert, 'Feminism in your face', *Village Voice*, 9 June 1992.
16. Kate Muir, Life & Times, *The Times*, 8 July 1992.

CHAPTER THREE: My heart belongs to Daddy . . . ?

1. 'Our Divorce Despair', *Daily Express*, 17 June 1992.
2. National Children's Homes Fact File: Children in Britain 1992.
3. Annabel Ferriman, 'Children Carry Scars of Divorce into Middle Age', the *Observer*, 15 September 1991.
4. Jonathan Bradshaw and Jane Millar, *Lone Parent Families in the UK, Department of Social Security Research Report No. 6* (HMSO, 1991).
5. Flora Davis, *Moving the Mountain: The Women's Movement in America Since 1960* (Simon & Schuster, 1991), p. 228.
6. Sarah Nelson, 'Power Failure', *Social Work Today*, 11 June 1992. Conference organised by the Scottish Council for Single Parents, 13 Gayfield Square, Edinburgh EH 3NX.

7. *Stepladder*, issue 7, 1992, published by National Stepfamily Association, 72 Willesden Lane, London NW6 7TA.
8. *The Times*, 12 December 1990.
9. *The Times*, 20 December 1990.
10. 'English Mother Wins Court Fight for Daughter', the *Daily Telegraph*, 9 July 1992.
11. Hugh Dehn, 'Unfair for Fathers', the *Guardian*, 8 July 1992.
12. ibid.
13. Roger Bird, *Child Maintenance: The New Law: The Child Support Act 1991* (Family Law, 1991).
14. Jessica Davies, 'Why are mothers becoming less caring?', *Daily Mail*, 14 July 1992.

CHAPTER FOUR: Just wait until your father gets home . . . ?

1. David Cohen, 'Left Earning the Money and Holding the Baby,' the *Independent*, 25 February 1992.
2. Jonathan Bradshaw and Jane Millar, *Lone Parent Families in the UK, Department of Social Security Research Report No. 6* (HMSO, 1991), p. 55.
3. 'Token New Man', the *Guardian*, 16 September 1991.
4. Yvonne Roberts, *Man Enough* (Chatto & Windus, 1984), p. 79.
5. Paul Morrison, 'Men and Change', in Victor J. Seidler, *The Achilles Heel Reader* (Routledge, 1991), p. 103.
6. Keith Bremner, 'Father and Son Reunite', *Concern*, Quarterly Magazine of the Children's Bureau, Spring 1992.
7. Susie Orbach and Luise Eichenbaum, *What Do Women Want?* (Michael Joseph, 1983).
8. Jessica Davies, Interview with Lady Fiona Fowler, *Daily Mail*, May 1992.
9. David Cohen, 'The Baby Came but the Sex Went', the *Independent*, 8 July 1992.
10. Richard Ehrlich, 'When Father Rules the Roast', the *Daily Telegraph*, 29 May 1992.
11. Jessica and Philip Norman, 'Springtime for Parents', the *Guardian Review*, 25 March 1992.
12. Linda Grant, 'A Woman, No Man and a Baby', *Independent on Sunday*, 14 June 1992.
13. Bryan Appleyard, 'Only Nuclear Families Can Defuse This Social A Bomb', the *Sunday Times*, 24 October 1991.
14. 'Token New Man', the *Guardian*, 16 October 1991.
15. *Lone Parent Families in the UK*.
16. Richard Ford, 'Divorce Risk Greater for Trial Marriage Couples', *The Times*, 19 June 1992.
17. 'The Caring Face of Capitalism', *The Director*, 1990; quoted in

Work versus Family (Dawliffe Hall Educational Foundation, 1991).

CHAPTER FIVE: I don't take the welfare to bed

1. Celia Hall, 'Poverty rose faster in Britain than in any other EC state', the *Independent*, 6 June 1990.
2. Michael Meacher, analysis of government statistics supplied in parliamentary written answer (Hansard, 6 March 1991).
3. Brian Donnelly, *Self-Help Projects for Families and Children: Panacea or Placebo?* (National Children's Bureau, 1989), p. 9.
4. Ruth Cohen, Jill Coxall, Gary Craig and Agra Sadiq-Sangster, *Hardship Britain: Being Poor in the 1990s* (Child Poverty Action Group, 1992), p. 75.
5. David Brindle, 'Huge Cut in Income for Poorest', the *Guardian*, 16 July 1992.
6. G. Davy Smith, M. Bartly and D. Blane, 'The Black Report on socioeconomic inequalities in health: 10 years on', *BMJ*, vol. 301, 18–25 August 1990; quoted in Cary Oppenheim, *Poverty: The Facts* (CPAG, 1990).
7. Charles Murray, 'Underclass: A Disaster in the Making', *Sunday Times Magazine*, 26 November 1989.
8. Oliver James, 'Crime and the American Mind', the *Independent*, 21 May 1990.
9. Figures supplied by Child Poverty Action Group.
10. David Brindle, 'Official Enquiry Tolls Knell for Lottery of Social Fund', the *Guardian*, 7 September 1991.
11. ibid.
12. Saul Becker, *Windows of Opportunity: Public Policy and the Poor* (CPAG, 1991), p. 44.
13. Lynda Bransbury, writing in *Benefits*, a journal of social security, research, policy and practice (Issue 2, September/ October 1991).
14. Gisela Kaplan, *Contemporary Western European Feminism* (UCLA Press, 1992).
15. ibid., p. 63.

CHAPTER SIX: A bit of a domestic

1. Evelyn and Barry M. Shapiro, *Women Say, Men Say: Women's Liberation and Men's Consciousness* (Delta Special, published by Dell Publishing Co. Inc., 1979).
2. See Annual Reports of Welsh, English, Scottish and Irish Women's Aid Federations, 1991.
3. Lorna J. F. Smith, *Domestic Violence, Home Office Research Study (1989) 107*, p. 6.

4. London Strategic Policy Unit (1986), *Police Response to Domestic Violence*.
5. *The Times*, 4 October 1983.
6. Tamar Lewin, 'Feminists Wonder If It Was Progress To Become Victims', the *New York Times*, 10 May 1992.
7. ibid.
8. Anthony Doran, 'Battered Husbands', *Daily Mail*, 24 July 1992.
9. *Domestic Violence Home Office Research Study 107*, p. 49.

CHAPTER SEVEN: Who's the boss's darling?

1. Fay Inchfawn, 'Women in Britain', in Jane Waller and Michael Vaughan-Rees, *Women in Wartime* (Optima, 1987), p. 63.
2. ibid., p. 59.
3. James Buchan, 'The Redundant Male', *Daily Mail*, 24 July 1992.
4. Janice Walmsley, 'The Mothering Wars', *Daily Mail*, 5 May 1992; Lynda Lee Potter, 'Can a Good Mother Ever Make a First-Rate Boss?', *Daily Mail*, 4 March 1992; Jacki Davis, 'Downfall of the Woman Boss Who "Frightened" Top Men at British Gas', *Daily Mail*, 11 March 1992 and 'The Woman at War', *Daily Mail*, 21 November 1991; Vikki Orvice and Janice Walmsley, 'The New Spinsters', *Daily Mail*, 26 March 1992; 'Tyranny of the Woman Boss', *Daily Mail*, 17 June 1992; Diane Hutchinson, 'Beware the Single Girl', *Daily Mail*, 21 May 1992.
5. Caroline Davies, 'Why Don't Daughters of Working Mothers Want Children?' the *Standard*, 23 January 1992.
6. *Today*, 15 February 1990.
7. The *Guardian*, March 1990.
8. Kevin Maguire in the *Daily Telegraph*, 30 January 1992; Anne Steele, *The Times*, 26 February 1992.
9. Richard Savill, '£8,000 award for pregnant Director who was sacked', the *Daily Telegraph*, 28 April 1992.
10. Anna Quindlen, 'The Glass Half Empty', the *New York Times*, 22 November 1990.
11. Neil Lyndon, 'The Wrongs of Women', the *Spectator*, 23 November 1991.
12. Barrie Clement, 'Figures "Shock" a Minister', the *Independent*, 21 May 1992.
13. *The Female Resource – An Overview*, devised by Women in Management Association and Girls' School Association.
14. David Jack, 'Career Women Aiming High for Their Children', 3 March 1992.
15. Gervase Webb, 'Five Star World Makes Room at the Top for Dagmar', the *Standard*, 27 May 1992.

16. Angela Lambert, 'There's nothing wrong with success, power and riches', the *Independent*, 18 June 1992.
17. Valerie Hammond, *Women in Management: Optimising the Potential*, papers from the 1987 Study Tour to New Orleans and New York (May 1988), Ashridge College.
18. Cynthia Enloe, *Bananas, Beaches and Bases: Making Sense of International Politics* (Pandora, 1989), p. 194.
19. Stewart Fleming, 'US accepts a woman's place is in the economy', *Financial Times*, 12 April 1989.
20. Jeremy Laurence, 'Motherhood Costs Women £224,000 in lost earnings', *The Times*, 24 February 1992.
21. Viki Holton, *A Balanced Workforce? Achieving Cultural Change for Women: A Comparative Study*, Ashridge Management College (1991).
22. John Arlidge, 'Women key to working future', the *Independent*, 4 July 1992.
23. Kevin Banham and Clive Rassam, *Shaping the Corporate Future: Leading Executives Share Their Vision and Strategies* (Unwin Hyman, 1989).
24. Yvonne Roberts, 'Down By Law', the *Guardian*, 16 January 1990.
25. *Shaping the Corporate Future*.

CHAPTER EIGHT: Sleeptime, worktime, overtime, Rock

1. 'Women and Ethnic Minorities in the T & G', *T and G Equality Fact Pack*, p. 15.
2. ibid.
3. *T & G Women*, issue 6, 1990/1, p. 12.
4. Barbara Drake, *Women in Trade Unions* (reprinted Virago, 1984).
5. Gisela Kaplan, *Contemporary Western European Feminism* (UCLA Press, 1992), p. 73.
6. Gough Whitlam to his supporters when he was dismissed as Prime Minister by the Govenor general of Australia in the 1970s.

CHAPTER NINE: Happy ever after?

1. *Daily Express*, 29 July 1992. Front page.
2. Judy Jones, 'Children denied proper sex education', the *Independent*, 10 June 1992.

Also of interest

SLOW MOTION
Changing Masculinities, Changing Men

Lynne Segal

**'An enormously thoughtful and well-researched work . . .
A book I'd like everyone to read'
– Jane Dibblin, *City Limits***

'Women do not write books about men,' wrote Virginia
Woolf. Neither, until recently, did men. Throughout the 1980s
questions concerning the changing nature of men's lives and
experiences have been debated with new passion and concern.
From the exploration of sex roles to the study of gender and
power, the psychology of men has emerged fraught with strain
and crisis. Ironically, the thoughts of those seeking a sexual
politics to undermine men's power over women remain
consistently gloomy, while the category of masculinity remains
deeply obscure.

Slow Motion, by the author of the highly acclaimed *Is the Future
Female?*, approaches the 'problem of men' in a new way, by
looking not at masculinity, but at specific <u>masculinities</u>. From
tough guys and martial men to camp, gay, black-macho and
anti-sexist men, their competing images and roles are
analysed. From the complex and contradictory web of
different identities a new approach to sexual politics begins to
emerge.

Lynne Segal's forceful and perceptive analysis of this
uncharted territory moves beyond cynicism to create a new
sexual agenda for the 1990s.